The Best Book of

Microsoft Windows 3

Carl Townsend

SAMS

A Division of Macmillan Computer Publishing
11711 North College, Carmel, Indiana 46032 USA

International Standard Book Number: 0-672-22708-8
Library of Congress Catalog Card Number: 90-61474

Publishing Director: *Richard K. Swadley*
Product Development Specialist: *Linda Sanning*
Manuscript/Production Editor: *Diana Francoeur*
Coordinating Editor: *Andy Saff*
Technical Editor: *Russell A. Williams*
Indexers: *Hilary Adams, Joelynn Gifford, Sharon Hilgenberg*
Production Coordinator: *Steve Noe*
Production: *Claudia Bell, Sally Copenhaver, Travia Davis,
Jill Glover, Jodi Jensen, Mae Louise Shinault, Bruce Steed*
Cover Concept: *DGS Group*
Cover Photography: *Cassell Productions, Inc.*

Printed in the United States of America

Overview

P   A   R   T

P A R T

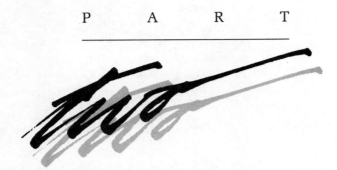

P A R T

P   A   R   T

Contents

Introduction, xxi

P   A   R   T

Exploring Microsoft Windows

P   A   R   T

Using Windows Applications 85

P   A   R   T

Advanced Techniques

P A R T

Four

Appendixes 349

Introduction

Windows 3.0 is probably the most important software product of 1990. It gives you the ease of use, standard conventions, and graphical user interface of earlier versions. In addition, with the new version 3, you get megabytes of virtual memory, more icons, and better file and program management tools. In short, Windows 3 is fun and powerful.

To take full advantage of this new product, you will need a 386 or 486 computer. You will also need plenty of extended memory and extensive disk space.

The Best Book of Microsoft Windows 3 is designed to show you how to get the most out of this product. It provides a tutorial overview of the various components of Windows. Examples of actual screen displays help to reinforce the text. You will also find notes, tips, and other interesting facts about the product.

Using This Book

The book is divided into four parts. *Part One* introduces you to the graphical user interface concept and some of the Windows vocabulary, and explains Program Manager and File Manager. *Part Two* describes how to use the various applications provided with Windows, such as the Calendar and the Notepad. *Part Three* is a collection of more advanced techniques. It explains how to control the printer, add soft fonts, run non-Windows applications, customize Windows, and more. *Part Four* is an extensive set of appendixes with valuable information on installation, memory management, troubleshooting, and other topics.

Terms and Conventions

As you read, you will see certain terms used frequently:

- *Windows* (with a capital *W*) refers to Microsoft Windows version 3.0.
- The word *window* (with a lowercase *w*) refers to a window that is displayed on a screen by a program.
- *Clicking the mouse* means to press and release the left button of the mouse unless otherwise specified.
- *Dragging the mouse* means to press the left button and drag the mouse; then release the button.

Menus, button and command names, dialog box text, and technical terms have distinctive treatment:

- The names of menus, such as the File menu or the Options menu, have one letter underlined. This letter is a mnemonic and can be used with the Alt key as a shortcut to access the menu options.
- Choices, or commands, that you can select from the menu are boldfaced. If the command has a mnemonic, it is underlined, such as the **Exit** command on the File menu.
- Menu items and text in dialog boxes (rectangular boxes in which Windows asks you for information or provides you with information) are spelled as they appear on the screens in Windows. For example, when you use MS-DOS File Manager to format diskettes, the message **Select the diskette to format** appears in a dialog box.
- Text and button labels that appear in a dialog box are boldfaced, and any mnemonics are underlined, for example, the **Cancel** button.
- Technical terms that may be new to you are italicized and defined the first time they are used.
- Text that you type from the keyboard appears in a special computer typeface. For example, to start Windows, type `WIN`. You type the letters *W I N*.

Key combinations that you press from your keyboard are represented in a special way:

■ Key combinations that are separated by spaces are pressed in sequence. Alt Spacebar means to press Alt, release it, and then press Spacebar.

■ Keys separated by a plus sign are pressed simultaneously. Alt + F4 means to press and hold down the Alt key while pressing the F4 key.

Icons, Notes, and Tips

Small drawings, called *icons*, appear in the left margin of the book. These icons help you quickly find instructions for using the mouse, the keyboard, or the 386 enhanced mode of Windows. In addition, **Notes** and **Tips** give you helpful suggestions, cautions, and information about using Windows.

Illustrations

The small screens in the left margin of the book are *pulldown menus*. These are lists of options from which you may make choices. When you select a menu by pressing the mnemonic for that menu (for example, the letter *F* for the File menu), a pulldown menu appears, showing the various choices that are possible for the File menu.

The larger screens in the center of the page that are shown as numbered figures represent actual windows that you would see in Microsoft Windows. Occasionally, these may not match your screen if you are using a version of Windows different from version 3. Also, if you are using a color monitor, the screen may not perfectly match.

Acknowledgments

The author gratefully acknowledges the help of many people in preparing this book. Special thanks to Tanya van Dam of Microsoft Corporation for supplying Microsoft Windows 3.0 and Microsoft Word for Windows software, to Russell Williams of DaVinci Systems Corporation for technical editing, and to Chris Doner of Access Softek. Thanks also to the many corporations that supplied beta copies of software. At Howard W. Sams & Company, thanks go to Linda Sanning, Diana Francoeur, Andy Saff, and the rest of the Sams staff for their teamwork in making this book a reality.

Trademarks

All terms mentioned in this book that are known to be trademarks or service marks are listed below. In addition, terms suspected of being trademarks or service marks have been appropriately capitalized. Howard W. Sams & Company cannot attest to the accuracy of this information. Use of a term in this book should not be regarded as affecting the validity of any trademark or service mark.

Apple is a registered trademark of Apple Computer, Inc.

Arts & Letters is a registered trademark of Computer Support Corporation.

CROSSTALK is a registered trademark of Digital Communications Associates.

dBASE IV is a trademark of Ashton-Tate Corporation.

Hayes is a registered trademark of Hayes Microcomputer Products, Inc.

Hercules is a trademark of Hercules Computer Technology.

Hewlett-Packard and LaserJet are registered trademarks of Hewlett-Packard.

HiJaak and Inset are trademarks of Inset Systems.

HOTSHOT is a registered trademark of SymSoft Corporation.

IBM and PC are registered trademarks, and OS/2 and PC DOS are trademarks, of the International Business Machines Corporation.

Intel is a registered trademark, and 386 is a trademark, of Intel Corporation.

Lotus and Lotus 1-2-3 are registered trademarks of Lotus Development Corporation.

Microsoft, Microsoft Word, and MS-DOS are registered trademarks, and Windows is a trademark, of Microsoft Corporation.

PageMaker is a registered trademark of Aldus Corporation.

Paintbrush is a trademark of Zsoft Corporation.

PostScript is a registered trademark of Adobe Systems, Inc.

SideKick is a registered trademark of Borland International, Inc.

UNIX is a trademark of American Telephone and Telegraph Corporation.

WordPerfect is a registered trademark of MicroPro Corporation.

Exploring Microsoft Windows

Part One is a quick-start guide to using Windows. It will help you get up and running on Windows and will show you how to use Windows productively. If you are really eager to try out Windows, skip to Chapter 2, "Getting Started with Windows." Before going too far in the book, however, be sure to read Chapter 1, "Introduction to Microsoft Windows." It will give important insights into the concept behind Windows and its significance in the marketplace.

Introduction to Microsoft Windows

Before you start using Microsoft Windows, let's look briefly at what Microsoft Windows is, what a graphical user interface is, and why Windows is such an important software product.

Microsoft Windows: A Graphical User Interface

Microsoft Windows is an extension, or *shell*, for MS-DOS that supports a graphical user and programming interface. *Graphical user interfaces* (GUIs) are symbolic interfaces that improve the speed of communication between people and computers. More specifically, a graphical user interface is a user interface that runs in a computer's graphic mode.

Figure 1.1 shows a typical screen that you might see if you were using a graphical user interface shell. In particular, this screen is an example of using Microsoft Windows 3.0. It is much easier to start a scanner program by clicking a graphic symbol that looks like a small camera than to start a program by typing a program name such as SJGAL at the DOS prompt. Clicking a symbol also frees you from having to remember the name of the program you are trying to start. And, since you are clicking, not typing, you do not make any typographical errors when entering the program name. Clicking is a natural type of action, like touching an object to initiate an action. You don't need directions or a manual.

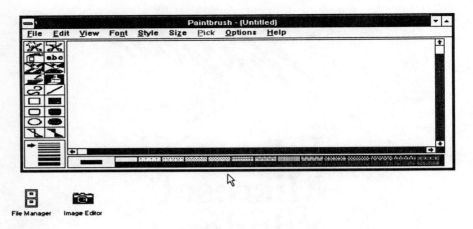

Figure 1.1 A graphical user interface.

The Desktop Metaphor

Microsoft Windows, like most graphical user interfaces, uses the *desktop metaphor*. With the desktop metaphor, the screen represents the top of a desk. Programs currently in the computer memory are represented by *windows* (rectangular areas of the screen) and have dropdown menus, dialog boxes, and icons. *Icons* are small symbols that are used to represent files, programs, a cursor, or program tools. Icons can even be used as parts of a menu in a window to initiate action.

Figure 1.2 shows a typical screen when running Microsoft Windows. In this case, two application programs are in memory, each represented by a window. The first is the Windows 3.0 Program Manager. The second is Windows Paintbrush. The top window represents the currently active program. At the bottom of the screen, three application icons are used to represent inactive programs you have temporarily put aside. These are probably still in memory in whatever state you last used them if you have Windows 3.0, an 80386 processor, and plenty of physical memory. Otherwise, they may have been temporarily swapped out to a disk. In either case, they are only a few keystrokes (or mouse clicks) away from being used again.

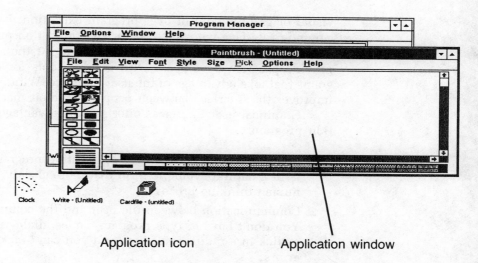

Application icon   **Application window**

Figure 1.2 A typical Windows screen.

Advantages and Disadvantages of a Graphical User Interface

Graphical user interfaces, or GUIs, are important for computer systems because they are symbolic interfaces. One way that human beings communicate is by telling stories, and the stories involve symbols. The success of today's films, television programs, books, and theme parks is based on a very simple premise—people need to hear stories. Even when we hear words, the words are symbols for images, and the words actually invoke images in our mind that form the story. A camera image on a computer screen, for example, is easily assumed by the user to represent some kind of scanning program. A story forms in our mind about this image.

Note: When a programmer develops a Windows program, the environment and programming interface don't automatically give the programmer a natural application program, or one that is easy to use. It's still up to the programmer to create a good "story." Some Windows programs are better than others in this respect, even for the same application.

Graphical user interfaces make communication with a computer possible by means of symbols, stories, and metaphors familiar to humans. Windows is a graphical user interface that gives the user visual or graphic control over program execution. It also provides a common interface with the user for all application programs, making it easier to learn new application programs. At the same time, GUIs provide program developers with graphic tools for developing programs that take advantage of the user interface. Windows is a tool that improves the interface between people and their machines.

Graphical user interfaces offer several advantages to an application program:

■ Communication between the application program and the user is in a natural symbolic form that more closely resembles the human thinking process.

■ Communication between the user and the computer is faster. You don't have to type program names, dialog is often merely a click in a multichoice box, and you can't make spelling errors.

■ The learning process for programs is faster, since the communication is more natural and symbol oriented.

■ Programs can be more powerful. In a conventional program, intricate operations that are generally difficult for the user and that are often purposely omitted by the program designer are now feasible. With a GUI, complex operations can be done with a few clicks of the mouse.

■ With Windows 3.0, the program now has access to all of your extended memory (2 megabytes or more) instead of the 640K available to conventional programs.

Because of all these advantages, most developers believe that graphical user interfaces will be the primary interfaces used by application programs in the future.

However, the graphical user interface does have some disadvantages with respect to today's hardware and software:

■ The amount of memory and disk space needed to support the graphic environment is much larger than that needed for conventional (or text-oriented) environments. In addition, faster processing speeds are required by the processor and disk interface. Printing of graphic images is slower because more information must be sent to the printer. Windows is particularly slow in comparison to many other GUIs.

■ Since hardware must be faster and contain more memory, hardware costs are higher.

■ The amount of programming support needed for a graphic environment is more extensive, particularly until tools are developed for this environment. Often a programmer must go through a relearning process. In the future, many programs that will be written for graphical user interfaces will need to support object-oriented programming and some level of artificial intelligence.

■ The GUI lacks support for the handicapped. If you can't work a mouse or have visual problems, the GUI is very difficult to use.

According to Microsoft, a true GUI meets fourteen requirements:

1. The screen is a true representation of what will be printed.

2. The user interface is graphically oriented, making extensive use of *icons* (graphic symbols that represent a file, a program, or a menu option).

3. The user interface permits direct manipulation of screen objects. For example, you can change a window's size by clicking the border and dragging it.

4. The screen is aesthetically pleasing and is a pleasure to use.

5. An object-action paradigm is used; that is, you select the object first and then select the action. This permits you to move on to the next task while the action is being completed.

6. Standard elements (resources) are used across all applications. Examples include menus, dialog boxes, and windows.

7. The interface is consistent across platforms (MS-DOS, OS/2, UNIX, etc.).

8. A strong set of tools is provided for developing to the environment.

9. The user must be able to personalize (customize) the interface.

10. Information is communicated through graphics.

11. The interface is flexible, supporting mice, keyboards, and other peripherals.

12. It is easy to install, configure, and use.

13. The interface supports multiple applications at once.

14. It supports interapplication communication.

The History of Microsoft Windows

One of the first GUIs to use the desktop metaphor was the Xerox Star. The Star was a computer system that came out of research work done at the Xerox Palo Alto Research Center (PARC) in the late 1970s. The system was ahead of its time in many ways, but it was also expensive. The Star never realized success as a commercial product.

In 1983 Apple Computer introduced the Lisa computer which, like the Star, used the desktop metaphor as a graphical user interface. In 1984, Apple released the Macintosh, a smaller version of the Lisa.

Microsoft began work on the Microsoft Windows product in early 1983. The first retail version, version 1.0, did not appear in stores until November 1985, over two years later. Unlike the current version of Windows, version 1.0 used *tiled* windows—windows that were adjacent and did not overlap.

Microsoft Windows version 2, released in 1988, was developed by both Microsoft and the IBM Corporation. Unlike version 1, version 2 supported overlapping windows and was designed to provide a user interface similar to the OS/2 Presentation Manager. Microsoft Windows version 2 was supplied in two special versions: Windows/286 designed for the 286 processor and Windows/386 designed for the 386 processor. In both cases, the user interface was identical, but each version exploited the special features of the faster microprocessor.

Windows 3.0, released in 1990, provided a graphical user interface that is identical to that of the OS/2 Presentation Manager, including proportional display fonts. In addition, Windows 3.0 provided virtual memory support. This meant that Windows application programs were no longer limited by the 640K bytes of the DOS conventional memory.

What Is Microsoft Windows?

Now that you have been introduced to Microsoft Windows and to GUIs, let's look more closely at Microsoft Windows and at its advantages to you as a user. We'll begin by reviewing the five basic classifications of all software: application programs, operating systems, utilities, development software, and environments.

Application Software

For most users, *application software* is perhaps the most important class of software. Application software is the software that really does the work. It's why you have a computer in the first place. Spreadsheets, word processors, and database managers are all examples of application software. You use application software to accomplish your objectives and to solve problems.

Operating Systems

Operating systems are a class of programs that manage the resources of the computer (hardware and software), process commands, and control program execution. You need some type of operating system to run application software.

Computers generally use a single operating system program. It is the foundation program for all computer operations, and is loaded automatically at start-up or when the computer is booted. For Microsoft Windows, the supporting operating system must be MS-DOS.

Utilities

Utility programs are those that permit you to manage files and other system aspects. Utility programs are often sold as components of the operating system. Utility programs permit you to copy files from one directory to another, print files, check the disk status, set the system date, format disks, and delete files. PC-Tools is an example of a utility product.

Development Software

Development software is used by professional programmers to develop application programs, utilities, and operating systems. Examples of development software include compilers, linkers, debuggers, and the Windows Software Development Kit. The Windows Software Development Kit, or *WinSDK*, is used for developing Windows application programs.

Environments

Environments include shells and other resources that are used with operating systems to change the user interface or the programming interface. Environments can be text-oriented (DESQview, PC Tools, or HyperPad) or graphic (Windows). Text environments are not GUIs, but they do have a speed advantage over GUIs.

Several GUI environmental products are available for use with MS-DOS. Besides Microsoft Windows, other examples of graphical user environments are DeskMate, GEM, and other related commercial products.

The Microsoft Windows Environment

Microsoft Windows is a software product that is used as an environment shell with MS-DOS. Once loaded into the computer's memory, it provides a graphical user interface for Windows application programs (see Figure 1.3). It also provides a programming interface for Windows applications.

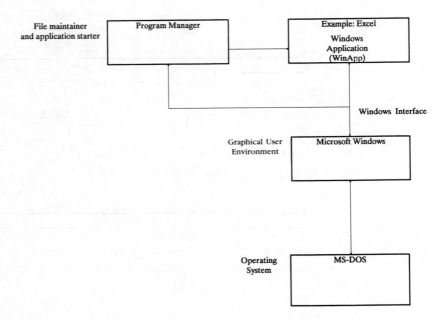

Figure 1.3 System organization with Windows.

Windows Applications

Windows applications, or *WinApps*, are programs specifically designed to run in the Windows environment. Windows must be loaded first or the WinApp will not run. Examples include the Windows applications provided with Windows and various commercial products such as Microsoft Excel and Aldus PageMaker. Over a hundred commercial Windows applications already exist (see Appendix G).

Note: To take full advantage of the features of Windows 3.0, the application program must be specifically written for that Windows version. WinApps written for older versions may not run at all, may run with problems, or may run limited to 640K in Windows 3.0.

In the default Windows installation, the Program Manager application is automatically loaded when Windows is started. Program Manager is used to start other Windows application programs.

Advantages of Microsoft Windows

The Windows applications have distinct advantages over their non-Windows competitors. In fact, almost every major product developer is working on a Windows version of its product. Let's look at some of the advantages of programs that use the Microsoft Windows environment.

Standard Graphical User Interface

One advantage of the Windows environment is that the graphical user interface is the same regardless of the application program being executed by the user. Basic operational concepts always remain the same. File opening, saving, and data editing are always the same.

Easy to Learn and Use

Windows application programs can be used by anyone with relatively little computer experience. There are no MS-DOS commands to learn. The Windows pulldown menus, dialog boxes, and other aspects of the screen always work the same way. The story on the screen conveys a degree of security to the user. The user can use any Windows application program productively with very little training.

Programs Work Naturally

The screen tells a story. The user is managing symbols rather than words. The program functions much like the human mind. As a result, using the application program is more natural.

Device Independence

All the drivers for the various output and input devices are installed as part of Windows. As a result, all Windows application programs use printers, mice, a keyboard, terminals, and other devices in the same way. For example, adding a new font to Windows means that the font is immediately available to every Windows application program that you have installed. Adding a new printer makes the printer available to all Windows programs. In contrast, adding a new printer for non-Windows programs means reinstalling each program. For a typical user, this would mean reinstalling WordPerfect, Ventura, dBASE IV, and others.

Multitasking Support

With Microsoft Windows, you can execute two or more programs at the same time. Each program has its own window area on the screen display. You could have a communication program that is downloading a file at the same time that you are working on a spreadsheet. You can even have multiple executions of the same program. For example, if you are creating a document with PageMaker and need to paste in a picture, you could start the scanner in another window and scan the picture needed. You could then paste into your document the picture you have just scanned.

Data Transfer Standards

Programs written to execute specifically under Windows, or WinApps, support three methods of transferring data between programs: transfer through files, transfer through the Clipboard, and

Dynamic Data Exchange (DDE). The *file transfer* method can be used with either WinApps or standard applications. This method simply involves writing the data to a file and then reading the file with another program. Since Windows supports multitasking, both applications can be in memory at the same time if there is sufficient memory.

The second method, the *Clipboard* method, uses the Edit menu in the Windows application to move or copy text or graphics from the source application to the Windows Clipboard. Then you can make the second application active and use the Edit menu in that application to paste the text or graphics from the Clipboard to the desired location. You can also use the Clipboard with non-Windows applications to copy and move.

The third method, *Dynamic Data Exchange* (DDE), is supported by many WinApps. Using the Windows DDE protocol makes it possible for applications to share data dynamically. For example, a communication program can receive data, process it, and then transfer the data to a spreadsheet program that is also in memory at the same time. In essence, the spreadsheet and communication programs appear to be sharing the same data. Similarly, a chart created with Microsoft Excel could be used in a word processing document, and the document would be instantly updated if the spreadsheet were changed.

Memory Management

Microsoft Windows can manage memory for a WinApps on a *dynamic* basis. That is, the program can seem to access and use more memory than is physically available. Only a portion of the program needs to be in memory at a time. Program resources can be shared between programs that are in memory at the same time. In addition, with Windows 3.0, programs address a *virtual* (not real) memory of almost 16 megabytes. This compares with the 640K memory limit of most conventional DOS programs. To use this feature, however, the program must be specifically written for Windows 3.0 and the extended memory must be available.

Looking at Windows 3.0

Windows 3.0 offers an extensive array of features over the earlier versions:

■ Screen fonts are proportional.

■ Dialog box controls and other objects appear three-dimensional.

■ The Executive has been replaced by three new applications: Program Manager, File Manager, and Task List. These provide much better control over file management and program execution.

■ For the 386 user, a virtual memory is supported. If you have applications that need more than 640K, Windows uses the extra memory transparent to the user. You can also run multiple applications, each with its own virtual processor and memory.

■ Icons are used to represent programs and program groups. Icons can also be used for file management.

■ File management is improved. For example, you can copy or move files by dragging icons.

■ The user has more control over customization of the system.

■ Installation is simplified, and displays and mice can be changed without a complete reinstallation.

■ Control Panel has been improved.

■ A Recorder application has been added for creating macros.

■ Paintbrush features have been upgraded, and color is now supported.

■ The Terminal application features have been expanded to support binary file transfers and other features.

■ Improved help support is available for applications.

■ Menus are supported to a deeper level.

■ Three rich color schemes are supported, including patterned backgrounds and 256 colors (on a VGA) for each window element.

Summary

Graphical user interfaces will almost certainly be the primary interfaces of the future. They offer the advantage of a natural communication between the user and the computer.

Microsoft Windows is currently the leading GUI environment for MS-DOS programs and has the following advantages over competing products:

- Standard graphical user interface for all programs.
- Natural user interface that is easy to learn and use.
- Programs that are independent of system devices.
- Multitasking support.
- Support for Dynamic Data Exchange.
- Virtual memory management supported to 16 megabytes of address space.

Getting Started with Windows

In this chapter you will learn the basic elements of the Windows environment. You will learn how to start Microsoft Windows, the chief visual components of a window, and how to quit Windows. Most of what you learn in this chapter will be common to all Windows applications.

Installing Windows

If you haven't done so already, install Windows by following the directions in Appendix A of this book. If you have already installed Windows, you might wish to refer to this appendix for ideas and tips that you can apply to your own system. Take the time to carefully plan your installation: which directory you will use for Windows, how your disk directories should be organized, and whether you need more than one copy of Windows on your hard disk. For some hardware systems, you may need a special copy of Windows.

Starting Windows

When you start Windows, you are installing a DOS environment and initiating one or more applications. The following sections will explain how to start Windows with the Program Manager or with an application, how to determine which of three modes to use, and how to use start-up options.

Starting Windows with the Program Manager

You can start Windows with the Program Manager by simply typing WIN from any directory. This will start Windows and also initiate execution of the Windows Program Manager application program.

Note: If typing WIN with the Program Manager fails to start Windows, the PATH command in the AUTOEXEC.BAT file is not set properly. See Appendix A.

Note: Windows displays a small hourglass when it is busy. You should not attempt to use the mouse or keyboard during this time.

Starting Windows with an Application

To start Windows with a specific application, you need only go to the directory in which the application is stored and enter WIN xxxx, where xxxx is the name of the Windows application program. For example, to start Microsoft Excel (a Windows application), go to your directory with Excel and type the command WIN EXCEL. If the application directory is in the current path string, you do not even have to go to that directory.

Operating Modes

Windows always starts in one of three modes: real, protected, or 386 enhanced. When you install Windows, it is normally configured to support the most appropriate mode for the existing hardware. You can always find out which mode Windows is in by selecting **About Program Manager** from the <u>H</u>elp menu of the Program Manager.

386 Enhanced Mode

The *386 enhanced mode* is the most advanced Windows mode. Many Windows features are supported only when executing in this mode. To use this mode, you must have a 386 or 486 processor and a total of 2MB or more of memory, including 1MB or more of extended memory. In this mode the processor is supporting multiple *virtual* processors, each running in its own protected memory with its own application.

386 Features that apply only to the 386 enhanced mode are marked with this icon in the text.

Standard Mode

Use the *standard mode* if you have a 286, 386, or 486 processor and at least 1MB of memory (including 384K extended). When using 2 to 3MB of memory with Windows applications only, you may find that this mode is faster than 386 enhanced.

Real Mode

Use the *real mode* if you are using an 8086 or 8088 processor or if you lack at least 384K of extended memory. You also must use this mode when executing Windows applications that have not been converted to Windows 3.0. In real mode, Windows will support any installed expanded memory.

Using Start-up Options

You can alter the installed mode by using command-line options when you start up (see Table 2.1). For example, if you have a 386 with 3MB of memory and you need to run a Windows 2.0 application, you could use the following command:

```
WIN /r
```

This command would start Windows in the real mode. To start Windows with a Windows 2.0 version of an application, use the application name in the command line with the mode option:

```
WIN EXCEL /r
```

Table 2.1 Windows Command-Line Mode Options

Option	Windows Mode
/r	Real
/s	Standard
/3	386 Enhanced

Getting Started

For the moment, type

`WIN`

This command will start Windows, display a Microsoft logo, start an application called Program Manager, and open a Main document window. Figure 2.1 shows the resulting screen.

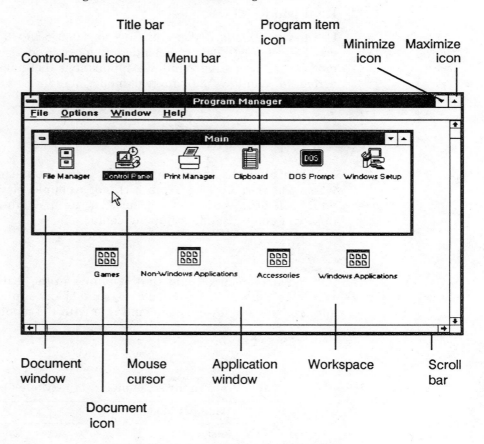

Figure 2.1 Starting the Windows Program Manager.

Note: Since Windows can be customized, your screen may not look exactly like this. You should, however, be able to identify the individual window elements described in these sections.

Elements of a Window

Now let's look closely at Figure 2.1. A single application program is executing: Program Manager. The program has its own single application window. On top of the application window are zero, one, or more document windows for the application. A *document window* is a window within an application window. It contains data that you can create or modify by using the application. In Figure 2.1, a single Main document window is displayed. Other applications can have multiple document windows. For example, Excel can have several spreadsheets open at a time, each in its own document window. Each open application has a single application window. Multiple applications can be opened at a time, each with its own application and document windows. Application and document windows overlap each other on the *desktop* (the screen background).

Note: If some of the document windows for Program Manager are not open, they will be shown as small icons in the Program Manager application window. Double-click the **Main** icon to open the Main document window.

The Control-Menu Box

The *Control-menu box* is a small box with a horizontal bar in the upper left of the window. When activated, the control-menu box opens a menu containing several basic commands that are common to any Windows window.

 To open the Control menu with a mouse, click on the Control-menu box.

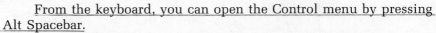 From the keyboard, you can open the Control menu by pressing Alt Spacebar.

Figure 2.2 shows the resulting Control menu that is displayed. Notice that it provides options for moving, sizing, minimizing, maximizing, restoring, and closing Windows. These options will be explained shortly.

Once the menu is displayed, you can either use the underlined letter or the mouse to activate any command of the menu. You can close the menu by pressing Esc or clicking anywhere in the window outside of the menu.

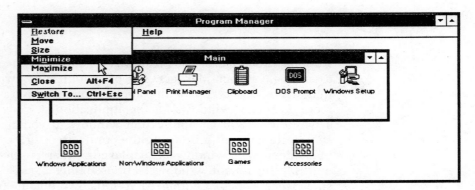

Figure 2.2 The Control menu.

The Title Bar

To the right of the Control-menu icon is a *title bar*. The title bar contains the name of the currently executing Windows application. If any files are open, this bar will also indicate the name of the open file. Figure 2.3 shows the Notepad open using the file `MEMO.TXT`.

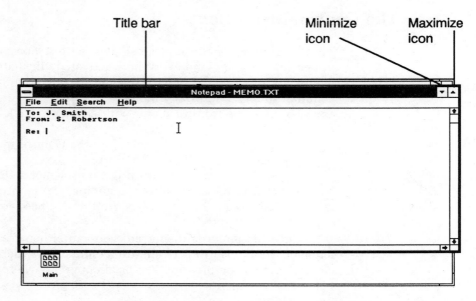

Figure 2.3 A title bar showing an open filename.

The Sizing Icons

In the upper right of the window are two small icons known as the *sizing icons*. The left one, the *Minimize* icon, reduces the window to an icon at the bottom of the screen (see the next section). The right icon, the *Maximize* icon, zooms the window to the full size of the screen. With a maximized window, the window borders are no longer visible. Once the window is maximized, the right icon changes to a *Restore* icon (see Figure 2.4). The Restore icon can be clicked to restore the window to its original size.

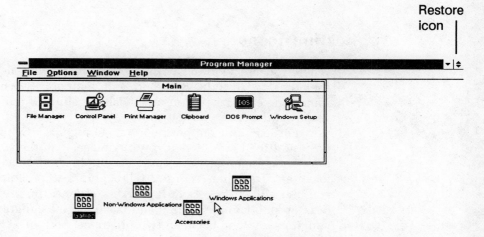

Restore
icon

Figure 2.4 The Restore icon.

The Menu Bar

Below the title bar of an application window is a line containing several menu options. This is the *menu bar*. For the Windows Program Manager, the menu bar includes the File, Options, Window, and Help options. Document windows have a Control menu but do not have a menu bar.

The Work Area

Below the menu bar is the *work area*, which is the area available to the user in the application program. For the Program Manager, the work area displays the document windows for various program groups that are currently open and displays small icons for the document windows that aren't. This is also called the *workspace* or *client* area.

Using Icons

Windows 3.0 supports three types of icons: application, document, and program item. We'll discuss each of these in turn.

Application Icons

When you are working with a program on your desktop, you may sometimes wish to leave the program temporarily while you work on something else. Later, you may wish to return to the document at the same point where you left it.

For example, suppose you create a graphic with a graphics program and then save it as a graphic image. You then switch to a desktop publishing program, import the graphic, and place it at the correct location. You then return to the graphics program, load another graphic, edit it, and save it. For the second time, you return to the desktop publishing program and paste the second graphic. In essence, you are switching between two programs, both of which require large amounts of memory space. With Windows, you can keep multiple applications in memory, limited only by the physical memory size.

You can also close a program's application window and store it either in memory or on disk, depending on the configuration. These are called *minimized* applications. Minimized applications are in the same state as you left them. The same document is open, the cursor is at the same place, and the document view is the same.

Windows indicates minimized applications by showing this program as an *application icon* at the bottom of the screen. Figure 2.5 shows three application icons at the bottom of the desktop.

At any given time you may have one, two, or more programs in the computer memory, each represented by a window on the screen. You can also have several additional programs set aside temporarily, each represented by icons at the bottom of the screen. Application icons can be dragged about on the desktop, but not into an open window. Normally, application icons are symbolic of the programs they represent.

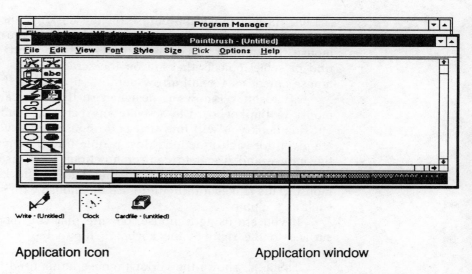

Figure 2.5 Typical Windows screen showing application icons.

Document Icons

Document icons represent document windows that are minimized.
Clicking a document icon opens the document window. For example,
the Program Manager has several document icons that represent each
program group. Four of these were shown in Figure 2.1. All of the
Program Manager's document icons are identical, and they can be
moved within the application window but not out of it.

Program Item Icons

Program item icons are exclusive to the Program Manager and represent programs that can be initiated from the Program Manager. Figure
2.1 showed six of these in the Main document window.

The Mouse

The *mouse* is a small device normally positioned next to the keyboard. It permits you to control the position of a pointer on the

screen. As you move the mouse on the desktop, the mouse pointer moves across the screen in the same direction you are moving the mouse. The mouse acts as an extension of the hand, enabling you to find or select objects that are on the screen. Figure 2.1 showed the mouse cursor as a small arrow pointing upward to the left.

Microsoft Windows is designed so that you can use either the mouse or the keyboard to activate any particular function. Throughout this book you will find that both mouse and keyboard directions are given for each function. Most people find it convenient to install the mouse and use it to control functions. The disadvantage, however, is that space is needed to the right of the keyboard for the mouse. This makes it difficult to use the mouse with some computers, such as a laptop.

If you are using a mouse, be sure that you have a clean, clear surface to the right of the keyboard (or to the left if you are left-handed).

Table 2.2 shows the various mouse terms used in this text. You use only the left button of the mouse when clicking or dragging. Windows makes no use of the right button.

Note: If you are left-handed and keep the mouse to the left of the keyboard, you may wish to use the right button of the mouse for all operations. You can use the Control Panel to switch the buttons (Chapter 17).

Table 2.2 Mouse Terms

Term	Meaning
Move	Move the mouse.
Drag	Press the left mouse button and hold it down while moving the mouse.
Point	Move the mouse so that the mouse pointer is over an object on the screen.
Click	Point to an object on the screen; then press and release the left mouse button.
Double-click	Point to an object on the screen; then quickly press and release the left mouse button twice.

The icon representing the mouse pointer can change shape depending on the current function of the mouse. Notice that the normal pointer is a small arrow pointing to the upper left. When you use the mouse to move the pointer to the right border of the window, the pointer changes to a two-headed arrow pointing to the left and right. If you touch the bottom border, the pointer changes to a two-headed arrow pointing up and down.

Using a Window

Now let's explore how to resize, move, enlarge, and close windows.

Note: Many of the shortcut keys available in previous versions are no longer active. Since most users have a mouse, this is a minor inconvenience. The remaining Control menu shortcut keys can be seen on the Control menu: Alt + F4 to close and Ctrl + Esc to change tasks.

Making a Window Active

Microsoft Windows permits you to load several programs into memory at once, but only one can be *active*, or in control of the processor, at a time. The number of programs permitted in memory depends on available memory and the size of the programs. Figure 2.6 shows the Calculator and Notepad windows. Although both programs are in the computer memory, only one can be active at a time. The active program is shown with a darker title bar. The other programs have a lighter title bar. In Figure 2.6, Notepad is the active application.

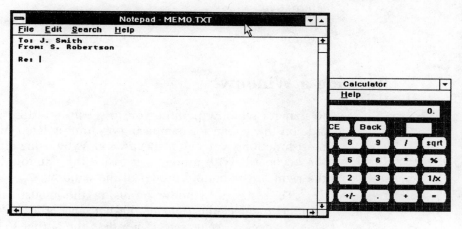

Figure 2.6 The Calculator and Notepad windows.

To change the active application or document window with the mouse, just click anywhere within the window that you wish to make active.

You can also change the active window from the keyboard. Even if you have a mouse, this is very important. If the active window is on top, you may not be able to see an inactive window that you wish to make active because it is under the foreground or active window. Assume, for example, that both Calculator and Notepad are loaded. If Notepad is the active window and completely covering the Calculator window, you would have to use the keyboard to switch windows. You can use Alt + Tab or Alt + Esc to change the active application window.

Alt + Tab is a *preview* mode. It rotates through all the programs (including the inactive programs represented as icons) in the order in which the programs were loaded. To properly preview, hold down the Alt key and press Tab until the desired title bar is highlighted. Then release both keys. The highlighted application will become active. For icons and hidden windows, you will see the title bar during the preview. Alt + Shift + Tab rotates through the available windows in the opposite order from which the programs were loaded. This works even for standard programs that are not Windows applications, as long as the Windows environment is active.

Alt + Esc is a more aggressive method of context switching: it immediately makes the next program active. Shift + Alt + Esc is the counterclockwise version of this command. This method is slower than Alt + Tab, since each application in the cycle is made active. If you have only two applications, however, this is often the better alternative.

For document windows, use Ctrl + F6 to change the document window.

Resizing a Window

Resizing a window permits you to set up multiple windows side by side on the screen for comparing or doing related functions. As with most functions, you can resize a window by using either the mouse or the keyboard. With either, you resize the window by moving either the right or the bottom border of the window.

 To resize a window by using the mouse, move the mouse pointer to select the right or the bottom border of the window (the icon changes on selection). Then drag the border to the new position to make the window either larger or smaller. As you drag the border, both the old and the new window sizes are shown. When you release the mouse button, the window will be shown in its new size. If you wish to change two borders at once, select the lower right-hand corner of the window. The cursor will now be a two-headed arrow pointing to the upper left and lower right. Drag the corner to create the new window.

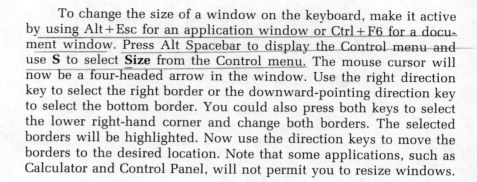

To change the size of a window on the keyboard, make it active by using Alt+Esc for an application window or Ctrl+F6 for a document window. Press Alt Spacebar to display the Control menu and use **S** to select **Size** from the Control menu. The mouse cursor will now be a four-headed arrow in the window. Use the right direction key to select the right border or the downward-pointing direction key to select the bottom border. You could also press both keys to select the lower right-hand corner and change both borders. The selected borders will be highlighted. Now use the direction keys to move the borders to the desired location. Note that some applications, such as Calculator and Control Panel, will not permit you to resize windows.

Moving a Window

You can move a window anywhere on the screen. This is useful if you need to move a window out of the way to see a window below it. Notice that as you move a window, Windows shows you both the old and the new location.

Windows can be moved with the mouse or the keyboard:

To move a window by using the mouse, select and drag the title bar.

To move a window from the keyboard, make the window active by using Alt+Esc for an application window or Ctrl+F6 for a document window. Press Alt Spacebar; then press **M** to select **Move** from the menu. Use the direction keys to move the window to the new location and then press Enter. You can use Esc to abort a move operation.

Enlarging a Window—Maximizing

Maximizing a window, or zooming it, changes the window so that it occupies the full screen. Maximizing a window minimizes distraction by temporarily eliminating other windows and icons on the screen. It also permits a larger display for viewing more of a worksheet or for word processing. The window borders are no longer visible.

Tip: In painting and spreadsheet programs, you will generally want to maximize windows to get the maximum working area. Chapter 18 describes how to maximize a program automatically on loading.

With the mouse, click the **Maximize** icon at the upper right of the window or double-click the title bar. The window will immediately zoom to the full screen.

From the keyboard, first make the window active. Then press Alt Spacebar and **X** for **Ma_ximize**.

Minimizing a Window

Minimizing, or shrinking, a window to an icon saves memory space in the computer and reduces clutter on the screen when you are using several programs. When minimized, the program is saved to a swap area of the disk or (if available) to memory.

To minimize a window with the mouse, click the **Minimize** icon in the upper right.

To minimize from the keyboard, first make the window active. Then press Alt Spacebar and press **N** for **Mi_nimize**.

Restoring a Window

The Restore function has two purposes. It can either restore a maximized window to its original state or restore an icon (minimized window) to an active window.

Restoring a Maximized Window to Its Former Size

To restore a maximized window to its former size by using the mouse, make the window active and click the **Restore** icon (double-arrow) in the upper right or double-click the title bar.

To restore a window from the keyboard, make the window active and press Alt Spacebar. Press **R** for **R_estore**.

Restoring an Icon to a Window

To restore an icon with the mouse, double-click the icon you wish to restore. Alternatively, click the icon you wish to restore once. This displays the Control menu for the icon. Then click **Restore**.

The keyboard is particularly useful if the icon is hidden by a window. To restore an application window, use Alt + Esc to rotate until the icon is highlighted. For a document window, use Ctrl + F6. Use Alt Spacebar to see the Control menu. Press **R** to restore.

Closing a Window

You can close a window with the mouse or the keyboard. In either case, if an application window is to be closed and any application program files are open and changed, Windows will query about each and ask if you wish the files saved. Figure 2.7 shows the Notepad window being closed.

To exit and close a window (application or document) with the mouse, double-click its Control-menu box. The window is now removed from the desktop.

To close a window from the keyboard, make the window active and use Alt+F4. Alternatively, use Alt Spacebar and press **C** for **Close**.

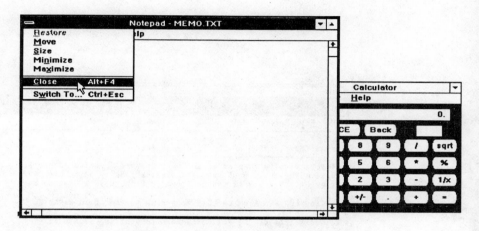

Figure 2.7 Closing a window.

Using the Scroll Bars

Some windows have *scroll bars* at the right or bottom that can be used to scroll the window over a larger area (see Figure 2.8). Typical applications with scroll bars include spreadsheet programs, word processors, painting programs, and desktop publishing programs.

The scroll bar includes arrows at the ends, with a small *scroll box* in the scroll bar. This box is also called a *thumb box* or *elevator*.

To scroll with a mouse, use the following techniques:

■ Drag the scroll box in the bar to position the window to a desired place in the document.

■ To move a line at a time, click an arrow at the end of the right scroll bar.

- To move a window at a time, click just below the top arrow, above the lower arrow, or just inside of the arrows on the lower scroll bar.

- To scroll continuously, click and hold down the mouse button on an arrow until the text you wish to see is visible.

To scroll from the keyboard, use the direction keys to scroll in the desired direction. PgDn and PgUp move a window up or down. Ctrl + PgUp and Ctrl + PgDn move one window at a time left or right. Ctrl + Home moves to the beginning of the document and Ctrl + End to the end.

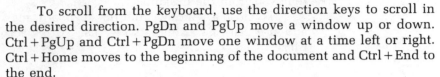

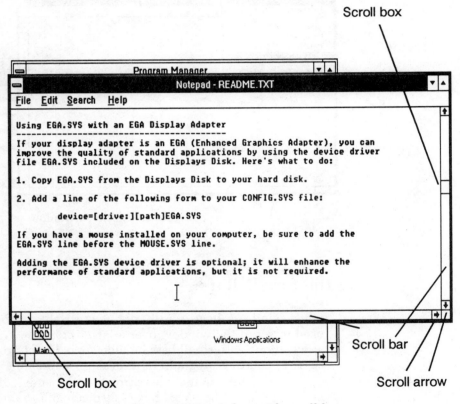

Figure 2.8 A window with scroll bars.

Terminating Microsoft Windows

You can exit Microsoft Windows by closing the Program Manager window.

 To exit and close Windows with the mouse, make the Program Manager window active and double-click its Control-menu box.

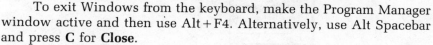 To exit Windows from the keyboard, make the Program Manager window active and then use Alt+F4. Alternatively, use Alt Spacebar and press **C** for **Close**.

In either case, Windows will prompt you to verify the closing. Click **OK** or press Enter. If any application program files are open and changed, Windows will query about each and ask if you wish them saved.

Tip: The quickest way to exit Windows is often without the mouse: press Alt+Tab to get the Program Manager; then press Alt+F4 and Enter.

Using Menus

You initiate action in a Windows application by using menus. The primary menu is displayed as a horizontal bar under the title bar, and the options can vary with the application. Secondary menus are displayed when a menu option is selected. A third level of menus, or a cascading menu, may appear in some applications.

The Control menu is common to all applications, but the options on this menu may vary. For many applications, the first options on the menu bar are File and Edit. Certain menu commands can be activated with the mouse or from a keyboard.

 To select a menu command using the mouse, click the desired menu option to see the menu. Pull down the mouse until the desired command is highlighted; then release the mouse button. To abort a menu, click the mouse outside of the menu.

 All Windows applications should provide keyboard access to the menu commands by defining unique characters in the menu bar options and menu commands. These are called *mnemonics* and are indicated with an underline. To activate a command from the keyboard, press Alt, press the letter for the desired menu option, and then press the letter for the command. For example, to activate a print command in most programs, press Alt **F P** (see Figure 2.9). To abort a command keystroke sequence, press Esc. If there is no character underlined in a menu option, press F10 to access the menu bar. Then use the arrow keys to select the option and press Enter.

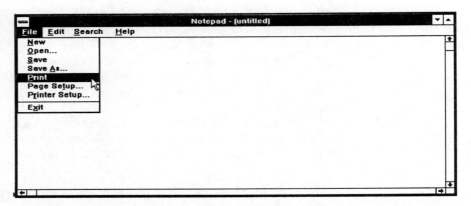

Figure 2.9 Activating a command from the keyboard.

Menu commands can be any of three types: direct, state setter, or extended (see Table 2.3). *Direct* commands initiate an action immediately, such as the **New** command of the File menu. *State setters* are often toggles, and the command is preceded by a check if the toggle is on. State setters can also be used to permit you to select from a list, such as a list of font attributes. In such cases, the menu list will be partitioned from the rest of the commands with a horizontal line (see Figure 2.10). *Extended* commands activate dialog boxes and are always followed by three periods. An example would be the **Printer Setup** command of the File menu (see Figure 2.11).

Table 2.3 Types of Menu Commands

Type	Description
Direct command	Initiates a command immediately
State setter	Alters a program state or selects one item from a list
Extended command	Displays a dialog box for additional information

Menu items may be enabled or disabled. *Enabled* menu items are shown in black and can be selected. *Disabled* menu items are grayed, and cannot be selected. Menu-item disabling in Windows is *dynamic*; that is, item disabling may change while the program is executing, based on the program state. For example, Figure 2.12

shows the Edit menu in Notepad. Since no text has been entered or selected yet, most editing commands are disabled.

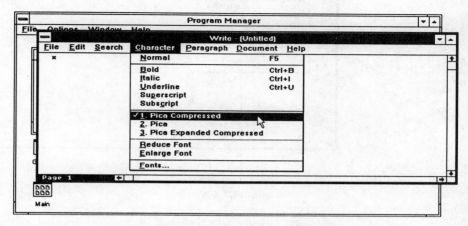

Figure 2.10 A state setter menu option.

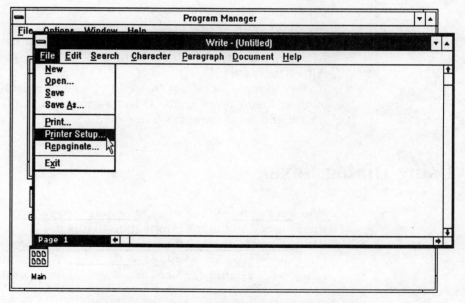

Figure 2.11 An extended menu command option.

Menu commands may have shortcuts, or *accelerator keys*. Accelerator keys permit you to initiate the command quickly from the key-

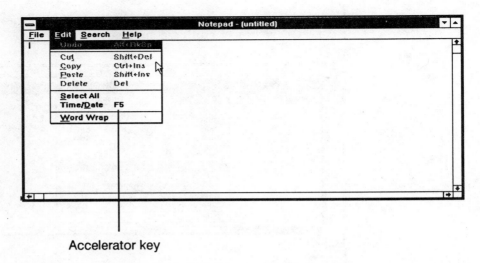

Accelerator key

Figure 2.12 Notepad's Edit menu showing disabled items.

board without using the mouse. If an accelerator key exists for a command, it is generally best to use the accelerator key instead of the mouse or normal keyboard commands. Notice that the Edit menu of Notepad shown in Figure 2.12 has six accelerator keys. You could, for example, initiate the **Undo** command by using the accelerator key Alt + Backspace.

A triangle located at the right of a menu selection indicates that another menu level exists. Selecting this command will display the next menu level, or a *cascading* menu.

Using Dialog Boxes

Windows applications use *dialog boxes* to request information from the user and to output information that is not part of the normal data file. A special type of dialog box, a *message box*, is used to display error messages and warnings to the user. When a menu item has an ellipsis (. . .) after the command, it initiates the display of a dialog box.

Like any other window, dialog boxes can be moved by dragging the title bar. Although dialog boxes have no menu bar, there is often a Control-menu box that permits the normal control options, such as closing, moving, and sizing.

Dialog boxes contain one or more special *controls*—objects having predefined behaviors that are consistent for all Windows applications. Dialog boxes can support any of five types of controls (see Table 2.4). Figures 2.13 and 2.14 show dialog boxes with examples of each type of control.

Table 2.4 Types of Dialog Box Controls

Control Type	Description
Command button	A command button that is labeled to define the action it controls, for example, the **OK** and **Cancel** buttons. The button is displayed as a rectangle. If the button has an ellipse, it activates another dialog box. If the label has an underlined letter, it can be activated from the keyboard by using Alt + *<letter>*, where *<letter>* is the underlined letter.
Option button	A round button permitting the user to select one item from a group. It is displayed as a small circle. You can select the option with a mouse click or with the direction keys and the Spacebar.
Check box	A toggle that can be turned on or off. It is displayed as a small square. You can toggle it with a mouse click or the Spacebar.
List box	A box showing the available choices. Use the mouse or direction keys to highlight a selection and double-click or press Enter, or click a command button. You can also press a letter to move the highlight to the first selection starting with the letter. For long lists, a vertical scroll bar at the right simplifies movement to the item. If the list supports multiple selections, use the direction keys and the Spacebar to select other items after the first. In small dialog boxes, a dropdown list box is used to conserve space. It's opened from a single-line list box with an arrow in a square box at the right. Click the arrow to open the box and select with a mouse. From the keyboard, use Alt + ↓ to open the box. Select the option with the direction keys and press Alt + ↓ again.
Text control	A box for entering text information. Also called a text control box. When selected, an insertion point appears in the box. Text can be entered or edited. Use Shift with a direction key to extend the selection if you need more space.

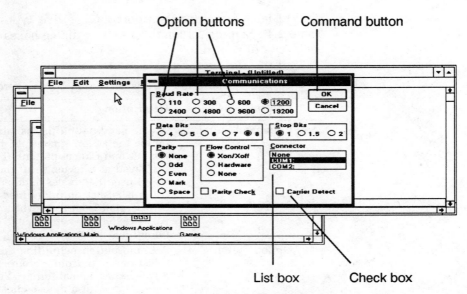

Figure 2.13 A dialog box showing four types of controls.

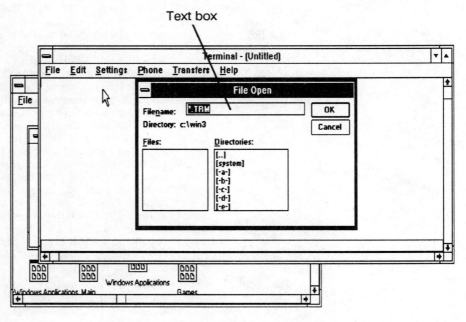

Figure 2.14 A dialog box with a text box.

You can use the mouse or a keyboard to move around in a dialog box and choose options. The display defaults to the first control of the dialog box.

With the mouse, click the desired option to select the option if it is not already selected.

From the keyboard, use Tab or Shift + Tab to select the desired option.

After you have chosen an option, use Table 2.4 to guide you in using the option.

Running Applications

Windows permits you to run multiple applications (or *tasks*) simultaneously. Programs can be started from the Program Manager or the File Manager, using either the mouse or the keyboard.

Starting Programs from the Program Manager

If the program has been installed as part of a group, you can start the program from its group document window.

To use the mouse to start an application from the Program Manager, double-click the group icon to open the document window for that group if it is not already open. Then double-click the icon for the application you wish to start.

From the keyboard, open the document window that contains the application you wish to start. Use the direction keys to highlight the icon for the desired application. Press Enter.

Another alternative with the Program Manager is to select the **Run** command from the File menu. Enter the program name with its full path and extension in the dialog box and press Enter or click **OK**.

A third method is also available: select the **DOS Prompt** icon from the Main document window. This returns you to the familiar DOS prompt, from which you can enter a command. To return to Windows, type exit.

Note: Some DOS programs should not be started from the Windows environment. These include CHKDSK (when the /F option is used), JOIN, and any others that modify the FAT table. Avoid similar utilities, such as Norton's SD. Exit Windows to use these.

Starting Programs from the File Manager

You can also start applications from the File Manager. Start the File Manager from the Program Manager by using the Main document window and selecting the **File Manager** icon.

Using the mouse, double-click the subdirectory of the application to open the directory window. Double-click the application filename. With some programs, you can start a program with a data file by double-clicking the icon for the data file.

From the keyboard, use the direction keys to select the directory and press Enter to open the directory window. Use the direction keys to select the application filename or data filename and press Enter.

Another alternative with the File Manager is to select the **Run** command from the File menu. Enter the program name with its full path and extension in the dialog box and press Enter or click **OK**.

Getting Help

Applications may vary in the type and level of help supported. Four types of help level are supported, and a Windows application developer may choose to use one or more of these levels:

■ A Help option is available on some menus. Selecting this option by clicking it or by using Alt H gives you access to a variety of help topics (see Table 2.5).

■ You can also use F1 to display a help dialog box (see Figure 2.15). From this you can choose the desired option. You can either use the index or the search option to find the desired information.

Table 2.5 Help Menu Options

Menu Item	Information Provided
Index	Alphabetical list of help topics for the current application
Keyboard	Key combinations available for an application
Commands	Command descriptions
Procedures	How-to steps for an application
Using Help	Help tutorial
About	Information on an application

■ Some dialog boxes support a help option button. Use this to get help for a specific dialog box.

■ Many dialog box options support a context-sensitive help. Highlight the option and then press F1 to get more information on that option.

Tip: If you need help frequently for an application, keep the Help window open and switch to it as necessary.

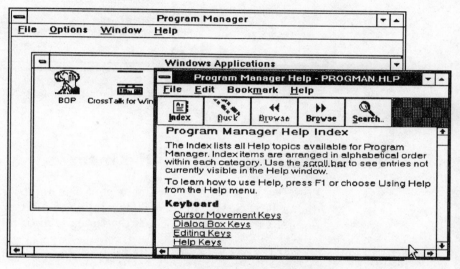

Figure 2.15 Getting help.

Finding Information by Searching

Press F1 to get the Help dialog box and select the **Search** icon. When the Search dialog box appears (see Figure 2.16), enter the desired topic and select **Search**. Topics found are displayed at the bottom of the dialog box. Select **Go To** to go to the topic.

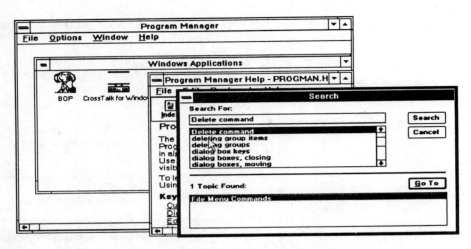

Figure 2.16 Searching for help.

Finding Information from the Index

Press F1 to get the Help dialog box. The index is displayed in the dialog box. Scroll and select the topic of interest when the mouse pointer turns to a hand. Click the **Index** icon to return to the index.

Switching Application Windows

Windows supports a type of multitasking in which multiple application windows can be open on the desktop, with the user able to switch between applications with a simple click of the mouse. Only one window can be active at a time; that is, only one window can own the keyboard at a time. The active window is shown with a dark title bar.

Other applications may run in the background without keyboard access, such as a communications program that is downloading a file while you continue with other work. The Clock application continues to run as an icon, with the Clock continuing to show the correct time.

You can switch applications with a mouse or the keyboard:

Using the mouse, the easiest method of switching applications is to click anywhere in the window you wish to make active.

From the keyboard, you can use Alt + Tab or Alt + Esc to switch applications (see "Making a Window Active").

Windows also includes a Task List application. If you wish, you can use it to switch applications. To initiate this application, you can use the mouse or the keyboard:

To activate the Task List with the mouse, double-click anywhere on the desktop or click **Switch To** on any Control menu.

To activate the Task List from the keyboard, press Ctrl + Esc or choose **Switch To** from any Control menu.

Once the Task List is displayed (see Figure 2.17), select from the list box the name of the application you wish to switch to and select **Switch To** (or press Enter). Alternatively, you can double-click the desired task.

The Task List application can also be used to arrange the desktop. Use the **Cascade**, **Tile**, or **Arrange Icons** buttons for rearranging windows or icons. Choose **End Task** to remove an application from memory.

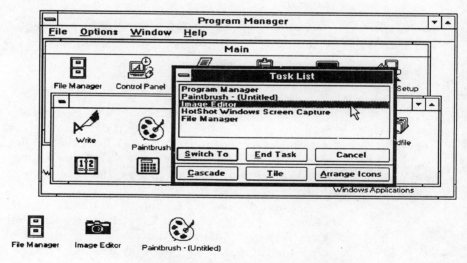

Figure 2.17 The Task List application.

Tip: If you need to see which programs you have loaded (including minimized programs), using Task List is an easy way to find out.

Using the Clipboard

Microsoft Windows contains a Clipboard that acts like a common area of memory for all programs. The Clipboard permits you to move and copy data within a program, between programs, or even to or from some non-Windows applications.

The Clipboard is usually modified by using the Edit menu of Windows applications or the Control menu with non-Windows applications. With Windows applications, the Edit menu will become very familiar, since it is almost identical in all applications. You will usually see **Copy**, **Cut**, and **Paste** commands. The **Cut** command deletes the data from the current location and places it in the Clipboard. The **Copy** command creates a copy of the current data and places it in the Clipboard. The **Paste** command copies data from the Clipboard to the current location in the application program. The following keyboard shortcuts are also available and are common to all application programs:

Command	*Shortcut*
Cut	Shift + Del
Copy	Ctrl + Ins
Paste	Shift + Ins

The Clipboard can store only a single item at a time. As you put something else in the Clipboard, it deletes what is already there. You can, however, do multiple pastes from the Clipboard, since pasting does not clear it. The only way to clear the Clipboard is to exit Windows. Once you close Windows, the contents of the Clipboard are lost.

You can view the Clipboard at any time by using the Clipboard program. Start the program by selecting the **Clipboard** icon of the Program Manager's Main window. As an experiment, start Windows and click the **Clipboard** icon from the Program Manager's Main document window to display the Clipboard. The Clipboard contents will be empty because nothing has been moved to it. Notice that the window can be resized like any other Windows application and that it contains a Control menu. Horizontal and vertical scroll bars permit you to scroll within the Clipboard contents. The Clipboard is capable of storing data in many formats.

Now load Notepad and try a simple paste. To load Notepad, first press Alt + Esc or Alt + Tab to get the Program Manager. Open the Accessories window. Select the **Notepad** icon and start it. Enter some text. Select some text by dragging the cursor over the characters until the text is highlighted. Select **Copy** from the Edit menu. Now press Alt + Esc and look at the Clipboard window. The copied text appears in a Clipboard (see Figure 2.18).

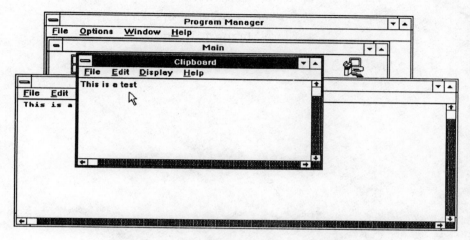

Figure 2.18 Opening the Clipboard application.

You can place a snapshot of the screen into the Clipboard by using PrtScrn. The screen can then be pasted from the Clipboard to another program, such as a word processor.

In the 386 enhanced mode, you can also use Alt + PrtScrn to capture the active window contents to the Clipboard.

Summary

This chapter introduced Windows and guided you through the basic techniques of starting Windows, using windows, and using the Control menu and Clipboard. If you haven't already started Windows, do so now and try some of the commands and features mentioned in this chapter. You should be able to

- Start Windows.
- Maximize a window to full-screen.
- Restore the window to its normal size.
- Minimize a program to an icon.
- Make a program inactive or active using several methods.

- Rotate between active or inactive programs.
- Move windows.
- Resize windows.
- Do basic Clipboard operations.
- Close Microsoft Windows.

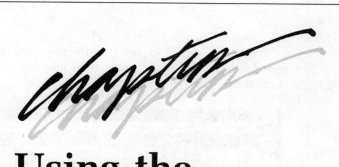

Using the Program Manager

Program Manager is the supervisor for using Windows. If you are using the default configuration, the Program Manager application is started each time you start Windows. From Program Manager, you can execute other programs simply by selecting icons from Program Manager's windows. This chapter will show you how to use Program Manager effectively.

Introduction to the Windows Program Manager

Program Manager is used to launch the application of other programs. Program Manager will start each time you start Windows unless you install Windows otherwise. If you start Windows with another application (such as Excel with the command **WIN EXCEL**), Program Manager still loads, but it is minimized as an icon at the bottom of the desktop.

Note: Windows can be customized to start in many ways. For example, you could start Windows with the File Manager or your own application instead of Program Manager. Chapter 18 describes how to do this.

To simplify management of program execution, Program Manager partitions programs into groups, with each group managed from its own document window. When you start Windows the first time, the Main document window is opened, with other groups represented as document icons at the bottom of the Program Manager application window (see Figure 3.1). All of the document icons are identical except for their labels. In the document window, application programs are represented by program item icons. You launch (start) programs from the program item icons.

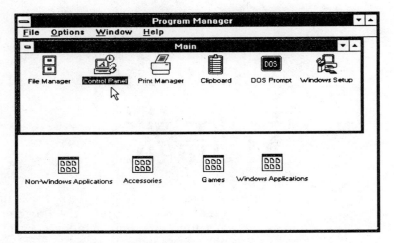

Figure 3.1 Starting the Program Manager.

Note: The grouping of programs has nothing to do with how your hard disk or your directories are organized. Programs in a group can be on different directories, and the same program may be on a disk once but launched from several document windows.

The document icons can be moved within the application window, but not outside of it to the desktop. If you try to move a document icon into a document window, it may appear to be in the document window. In reality, it is still on the underlying application window. If you make the document window active, the document icon will be hidden. The program item icons can be moved only within the document window.

You can define the groups you wish to use and the programs for each group. Program Manager is initially defined with five groups:

1. *Main* contains the Windows systems applications such as File Manager, Control Panel, Print Manager, Clipboard, DOS Prompt, and Setup.

2. *Accessories* contains a collection of Windows applications provided with Windows. The group contains a small word processor, a paint program, a communications program,

appointment calendar, clock, calculator, card file, and other tools.

3. *Games* includes two simple games for entertainment: Reversi and Solitaire.

4. *Windows Applications* contains the Windows applications that you install. Examples might include Excel, Crosstalk for Windows, and Arts and Letters.

5. *Non-Windows Applications* includes applications that you install that are not designed specifically for the Windows environment. Examples might be Ventura, Microsoft Word, and dBASE IV.

You can add or delete groups (including these), and add or delete programs within the groups. It is not necessary for a program to be in a group to start it from Windows. The Program Manager only makes it easier to start the program. You can also start a program from the DOS Prompt of the Main group or from the File Manager of the Main group.

Program Manager provides several conveniences over the DOS prompt:

■ You don't have to remember how to spell a program name or take a chance at misspelling it.

■ Programs can be started faster, with nothing more than a click of the mouse.

■ Programs are organized in groups the way you use them.

■ The user interface is easy to use. You don't need a DOS manual, and learning time is less.

■ You don't have to remember where the program is located.

To terminate a Windows session, you must always return to the Program Manager. You can then exit Windows by quitting the Program Manager.

Using Groups

Groups provide a method of organizing the programs on your desktop. The desktop would be very cluttered if all of your programs were represented on the desktop at one time. Program Manager permits you to organize the programs into logical group units the way you want to use them.

Tip: Organize your groups in a logical manner that meets your needs. For example, if you do desktop publishing, you may wish to put a paint program, word processor, and desktop publishing program in the same group. You can put the same program in multiple groups if you wish. This doesn't mean that multiple copies of the program are on the disk; it means only that the program can be launched from several groups. You can also mix Windows and non-Windows applications in a group. Keep a maximum of about twelve programs in a group so that you can see all the program item icons when the window is opened. If several users share the system, you might want to set up special groups for each user.

Rearranging Group Windows

If several group windows are open, it becomes difficult to see title bars and icons when you try to shuffle the windows on the desktop. Program Manager provides two commands to rearrange group windows: **Cascade** and **Tile**.

If you select **Cascade** from the Window menu, the group windows are cascaded and overlapped, with all title bars showing (see Figure 3.2). If you select **Tile**, the windows are placed side by side on the desktop as tiles (see Figure 3.3). All windows are visible, but some program item icons may not be visible. The windows with missing icons have scroll bars so that you can scroll to the hidden icons.

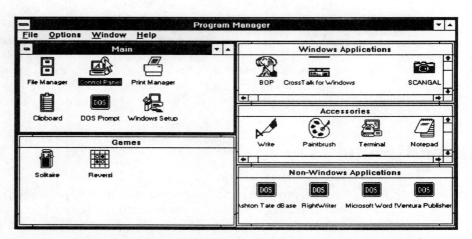

Figure 3.2 Cascaded windows.

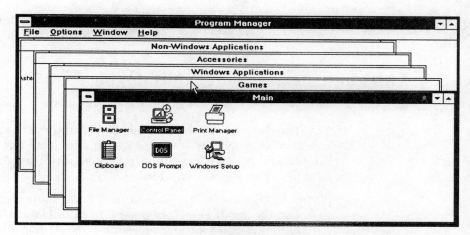

Figure 3.3 Tiled windows.

Notice that each of these commands has an accelerator key.
Shift + F5 will cascade; Shift + F4 will tile.

Using Group Windows

Group windows behave like document windows. Learning how to use
group windows will give you experience for using document windows in other applications. The following sections will show you
how to open and close windows, size and move them, rearrange
icons, and modify groups.

Opening Group Windows

 To open a group window with a mouse, double-click the group's
icon.

 To open a group window from the keyboard, press Ctrl + Tab or
Ctrl + F6 until the desired icon is highlighted; then press Enter.

Closing Group Windows

 To close a group window with a mouse, click its **Minimize** icon or
double-click the Control-menu box.

To close from the keyboard, press Alt + Hyphen(-) to open the group window's Control menu. Select **Minimize**.

Maximizing, Resizing, and Moving Group Windows

You can maximize, resize, and move group windows just as you would other windows (Chapter 2). To maximize with a mouse, click the Maximize box. Drag the title bar to move the window. Drag borders to resize a group window.

Note: Making a window smaller may make some icons no longer visible. Use the scroll bar, if necessary, to find icons in a small window. Alternatively, you can rearrange the icons if the window is not too small (see the next section).

Rearranging Icons

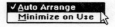 If you resize a window to make it smaller, some icons (either program item or document icons) may no longer be visible. If **Auto Arrange** on the Options menu is toggled on, the window will automatically be arranged. In this case, Windows tries to put everything in the new windows. If **Auto Arrange** is not toggled on (checked), rearrange by selecting **Arrange Icons** from the Window menu. You can also arrange icons by dragging them with a mouse.

You can also move a document icon by opening its Control menu (click the Control-menu box) or by using Alt + Hyphen(-) and selecting the **Move** command.

Adding Groups

 To add a new group to the Program Manager, select **New** from the File menu. The dialog box of Figure 3.4 will be displayed. Select the **Program Group** option and **OK**. The Program Group Properties dialog box will be displayed (see Figure 3.5). Type the name of the new group as a description. Keep the name short, since it will be attached to the icon as well as appear in the document window's title bar. You do not need to enter a filename. Click **OK** or press Enter.

Figure 3.4 Starting to add a new group.

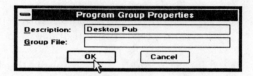

Figure 3.5 Defining the new group.

Adding Programs to a Group

After creating a group, you will probably want to add programs to the group. Programs can be added from the Program Manager, the File Manager, or the Setup program of the Main window.

To add a program to a group from Program Manager, first open the group window to which you wish to add the application. Select **New** from the File menu. When the dialog box is displayed, select **Program Item** and **OK** (see Figure 3.6). The Program Item Properties dialog box will be displayed. Enter an optional description. The description is used for the program item icon. In the command line, enter the program start-up line with the path, program name, extension, and start-up parameters (see Figure 3.7). Notice that you can browse executable files on the current directory or select another icon for the program from this dialog box. Click **OK**.

Figure 3.6 Starting to add a program to a group.

Figure 3.7 Adding a program.

Tip: Keep the description short so that it fits on the document window and uses minimal space.

Tip: You don't need to enter the full pathname if the program is in the current directory or if the path is specified in AUTOEXEC.BAT. You can also specify the directory of the data file if the program is in the AUTOEXEC.BAT path. If the WIN.INI file is set correctly (Chapter 18), you can start a program with a data file from a program item icon. For example, specifying `D:\WP\LETTER1.DOC` as the command line for a group item would permit you to start Microsoft Word with `LETTER1.DOC` from the program item icon. The WIN.INI file tells Windows that all `DOC` files require Microsoft Windows. Be sure to enter the file extension.

The program item icon defaults to one chosen by Windows. You can change this by selecting the **Change Icon** button of the Program Item Properties dialog box and selecting a different icon (see Figure 3.8). Select **OK** to exit the dialog boxes. Figure 3.9 shows the new group with the new program.

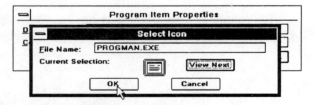

Figure 3.8 Changing the icon.

To add a program to a group from the File Manager, first open the File Manager from the Main group (Chapter 4). Then position the group window and File Manager on the desktop together (see Figure 3.10). Be sure that the document window with the file you wish to add to the group is open. Drag the program icon from the File Manager's document window to the group window. The group now contains a program item icon for the new file (see Figure 3.11).

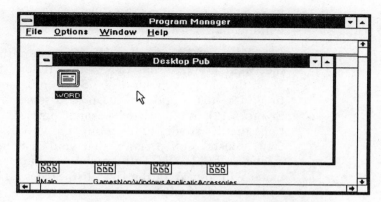

Figure 3.9 The group with a new program.

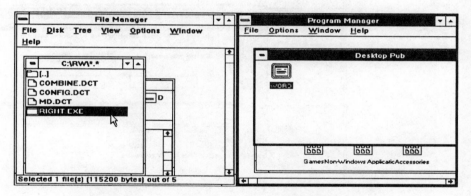

Figure 3.10 Starting to add a program from File Manager.

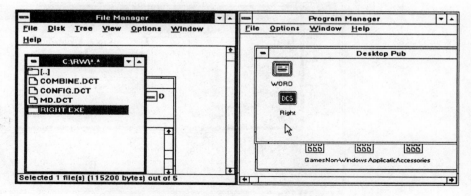

Figure 3.11 The result after adding the program.

Tip: Tile the windows first by using Ctrl + Esc to get the Task List window and select **Tile**.

You can also add programs to a group from the Setup program of the Main group. From the Main window, select **Windows Setup**. From the Options menu of the Setup program, select **Setup Applications**. Use the dropdown list box to select the drives to search (see Figure 3.12). Windows will search the specified drives for applications that it can add to the group and will display the list (see Figure 3.13). Select each program that you wish to add (click or use the arrows and Spacebar) and then click **Add** or press Enter. The program name will appear in the right list. Select all the programs you wish and then select **OK**.

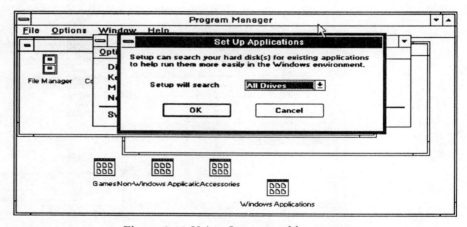

Figure 3.12 Using Setup to add a program.

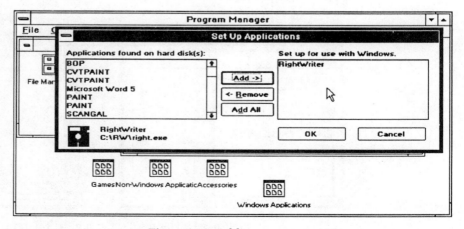

Figure 3.13 Adding a program.

Note: Using Setup will add the program only to the Windows Application group or to the Non-Windows application group, as appropriate.

Deleting Programs from a Group

To delete a program from a group, first open the group window. Select the item to delete by using the direction keys or by clicking. Select **Delete** from the File menu. A Delete dialog box will be displayed to confirm the deletion. Select **Yes** or press Enter.

Note: Deleting a program from a group does not delete the program from the disk.

Deleting Groups

To delete a group with all of its program items, first select the group icon. Then select **Delete** from the File menu. A Delete dialog box will be displayed to confirm the deletion. Select **Yes** or press Enter.

Arranging Program Item Icons

To rearrange program item icons in a group window, select the window and then select **Arrange Icons** from the Window menu. You can also drag program item icons to position them where you want them.

Moving Program Items

To move a program from one group to another, open both group windows. Use the mouse to drag the program item icon from its current group to the new group. If you don't have a mouse, use the direction keys to select the program item icon and then select **Move** from the File menu. Select the name of the destination group and choose **OK**.

Copying Program Items to Another Group

You can also copy a program item to another group. To copy, first open both group windows. Hold down the Ctrl key and drag the icon from its current group to the new group. The program item will then be in both groups.

Editing Program Items

To change the properties of a program item, first select the program item. Then select **Properties** from the File menu. Make the desired changes and select **OK**.

Starting Applications

The primary purpose of the Program Manager is to initiate the execution of programs (see "Running Applications," Chapter 2). You can launch an application from the Program Manager in any of two ways.

Starting an Application from its Group

To start an application from a group window, double-click the program item icon. From the keyboard, you can start an application by selecting it with the direction keys and pressing Enter.

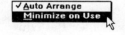

If you wish the Program Manager minimized to an icon when the program starts, select **Minimize on Use** from the Options menu before starting the program.

Starting an Application from the File Menu

To start an application from the File menu, select **Run** on the menu and enter the program name. Use this method if the program is not part of any group.

Exploring the Program Manager

As a starting tutorial, try starting the Clock program from Program Manager. Open the Accessories group window and then double-click **Clock** or select it with the direction keys and press Enter. The application window will open and display a clock (see Figure 3.14).

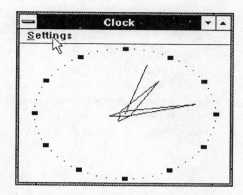

Figure 3.14 Displaying the clock.

If you prefer a digital display, click **Settings** on the menu bar and select **Digital** (or use Alt S D). This will change Clock to a digital display. Selecting **Analog** from the menu will return it to an analog display.

If you like to keep a clock handy while you work, click the **Minimize** box in the upper right corner. This will minimize Clock to an icon on the screen, but it will still display the correct time.

Tip: Chapter 18 describes how to start Clock (or any application) automatically with Windows, keeping Clock minimized as an icon.

Quitting the Program Manager

Quitting Program Manager will terminate Windows and remove the environment from memory. To quit Program Manager, use any of these methods:

- Select **Exit Windows** from the File menu.
- Double-click Program Manager's Control-menu box.
- Select **Close** from the Control menu.
- Press Alt + F4.
- Press Alt Spacebar C.

In all cases you will get a prompt asking if you wish to exit. Press Enter or click **OK**. The confirmation box also has a check box for saving changes. Select this if you wish to save the desktop. If any files are opened, you will be prompted with a query for saving each.

Summary

Program Manager is the main or supervisory program when you are using Windows. If no program is specified, Program Manager is loaded and started when Windows is initiated; that is, Program Manager is the default application. From Program Manager, you can start, or *launch,* other applications. Closing Program Manager terminates Windows and removes the environment from memory.

Using the File Manager

File Manager is a Windows application that supports file and disk management. Many of its operations are similar to the Executive program of Windows 2. However, File Manager now has an improved user interface with icons and includes a directory tree window. Here are a few of the things you can do with File Manager:

- View the directory tree or files in one or more directories.
- Initiate program execution.
- Name and rename files and directories.
- Create and delete directories.
- Search for files and directories.
- Move and copy files and directories.
- Print ASCII files.
- Modify file attributes.
- Format diskettes.
- Make system diskettes.
- Copy diskettes.
- Label diskettes.

File Manager is such a useful utility that you may wish to start Windows with it and terminate Windows from it (see Chapter 18). This chapter will describe how to use File Manager.

Introduction to the Windows File Manager

File Manager lets you work with files in the way they are organized on the disk. A typical disk may have thousands of files. To properly manage these files, MS-DOS (your operating system) permits you to organize a disk into directories. The files are stored in the directories. For example, all of the files associated with your word processor program might be stored in a single directory, perhaps called MW (if you are using Microsoft Word) or WP (for WordPerfect). If you are working on a project, you might have all of the files for that project in a single directory. The directories on the disk are arranged in a hierarchical structure, much like an inverted tree.

The topmost directory for a particular drive is called the *root directory* for that drive. You can assign your own names to other directories. File Manager permits you to view the directory tree structure for any drive and also view the files in any directory.

In working with File Manager, you are working with two types of document windows (see Figure 4.1). The first is the *Directory Tree window*, which shows the directories for the selected drive. You can also display one or more *directory windows*, each showing the files in a specified directory.

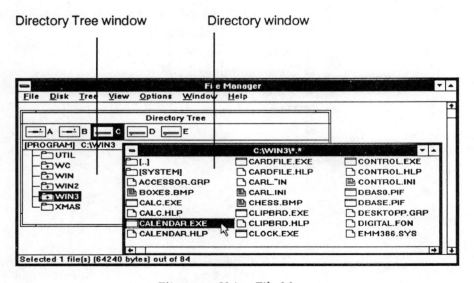

Figure 4.1 Using File Manager.

In Figure 4.1, notice the small icons that are used to represent the files and directories. File Manager uses the following icons in the document windows:

Icon	*Meaning*
🗁	Directory entry.
🗆	Program and batch files. You can use these to start applications.
🗎	Data files. Often you can start an application from these.
🗋	Other file types.

Starting File Manager

Like any other application, File Manager can be started from either the mouse or the keyboard:

To start with the mouse, double-click the **File Manager** icon on Program Manager's Main document window.

To start from the keyboard, use the direction keys to select the **File Manager** icon on Program Manager's Main document window and press Enter.

File Manager will start and display the Directory Tree for the current drive. In Figure 4.2, one document window is open—the Directory Tree window. Notice several features of the Directory Tree window. At the top, under the title bar, is an icon for each disk drive. The currently selected drive is highlighted. On the next line is the volume label for the current disk (**PROGRAM**), followed by the current path. Under this is a directory tree with the directories in alphabetical order. The current directory (the root) is highlighted. Commands on the File Manager's menu bar affect this directory. The directories are represented by directory icons beneath the root directory, much like an inverted tree. Only the first subdirectory level is shown. If a directory contains subdirectories, the directory icon will contain a plus (+) sign. If the window can't show all the directories, a vertical scroll bar will be at the right of the window. You can use this scroll bar to view the rest of the directory tree.

Disk Drive icon

Volume label   Directory path

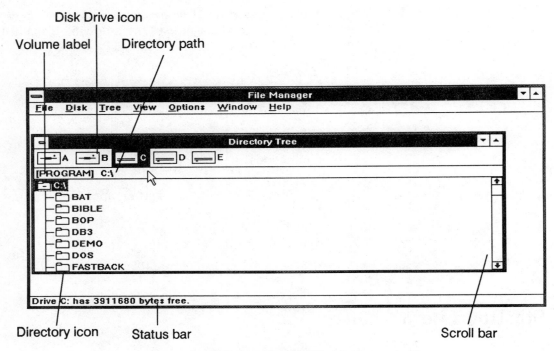

Directory icon   Status bar   Scroll bar

Figure 4.2 The File Manager windows.

The window behaves like a normal document window. It can be moved, resized, or minimized. It cannot be closed.

Note: If you prefer starting Windows from File Manager instead of from Program Manager, you can do so by editing the SYSTEM.INI file (Chapter 18).

Note: Sometimes a command may not update the display to reflect a change. If you need to update the display, choose **Refresh** from the Window menu or press F5.

Managing the Directory Tree

From the Directory Tree window, you can create, edit, move, and delete directories, as well as select directories for file viewing. The next sections will show you how to do these tasks. They will also explain how to change disk drives and directories and control the level of the directory display.

Changing Disk Drives

The selected drive determines from where the directory tree is displayed. It also determines the drive on which File Manager's commands will act. Changing the drive changes the directory tree. The current drive is highlighted.

To change the drive with a mouse, click the icon for the drive you wish to select.

To change the drive with the keyboard, tab to the disk-drive icon area and use the direction keys to select the desired drive. Press Enter. Alternatively, you can hold down the Ctrl key and press the letter for the desired drive.

Changing Directories

The selected directory determines from which directory the files will be displayed if a directory window is opened. It also determines the directory on which File Manager's commands will act. Changing the drive changes the directory tree. The current directory is highlighted. Only one Directory Tree window can be open at a time.

To change the directory with the mouse, click the directory to which you want to change.

From the keyboard, use the Up and Down arrows to select the desired directory. The Home key selects the root directory. You can also press any letter to go to the first directory containing that letter, if one exists.

Displaying Files on a Directory

To view files and subdirectories on a directory, you must open its directory window. You can have open any number of directory windows, each displaying the contents of a directory.

To use the mouse for displaying the files and subdirectories on a directory, double-click the directory icon in the Directory Tree window or a directory window. This will open a new directory window with the files and directories displayed in alphabetical order, as in Figure 4.1.

From the keyboard, you can open a directory window by using the direction keys to highlight the directory and then pressing Enter.

Controlling the Display Level

The default for the directory display shows the root directory and the first level. If any of the directories have subdirectories, their icons will be shown with a small plus (+) sign.

Expanding the Levels of the Display

You can expand a single directory to display all subdirectories or only the next level, or you can choose to expand the entire tree for all directories.

To expand one level, click the plus sign in the icon or select the directory and enter a plus sign from the keyboard. The sign in the directory changes to a minus (−) (see Figure 4.3).

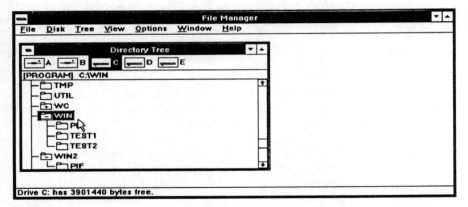

Figure 4.3 Expanding one level of the display.

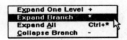

To expand a single directory for all levels, select the directory and then select **Expand Branch** from the Tree menu. From the keyboard you can use an asterisk (*) to expand a branch.

To expand the entire tree for all branches, select **Expand All** from the Tree menu or enter Ctrl + Asterisk (*).

Collapsing the Levels of the Display

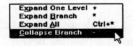

The directories can be collapsed by branch only. To collapse a branch, click the minus sign in the directory icon or choose the icon and press minus (−). You can also collapse a branch by selecting **Collapse Branch** from the Tree menu. When File Manager is started, all directories except the root are collapsed.

Creating and Deleting Directories

You can create and delete directories from File Manager. The result is the same as if you had used the MS-DOS commands MD (make directory) and RD (remove directory).

To create a new directory, select the directory in which you wish to place the new directory (the parent) and then select **Create Directory** from the File menu. In the dialog box (see Figure 4.4), enter the name of the new directory. Click **OK** or press Enter. Directory names can have from one to eight characters, and can also have an extension if you wish. After creating the new directory, you can add files to it.

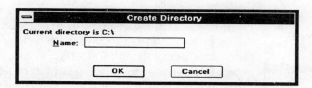

Figure 4.4 Creating a new directory.

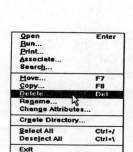

To delete a directory, select the directory to delete and then select **Delete** from the File menu. Unlike the RD command in MS-DOS, this will remove the directory and all files and subdirectories under it. You can use the Del key as a shortcut.

Note: Use caution in deleting. When deleting a directory with files, the directory and files are physically removed from the disk.

Tip: You can delete multiple directories with a single command. You can't do it from the Directory Tree window, but you can from a directory window. First, from the parent directory, open a directory window containing the directories to delete. In the new directory window, select the subdirectories to delete (see "Selecting Files" in this chapter). Then choose **Delete** from the File menu. Use caution because this action will delete the directories and the files in them.

Moving and Copying Directories

If you have a mouse, moving or copying a directory with all of its files involves nothing more than dragging an icon. To move or copy a directory with all of its files from one parent directory to another, first open the parent directory window for the directory to move. In the directory window, click to select the icon for the directory that is to be moved or copied. To move the directory, hold down the Alt key and drag the directory icon to the new location. You can drag it to a new parent in the Directory Tree window, to a disk icon, or to another directory window. To copy a directory, hold down the Ctrl key and move the icon.

To use the keyboard to move or copy a directory with all of its files from one directory to another, first open the parent directory window for the directory that is to be moved or copied. When the directory window is displayed, select the icon for the directory to move by using the direction keys. Select **Move** or **Copy** from the File menu. Enter the destination directory and select **Move** or **Copy** on the dialog box. This will move or copy the directory and all of its files to the destination directory. As a shortcut, you can use F7 for a move and F8 for a copy.

For example, in Figure 4.1 the directory window shows a SYS-TEM subdirectory in the WIN3 directory. To copy this subdirectory to a C:\WC directory, hold down the Ctrl key, select the **SYSTEM** icon, and drag the icon to the **WC** icon in the Directory Tree window. This creates a new SYSTEM subdirectory in WC with all of the SYSTEM files in it. Alternatively, you can select the **SYSTEM** icon, choose **Copy** from the File menu, and then enter the C:\WC directory name into the dialog box.

Tip: Dragging without pressing any key will initiate a Copy if the destination is a different drive and a Move if they are on the same drive. It's a shortcut, but it can be confusing.

Tip: Multiple directories can be moved in one operation. Select them the same as you would when selecting multiple files (see "Selecting Files").

Locating Directories

You can search a particular drive for a directory. Select the drive and, if desired, the directory to search. Choose **Search** from the File menu. In the dialog box that is displayed, enter the directory name (see Figure 4.5). You can use wildcard characters, such as asterisks or question marks, in the specification. Toggle the **Search Entire Disk** on or off, as appropriate and select **OK**. The result is displayed in a Search Results box (see Figure 4.6).

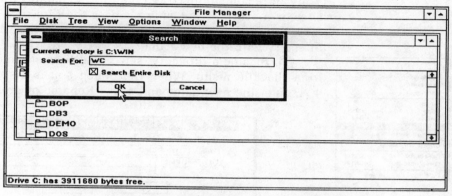

Figure 4.5 Initiating a directory search.

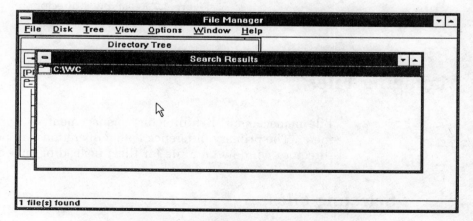

Figure 4.6 Displaying the search results.

Note: The Search Results window is not a directory window. You cannot move or copy files into the window. You can, however, select within the Search Results window and move, copy, or print from it by using the commands on the File menu.

Tip: If you have large disks with many directories and can't remember how you spelled a directory, the Search Results window is one way to find a list of possibilities.

Renaming Directories

You can rename a directory on a disk. Renaming a directory does not alter or move files but only changes the directory entry in the disk directory. The directory name changes, and the files will be in the directory with the new name.

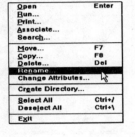

To rename a directory, select the directory and choose **Rename** from the File menu. When the dialog box is displayed (see Figure 4.7), enter the new name and select **Rename** or press Enter.

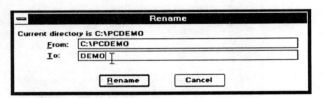

Figure 4.7 Renaming a directory.

Managing Files

File management, like directory management, is done from the File menu. The primary difference is that operations are performed from a directory window on a file (or files) instead of on a directory.

Selecting Files

To perform a file operation from a directory window, select the files on which to perform an action and then select the action. You can select a single file, a range of files, or files that are not adjacent in a file list. You can also select multiple groups of files. Making multiple file selections is called *extending* a selection.

To select any file, first open the directory window containing the file by double-clicking the directory icon or using the direction keys to highlight the directory and pressing Enter. Directory windows can be opened from the Directory Tree window or other directory windows. Then click or use the direction keys to highlight the file you wish to select.

To select a range of files, open the directory window for the file and use one of the following techniques:

With the mouse, click the first file in the range to highlight it. Hold down the Shift key and click the last file in the range. The entire range will be highlighted.

From the keyboard, use the direction keys to highlight the first file in the range. Hold down the Shift key and extend the range with the direction keys.

To select files that are not in sequence, open the directory window and use the Ctrl key:

With the mouse, click the first filename; then hold down the Ctrl key and click each additional filename.

From the keyboard, select the first file. Press Shift + F8, and the selection cursor will begin to blink. Use the direction keys to move the cursor to each file and press the Spacebar. When the selection is complete, press Shift + F8 again.

Note: All the files selected must be from the same directory window.

To select multiple groups, use both the Shift and the Ctrl keys:

With the mouse, click the first file of the first group. Hold down the Shift key and click the last file of the group. The first group is now highlighted. Hold down the Ctrl key and click the first file of the next group. Hold down the Shift + Ctrl keys and click the last file of the second group. Continue with as many groups as desired.

From the keyboard, select the first group by holding down the Shift key as you move the highlight over the group. Then press Shift + F8. Use the direction keys to select the first item of the second group. Press the Spacebar. Hold down the Shift key and use the direction keys to select all of the second group. Press Shift + F8 when finished.

To select all files in a directory, choose **Select All** from the File directory or enter Ctrl + /.

Open	Enter
Run...	
Print...	
Associate...	
Search...	
Move...	F7
Copy...	F8
Delete...	Del
Rename...	
Change Attributes...	
Create Directory...	
Select All	Ctrl+/
Deselect All	Ctrl+\
Exit	

To cancel a selection, you can use any of three methods:

1. Make another selection. If you reselect, it will cancel the first.
2. Choose **Deselect All** from the File menu or press Ctrl + \. This will clear all selections.
3. Deselect individual filenames from an extended list by holding down the Ctrl key and clicking the individual file. From the keyboard, you can do this by pressing Shift + F8 and using the direction keys to move the cursor to the file to deselect. Press the Spacebar, then Shift + F8 again.

Tip: To select a group of files with related filenames (such as all .BAK files), use the **Search** command of the File menu (see "Locating Directories" or "Locating Files"). You can then initiate a move, copy, or delete command from the Search results.

Renaming Files

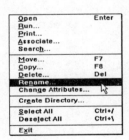

To rename files, first select the files to rename. Choose **Rename** from the File menu (see "Renaming Directories"). Enter the new filename and select **Rename**.

Tip: You can rename multiple files with a single command by using wildcard characters (see Figure 4.8). Use caution, however. The results may not be what you expect. For example, in Figure 4.8 if the **To:** box contained `WIN?.DOC`, you would have a problem. However, `WIN??.DOC` would work.

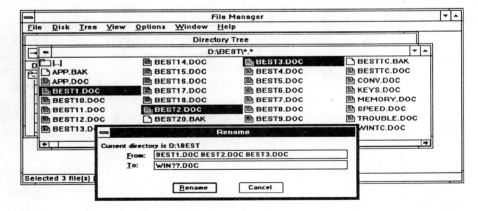

Figure 4.8 Renaming a file.

Locating Files

Locating files is exactly like locating directories (see "Locating Directories"). Select the directory to scan and then choose **Search** from the File menu. Enter the filename for which to search. You can use wildcard characters such as the asterisk (*) and question mark (?). The Search Results box will return all files matching the template. You can then select files from this box for moving, copying, or deleting.

Moving and Copying Files

If you have a mouse, moving or copying a file or group of files involves nothing more than dragging an icon. To move or copy a file or files from one directory to another, first open the directory window containing the files to move. In the directory window, select the files to move. To move the files, hold down the Alt key and drag any of the icons in the file group to the new location. You can drag the icon to a new directory in the Directory Tree window, to a disk icon, or to another directory window. To copy a file or file group, hold down the Ctrl key and move the file icons.

To use the keyboard to move or copy a file or group of files from one directory to another, first open the directory window for the files to move or copy. Select the files. Choose **Move** or **Copy** from the File menu. Enter the destination directory and select **Move** or **Copy** on the dialog box (see Figure 4.9). This will move or copy the files to the destination directory. As a shortcut, you can use F7 for a move and F8 for a copy.

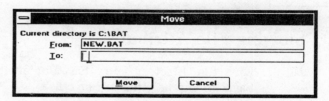

Figure 4.9 Initiating a move from the keyboard.

Tip: Dragging without pressing any key will initiate a copy if the destination is a different drive and a move if the files are on the same drive. It's a shortcut, but it can be confusing.

If you are moving or copying a group of files with related names, use the **Search** command of the File menu to locate all matching files. These are placed in a Search Results box. You can then initiate a move or copy from this box just as you would from a directory window; that is, you can drag the icons.

Deleting Files

To delete files, select the file or files to be deleted and choose **Delete** from the File menu. You can use the Del key as a shortcut.

If you are deleting a group of files with related names, use the **Search** command of the File menu to locate all matching files. These are placed in a Search Results box. You can then press the Del key to delete the files from the directory.

Printing Files

You can print text files directly from File Manager. Select the file to print and choose **Print** from the File menu. This technique should be used only with text files, such as the TXT files used with Notepad. You should not try to print files containing alphanumeric characters or control codes. In most cases, you should do your printing from the print option in the application program.

Changing File Attributes

Each file directory entry has four attribute bits associated with it. Each bit can be either on or off.

Bit	Description
R	*Read only.* If on, the file cannot be deleted or edited.
A	*Archive.* If on, the file has not been backed up since it was last edited.

H   *Hidden.* The file will not show up on an MS-DOS DIR listing.

S   *System.* One of the MS-DOS system files. Does not show up on an MS-DOS DIR listing.

In the default Windows display, the file attributes are not shown, and hidden or system files are not displayed in a directory window. You can see the current attributes for the files in a directory window by choosing **File Details** from the View menu. If you wish to see the hidden or system files, choose **Include** from the View menu and toggle on **Show Hidden/System Files**.

You can alter the file attributes for any file or group of files. To change a file's attribute, select the file and then choose **Change Attributes** from the File menu. A Change Attributes dialog box is displayed (see Figure 4.10). Toggle the desired attributes on or off, and then select **OK** or press Enter.

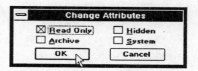

Figure 4.10 Changing file attributes.

Tip: To protect against viruses, it's a good idea to set the attributes of COMMAND.COM and the DOS system files to read-only. In this way, they can't be altered by any other program or user unless the bit is first turned off again.

Starting Applications from File Manager

You can start both Windows and non-Windows applications from File Manager.

To start an application from File Manager with the mouse, display the application's filename in a directory window and double-click the name.

To start an application from File Manager with the keyboard, select the filename in a directory window and press Enter.

You can also start an application by selecting the filename and choosing **Open** from the File menu. Another method is to choose **Run** from the File menu. When the dialog box is displayed, enter the full pathname of the file to execute. Programs can be started only from files with the following extensions: .COM, .EXE, .BAT, or PIF.

You can also start many programs with a document file (including non-Windows programs) by double-clicking or opening the respective data file. Alternatively, you can drag the data file icon to the program name icon or use the **Run** command from the File menu and enter the data filename in the Run dialog box.

Tip: It's easier to start programs from Program Manager. If you use a program often, add it to a Program Manager group by opening a Program Manager's document window for the group. Drag the filename to the group window. This will work only for executable files (.EXE, .COM, .BAT, and .PIF).

Windows comes with built-in links for starting many Windows applications from data files. As you install other Windows programs, in most cases the installation routine will add for you the linkages for that program (Chapter 18). For non-Windows programs, however, you must create your own links. With File Manager, you can create your own program/data file links so that you can start, say, your favorite word processor from a data file.

To create a program/data file linkage, first select a data file in a directory window for the program. Then choose **Associate** from the File menu (see Figure 4.11). Enter the name of the executable program or its batch file. Enter the full pathname if it is not in the current path. Click **OK** or press Enter. In Figure 4.11, all .DOC files are associated with the MW.BAT file, which starts Microsoft Word.

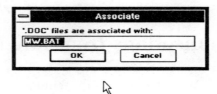

Figure 4.11 Building a program/data file linkage.

Note: A linkage may already be created during the installation of a Windows program. If it exists, it will be displayed in the Associate dialog box. You can edit it or cancel the request.

Diskette Management

File Manager supports a few commands that are specific to diskettes, such as formatting and copying.

Formatting Diskettes

To format a diskette, insert the diskette into any available drive and choose **Format Diskette** from the Disk menu. If you have more than one drive, a dialog box is displayed (see Figure 4.12). Select the drive containing the diskette and choose **OK** or press Enter.

Figure 4.12 Selecting the drive.

You will then see a confirmation box, verifying that the format will erase all data from the diskette. Select **Format**.

Another dialog box is displayed, showing a high-capacity option and a system disk option. If you are using a high-capacity drive and diskette, the **High Capacity** option should be on. If you plan to make this a system disk, toggle the **Make System Disk** option on (see Figure 4.13). Click **OK** or press Enter.

Figure 4.13 Initiating the format.

If you wish to make a *system diskette* (one that your system can boot from), first format a disk (see the preceding explanation) with the **Make System Disk** option toggled on. This will save space for the system files. Then choose **Make System Disk** from the Disk menu. If your system has more than one drive, select the drive on the next dialog box. On the next dialog box, select **Yes** on the confirmation box. File Manager will then copy the system files to the diskette.

Note: Formatting erases all data from a diskette. You cannot recover files from a formatted diskette.

Copying Diskettes

Note: This copy procedure does a sector and bit copy from the source to destination diskette. You can use this procedure only if both diskettes have the same capacity and are of the same type.

If you need to copy one diskette to another, it's quicker to copy the diskette than to copy files. To copy a diskette, use the following procedure:

1. Place the source diskette in the drive you wish to copy from.
2. Select the disk drive icon for this drive. The source drive icon should be highlighted.
3. Select **Copy Diskette** from the Disk menu.
4. If your computer has a dual-disk drive, select the destination drive in the next dialog box (see Figure 4.14).
5. A confirmation box is then displayed verifying the copy. Select **Copy**.
6. You will then see a box requesting the insertion of the source diskette. Select **OK**.

As the copy proceeds, File Manager will prompt as necessary for the changing of diskettes if you have only one drive.

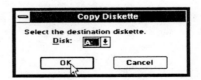

Figure 4.14 Initiating a diskette copy.

Note: All previous data on the destination diskette will be destroyed. If you wish to keep data already on the destination diskette, copy the files (see "Moving and Copying Files").

Tip: You do not need to format the diskette before copying onto it.

Tip: Don't try to copy a low-capacity disk in a low-capacity drive to a low-capacity diskette in a high-capacity drive. It may seem to work, but reading of the resulting diskette will be marginal. Instead, use the single low-capacity drive and use it as both the source and the destination drives. File Manager will prompt you when to change diskettes.

Labeling Diskettes

You can use File Manager to add an electronic label to any disk. To label a diskette, first select the icon for the disk you wish to label. Select **Label Disk** from the Disk menu. A Label Disk dialog box is displayed. Type (or edit) the label (see Figure 4.15). Choose **OK** or press Enter.

Figure 4.15 Labeling a disk.

Controlling the Display

File Manager provides several options for controlling the display. These are available from the View and Options menus. The View menu defines the information that is displayed and the order of the displayed files. The Options menu controls the display of confirmation messages, the lowercasing of text, and the status bar.

Controlling the Directory Window Display

The View menu controls the display of the files in a document window. In the default document window display, the filenames are displayed in alphabetical order with no detail information.

You can control which windows the View menu affects by controlling which window is active when you initiate a **View** command.

If the Directory Tree window is active, commands from the View menu will affect all subsequent directory windows, but not those already open. If a directory window is active, the commands affect only that window.

Many of the View menu command dialog boxes have a **Set System Default** option. If this option is toggled on, your selection will become the new default windows setting for all directory windows. It will also become the new default setting if you select the **Save Settings** option when you exit File Manager.

If **File Details** is toggled on, all detail information about the files is always displayed. If **Other** is selected, a dialog box is displayed from which you can select which details to display (see Figure 4.16). The following options are available:

Size	Size of file in bytes
Last Modification Date	Last edit date of file
Last Modification Time	Last edit time of file
File Flags	Attribute settings for file
Set System Default	Make options permanent whether or not Directory Tree window is selected

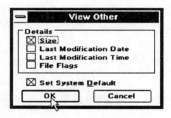

Figure 4.16 Selecting details for display.

The default sorting order for the files is the subdirectories first and then the files in alphabetical order. The next section of the View menu permits you to alter this sort order. You can select a **By Name** or **By Type** order directly from the menu. For other sort orders, select **Sort by**. This displays a dialog box (see Figure 4.17) from which you can select other sort orders.

Figure 4.17 Defining the sort order.

The default display is all files except hidden and system files. You can change this display by using the **Include** option of the View menu. This displays a dialog box (see Figure 4.18), from which you can select which files to display. The **Name:** text box permits you to define a template for the display, for example, display all .DOC files. The other options are as follows:

Directories	Displays all subdirectories in the directory
Programs	Displays all files with .EXE, .COM, .BAT, and .PIF extensions.
Documents	Displays text and graphics files
Other	Displays other files
Show Hidden/System Files	Includes hidden and system files
Set System Default	Applies to all directory windows

Figure 4.18 Defining which files to display.

If you wish to minimize the number of directory windows by closing old windows as you open new ones, select **Replace on Open** from the View menu. If you want new directory windows to overlay old ones, toggle this off.

Choosing Other Display Options

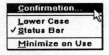

Other display options are available from the Options menu. **Confirmation** permits you to control which confirmation messages are displayed on various actions (see Figure 4.19). In the default setting, all messages are displayed.

Figure 4.19 Controlling the confirmation messages.

Lower Case is a toggle that permits the directory windows to display in lowercase. **Status Bar** toggles on or off the status information bar at the bottom of the windows. In a directory window, the status bar shows the number of files selected and the space occupied by them. On a Directory Tree window, the status bar shows the free space on the selected drive.

Minimize on Use shrinks the File Manager to an icon if you start an application from it.

Controlling the Windows

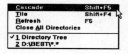

The Window menu permits you to control the arrangement of the windows. The familiar **Cascade** (Shift+F5) and **Tile** (Shift+F4) options permit you to cascade or tile the displayed windows. The **Refresh** option (F5) is useful for refreshing the screen if it is not automatically updated after an operation.

The normal procedure for closing a document window is to double-click its Control-menu box. You can also close a document window by using Alt+Hyphen(-) or by choosing **Close** from its Control menu. If you wish to close all directory windows, select **Close All Directories** from the Window menu.

Terminating File Manager

File Manager is terminated like any other Windows application: double-click the Control-menu box, or open the Control window and choose **Close**. Another method is to choose **Exit** from the File menu.

Summary

File Manager is a Windows application that supports file and disk management. Some examples of uses for File Manager are

- Renaming, moving, copying, and deleting files and directories.
- Formatting, labeling, and copying diskettes.
- Viewing the disk organization.
- Program launching.

Using Windows Applications

Microsoft Windows has a collection of applications that can make your work easier. You have already been very briefly introduced to the first of these, Clock. Part Two of this book will introduce you to nine additional Windows applications: Calendar, Calculator, Cardfile, Notepad, Terminal, Reversi, Solitaire, Write, and Paintbrush. Eight of the ten are accessible from the Program Manager's Accessories group window. The other two (the games) are accessible from the Games group window.

Using Windows Calendar

Windows Calendar is an electronic appointment book that you can use to keep track of your time and appointments. You can even set alarms for special appointments. You can set as many appointment calendars as you wish, since each is stored as a separate file on the disk. If you share a computer, each user can keep a separate appointment book.

Starting the Calendar

The easiest way to start Calendar is to double-click the **Calendar** icon in the Program Manager's Accessories group window (see Figure 5.1). If you don't have a mouse, use the direction keys to highlight the **Calendar** icon and press Enter. The Calendar window will open and display the current time and date below the title bar. As you can see from Figure 5.2, the rest of the work area looks very much like an appointment calendar. Notice that the default increment is one hour, but you can change the increment. The title bar contains the word (untitled), which indicates that no file (appointment book) is open. The insertion point is next to the first time period of the day, in this case, 7:00 AM.

A scroll bar is at the right of the work area. You can click the Up Arrow to move upward through the day's appointments or the Down Arrow to move downward. You can also drag the scroll bar to any area of the day's appointments. From the keyboard, you can get the same scrolling action by using the Down and Up Arrow keys, or PgDn

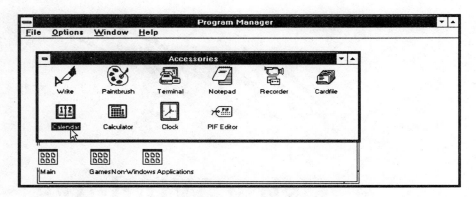

Figure 5.1 Starting Calendar.

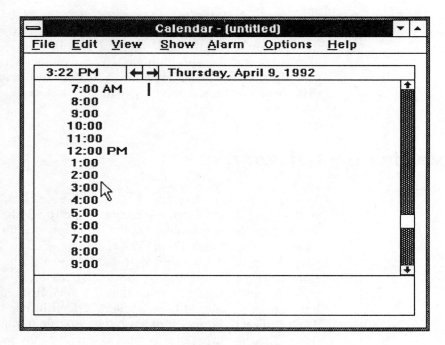

Figure 5.2 The appointment page.

and PgUp. You can scroll between days by clicking the Left Arrow and Right Arrow keys at the top of the work area. From the keyboard, you can scroll between days by using Ctrl + PgUp to move backward or Ctrl + PgDn to move forward. A quick scroll will show that the entire 24 hours is on the page, even though the window shows only part of the day and starts at 7:00 A.M.

Note: If the time or date is wrong, correct it before continuing. You can change the time or date by using Control Panel (Chapter 17) or by exiting Windows and using the DOS commands TIME and DATE.

Basic Calendar Operations

Text entered from the keyboard is always entered at the insertion point, which is shown as a flashing vertical line on the window. To enter an appointment for a particular day, use the direction keys or click the mouse to move the insertion point to the desired time and then type the appointment information.

For simple edits, use the Del key to delete the character to the right of the insertion point and use the Backspace key to delete the character to the left of the insertion point. For more complex editing, you should use the Clipboard (see "Editing Appointments—The Edit Menu"). The Clipboard is an area of memory in Windows that can be used to transfer data between Windows programs. The data can be text, numeric, or graphic.

At the bottom of the day's page is a scratch area. You can use the scratch area to enter notes that apply to the entire day, such as a note that it is your spouse's birthday or your anniversary. To use this scratch area, click the insertion point into the area or use the Tab key to move the insertion point. Then enter the text. Up to three lines of text can be entered if the Calendar window is as large as possible.

Calendar supports two views: a Day view and a Month view. To see the Month view, double-click the date at the top of the title bar (see Figure 5.3). The entire month will be shown, and the day of the month will be highlighted. The scratch area at the bottom of the Month view page is the same as the scratch area for the day that is highlighted; that is, you can enter the scratch area data from the Month view or the Day view. To switch back to the Day view (of any day in the month), double-click a day in the Month view. You can also use the View menu to switch between the Day and Month views.

Once you have completed your appointments, you should save your appointment calendar as a file. The first time you save your appointments, use the **Save As** option of the File menu. For subsequent saves, you can use the **Save** option. Enter the filename and click **OK** or press Enter.

Calendar - (untitled)

File	Edit	View	Show	Alarm	Options	Help

3:29 PM ← → **Thursday, April 9, 1992**

April 1992

S	M	T	W	T	F	S
			1	2	3	4
5	6	7	8	> 9 <	10	11
12	13	14	15	16	17	18
19	20	21	22	23	24	25
26	27	28	29	30		

Figure 5.3 Looking at a Month view.

Using the Menu Commands

The Calendar program contains six menus: File, Edit, View, Show, Alarm, Options, and Help.

Calendar File Management—The File Menu

The File menu is used for managing appointment files. It contains eight command options: **New**, **Open**, **Save**, **Save As**, **Print**, **Page Setup**, **Printer Setup**, and **Exit**.

Use the **New** command to create a new appointment file. **New** is most commonly used to delete all of the current appointments when you wish to start a new appointment file. It has the same action as restarting Calendar.

Use the **Open** command to open an existing appointment file. Calendar is often used with several appointment files. Once Calendar is started, use the **Open** option to open the desired appointment file.

The command displays a dialog box, as shown in Figure 5.4. In the upper left of Figure 5.4, you can define the template for the displayed files. Since Calendar files have a default extension, .CAL, the default template specifies .CAL.

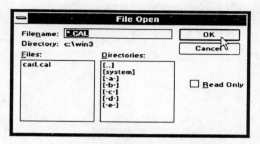

Figure 5.4 Opening a file.

 To open a file with the mouse, double-click the filename in the list box or click the filename once and click **OK**. Double-click in the directories list box to change directories or drives. Click the double periods in the directories list box to move up the directory tree.

 To open a file from the keyboard, use the Tab key to move the cursor to the list box. Use the direction keys to select a file. Press Enter. To change directories, tab to the directories list and use the direction keys to select a directory or drive. Press Enter. Select the double periods to move up to a parent directory.

If you wish to open a file for reading only, check **Read Only** in the box (tab to it and press the Spacebar).

You can use the scroll bars at the right of the list boxes to scroll the filenames in the list box. You can also use the direction keys to scroll the list boxes.

 Use the **Save As** command to save an appointment file for the first time. The command displays a dialog box for a filename (see Figure 5.5). Enter the filename and click **OK** or press Enter. When using the **Save As** command, you do not have to specify a file extension. The file extension .CAL is implied. After the file has been saved, the filename will be displayed in the title bar.

Use the **Save** command to save the current appointments in the file specified in the title bar. This command is used on subsequent saves after using **Save As** the first time. It can also be used at any time to save the currently open file.

Tip: Use the **Save** command every 15 to 20 minutes to save your current work.

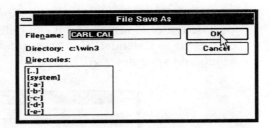

Figure 5.5 Saving a file.

Use the **Print** command to print the appointments. You can choose to print for one or more days. When the **Print** command is selected, a dialog box is displayed that requests the day range (see Figure 5.6). Enter the desired range. Calendar prints appointments for the single day specified by the **From:** box if the **To:** box is left blank.

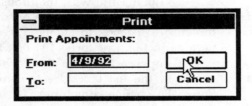

Figure 5.6 Printing the appointments.

You can use the **Page Setup** command to define the page layout (headings, footers, and margins). Figure 5.7 shows the dialog box for this command. In defining headers and footers, the following codes are available:

&c   Center the following text

&d   Current date

&f   Current filename

&l   Left-justify the following text

&p   Page number

&r   Right-justify the following text

&t   Current time

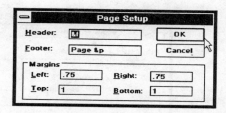

Figure 5.7 Defining the page layout.

If you need to change printers, use **Printer Setup** to select the printer. This displays a dialog box from which you can select a printer (see Figure 5.8). If you select **Setup** on this dialog box, a second dialog box is displayed from which you can select cartridges, orientation (Portrait/Landscape), resolution, paper, and more (see Figure 5.9). The options on this dialog box will depend on the printer you are using. Selecting **Fonts** in this dialog box displays a third dialog box for installing soft fonts (see Figure 5.10). Using this command is similar to using the identical dialog boxes from Control Panel (Chapter 17).

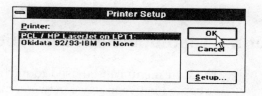

Figure 5.8 Selecting a printer.

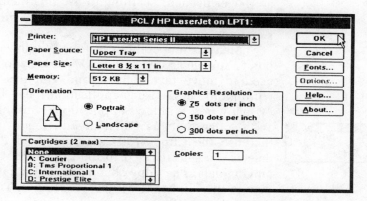

Figure 5.9 Setting up a printer.

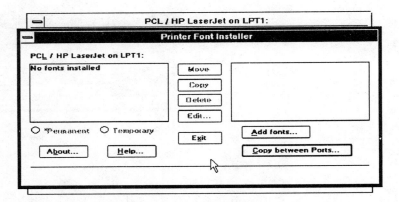

Figure 5.10 Font installation.

Use the **Exit** command to close and exit Calendar. It is the same as double-clicking the Control-menu box.

There is no option on the File menu to delete an appointment file. If you no longer need an appointment file, use the **Delete** option of the File Manager to delete the file or delete it by using the DEL command from MS-DOS.

Editing Appointments—The Edit Menu

The Edit menu can be used to move or copy data. Text can be moved or copied between days, between months, or to or from another application. Notice that each command also has a shortcut key. You can use the Edit menu to remove pages from an appointment file that are no longer needed. Learning to use this menu is extremely important, since there are similar commands and shortcut keys in almost all Windows applications.

Many Edit operations use the Windows Clipboard. This is a temporary storage area in Windows available to all applications. It can be used to move text, figures, and graphics between applications or within a file in the same application. The Clipboard can even be used by many non-Windows applications running under Windows.

Notice that the Calendar Edit menu contains three commands that use the Clipboard: **Cut**, **Copy**, and **Paste**. The **Cut** command deletes the selected text to the Clipboard. Use the **Cut** command for moving data. The **Copy** command copies data from the Calendar window to the Clipboard without deleting it. The **Paste** command copies data from the Clipboard to the Calendar window. When Calendar is first started, all three options are shown in gray. The Clipboard is

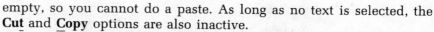

empty, so you cannot do a paste. As long as no text is selected, the **Cut** and **Copy** options are also inactive.

You can use the Clipboard with the mouse or the keyboard for editing:

To select text with the mouse, drag the cursor over the text to be edited (see Figure 5.11). To move the selected text, first select **Cut** from the Edit menu to move it temporarily to the Clipboard and then click the insertion point to the new location. Select **Paste** from the Edit menu. To copy the selected text, select **Copy** from the Edit menu, move the insertion point to the new location, and select **Paste** from the Edit menu. To delete the selected text without copying it to the Clipboard, press Del.

As with the mouse, you select the desired text (see Figure 5.11) and then perform the desired operation. To select the text from the keyboard, first move the insertion point to the beginning of the selected text using the Up, Down, Left, and Right Arrow keys. Hold down the Shift key and move the insertion point to select the text by using the direction keys. Release the Shift key. You can quickly select to the end of a line by using Shift + End or select to the beginning of a line by using Shift + Home. To delete the selected text, use the Del key.

To move the selected text, use Shift + Del to move the selected text to the Clipboard. Move the insertion point to the new location and use Shift + Ins to copy the text from the Clipboard to this location. To copy the selected text to a new location, select the text and use Ctrl + Ins to copy the text to the Clipboard. Move the insertion point to the new location and use Shift + Ins to paste the text from the Clipboard to the new location.

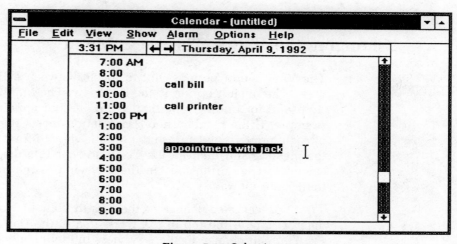

Figure 5.11 Selecting text.

For example, suppose you have an appointment set up for 3 o'clock with a client. The client calls and wishes to reschedule for 3 o'clock the next day. Select the 3 o'clock appointment that is currently scheduled, and choose the Edit menu and **Cut** option. To change to the next day, click the Right Arrow key to the left of the date at the top. Put the insertion point at 3 o'clock of this day and select **Paste** from the Edit menu.

You could also copy or move from your appointment calendar to another Windows program. For example, to copy from a scratch area for a day to Windows Write, select the contents of the scratch area and **Copy** from the Edit menu. Make Windows Write active and select **Paste** from the Edit menu of Windows Write.

The **Remove** command deletes pages from the appointment calendar. A dialog box requests the specific range of dates to delete (see Figure 5.12). If the second box is left blank, pages are deleted only for the single date specified in the **From:** box.

Tip: It is a good idea to periodically use the **Remove** command to delete appointment pages for previous days. This minimizes the size of the appointment file.

Figure 5.12 Removing appointment pages.

Changing the View—The View Menu

The View menu permits you to toggle between a Day and a Month view. The default option is the Day view. The Month view is primarily useful for finding a particular day in your appointment book. For example, if the neighborhood association meets the second Monday of each month, you can use the Month view to find the exact date for the meeting and then the Day view to schedule the meeting on your calendar. The current day in the Day view is the highlighted day of the Month view.

Tip: You can also change to the Month view by double-clicking the date or time at the top of the work area of the Day view or by using F9. You can change to the Day view by double-clicking any date on the Month view, or by pressing Enter or F8 with the date highlighted.

Changing Dates—The Show Menu

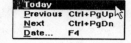

The Show menu has four commands: **Today**, **Previous**, **Next**, and **Date**. Use the **Today** command to return to the current day or month. This is a quick way to return to the current date if you have been looking at a previous or future date.

Use the Previous command for returning to the previous day from the Day view or previous month from the Month view. The keyboard shortcut for the **Previous** command is Ctrl+PgUp.

The **Next** command is the reverse of the **Previous** command, and is useful for switching to the next day from the Day view or the next month from the Month view. The keyboard shortcut is Ctrl+PgDn.

Tip: With a mouse, it's easier to click the Right and Left Arrows at the top when you want to move to the previous or the next day or month.

Use the **Date** command for showing a Day view of a specific date. A dialog box is displayed (see Figure 5.13), and you can enter any date from January 1, 1980 to December 31, 2099. Dates should be specified in an MM/DD/YY or MM-DD-YY form. Zeros are not needed on months and days. The years can be expressed with two or four digits. If a two-digit year is entered, the 20th century is assumed.

Figure 5.13 Requesting a specific day view.

Setting the Alarm—The Alarm Menu

The Alarm menu permits you to control the alarm feature of Calendar. With the Alarm menu, you can set an audio or visual signal for an appointment announcement.

The **Alarm Set** command or the F5 key will set an alarm on the appointment at the insertion point's current location (see Figure 5.14). A small bell will appear to the left of the time, indicating that the alarm is set for that time. The **Alarm Set** command and the F5 key act as a toggle, turning the alarm for that appointment on or off. To turn off an alarm, select the appointment and press F5 or choose **Alarm Set** again.

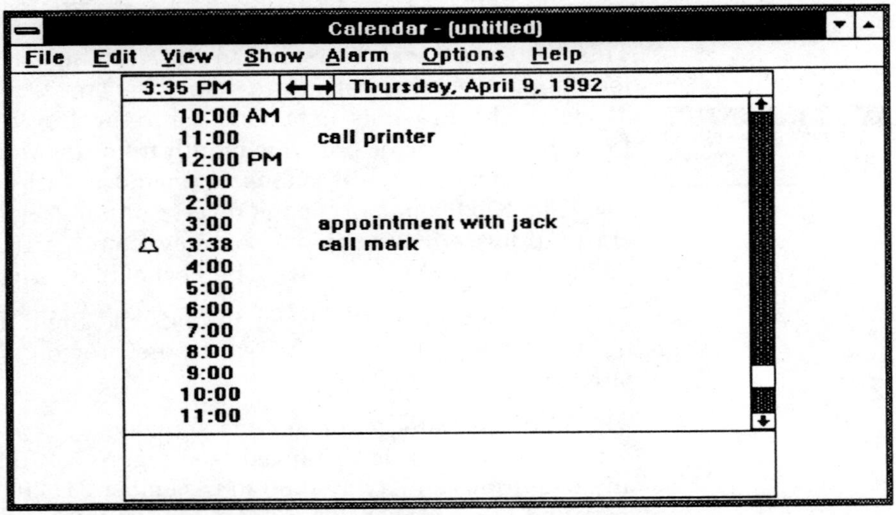

Figure 5.14 Setting an alarm.

For the alarm to work, Calendar must be loaded as an active window, inactive window, or icon. You must also have loaded with Calendar the file that contains the appointment having the alarm. If this is true, what happens at the alarm time depends on the status of the Calendar program. Here are the possibilities:

■ If Calendar is an active window, a dialog box is displayed with the appointment text and a beep is sounded (see Figure 5.15). Click **OK** or press Enter to continue.

■ If Calendar is an inactive window, the title bar will flash with the beep. You must make the window active to see the alarm window and message.

■ If Calendar is an icon, the icon will flash and a beep will sound when the announcement time is reached. To see the dialog box, you must press Alt Esc or click the icon to make Calendar active.

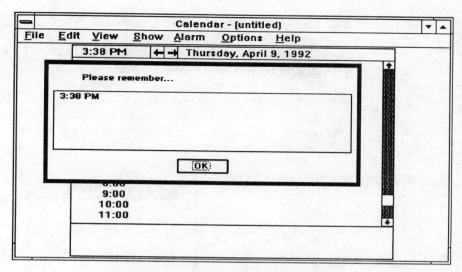

Figure 5.15 An alarm.

The **Controls** command permits you to set certain features of the alarm. **Early Ring** on the **Controls** dialog box (see Figure 5.16) permits you to beep or display the visual alarm for a specified number of minutes before the appointment time. The number of minutes must be entered in the text box. **Sound** permits you to toggle the audio alarm on or off. You can also toggle the audio by using Alt+S when the dialog box is displayed.

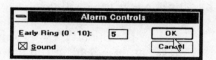

Figure 5.16 Setting the alarm controls.

Tip: Calendar is useful for monitoring your appointments and sounding alarms for specified appointments. If you keep it loaded as an icon when you are using Windows, the alarms will work and very little memory will be used.

Setting the Options—The Options Menu

The **Options** menu has three commands: **Mark**, **Special Time**, and **Day Settings**. Use the **Mark** command for marking special days in the Month view. To mark a day, use the cursor or the direction keys to select the day in the Month view and then select **Mark** in the Options menu or press F6. Both the **Mark** command and the F6 shortcut act as toggles. The command displays a dialog box from which you can choose the marking symbol (see Figure 5.17). The symbol you choose will mark the day in the Month view.

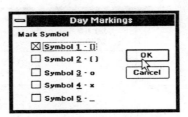

Figure 5.17 Marking a day.

The **Mark** command is very useful for marking certain days in the Month view. For example, you might wish to mark the date of your spouse's birthday or the date of an appointment for which you do not yet know the time. Select the month and then the date. Enter your notes about that day in the scratch area at the bottom of the page, and these will be attached to that day. The scratch area in the Month view is specific for each day and is the same as the scratch area for that day in the Day view.

Use the **Special Time** command to set appointments for special times that do not fit in the normal increments shown on the appointment page. For example, using this command you could set an appointment at 9:20 or 4:25 or any other specific time. The command is activated by using the Options menu and **Special Time** or by using the F7 shortcut key. A dialog box appears from which you can set the time (see Figure 5.18). The command is available only in the Day view.

Once a special time is entered, it appears on the appointment calendar with an insertion point. You can then enter the appointment information at the insertion point. To enter afternoon times, select the **PM** designator in the **Special Time** dialog box. To delete a **Special Time** appointment, put the insertion point on the line to delete and select the Options menu and **Special Time** or press F7. Then click **Delete** in the dialog box. You could also manually enter the time to

Figure 5.18 Setting a special time.

delete in the dialog box and click **Delete**. The keyboard shortcut is Alt + I to insert a **Special Time** and Alt + D to delete a **Special Time** when the dialog box is displayed.

The **Day Settings** command permits you to define how the appointment calendar is displayed (see Figure 5.19). The **Interval** option permits you to set the interval for the times on the appointment schedule. The **Hour Format** permits you to select between A.M./P.M. and military formats. **Starting Time** permits you to set the starting time of the display in the appointment calendar. The page will still contain appointments for earlier times. This option controls only the starting time for the initial display.

Figure 5.19 Defining the day settings.

Tip: You will probably wish to use the **Interval** option to start your appointment entries at the interval that meets your specific needs.

Getting Help—The Help Menu

If you need help in using Calendar, it's only a few keystrokes away. Use the Help menu to select the type of help you need and then select the topic (Chapter 2).

Summary

Calendar is a useful application for almost any computer user because with it you can manage your personal schedule and appointments.

You may wish to modify your Windows so that Calendar is automatically loaded as an icon with your personal appointment file (Chapter 18). This modification will permit your alarms to work for your appointments.

Using Windows Calculator

Windows Calculator is a small on-screen calculator much like the desk calculators you have probably already used. You work the calculator by clicking the appropriate buttons with the mouse or by entering the button labels from the keyboard. This chapter will show you how to use Calculator.

Starting the Calculator

To start Calculator the easiest way, select the **Calculator** icon in the Program Manager's Accessories group. Once started, the screen will display the Calculator image (see Figure 6.1).

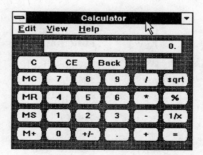

Figure 6.1 The Calculator.

Notice in Figure 6.1 that the window includes only a single Minimize icon in the upper right. You cannot resize the window, but you can minimize it to an icon. There is a small menu bar with three options: **Edit**, **View**, and **Help**.

Performing Basic Calculator Operations

Before trying to perform an operation on the Calculator, take a look at the keys that are available. At the top of the Calculator is a small display window that displays the steps and results of calculations. Below it is a small window that indicates whether any value is stored in memory. Keys for each numeric digit are in the second, third, and fourth columns. The keys in the fifth and sixth column are used for performing operations. In the fifth column, you will see the keys for the basic operations: divide, multiply, subtract, and add. The sixth column contains keys for performing two special operations: finding square roots and finding percentages. The equal sign in the lower right is used for displaying the results of a calculation. The top row contains keys for editing the display. The far left column manages the Calculator's memory.

You can use either the mouse or the keyboard to perform calculations:

To perform a calculation with the mouse, click on the appropriate numbers and operations.

To perform an operation with the keyboard, enter the numbers and operations from the keyboard. You may use either the numbers at the top of the keyboard or, if Num Lock is toggled on, the keyboard numeric pad. The operation keys are shown in Table 6.1.

Table 6.1 Calculator's Operation Keys

Key	Function	Keyboard Equivalent
+/−	Negate display	F9
/	Divide	/
*	Multiply	*
−	Subtract	−
+	Add	+
sqrt	Square root	@
%	Percent	%
1/x	Reciprocal	r
C	Clear calculation	Esc

Table 6.1 (cont.)

Key	Function	Keyboard Equivalent
CE	Clear display	Del
Back	Delete right digit	Backspace or ←
=	Return result	= *or* Enter
MC	Clear Memory	Ctrl + C
MR	Display Memory	Ctrl + R
MS	Store to Memory	Ctrl + M
M+	Add to Memory	Ctrl + P

Note: Many of these keys and functions have changed from Windows 2.0.

As an example of using Calculator, let's add 123 and 5. Click (or type) 1, 2, 3, then +, 5, and then =. The result, 128, is shown in the display window (see Figure 6.2).

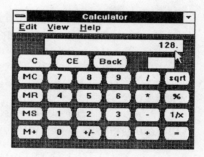

Figure 6.2 Displaying the results.

Using the Memory

Calculator also contains a single memory location that can be used to store results temporarily. The left column contains four memory operations available to the user:

Button	*Key*	*Action*
MC	Ctrl + C	Clear Memory
MR	Ctrl + R	Display Memory
MS	Ctrl + M	Store in Memory
M+	Ctrl + P	Add to Memory

To perform a memory operation with the mouse, click the appropriate memory button.

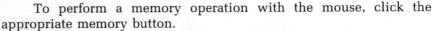

To perform a memory operation from the keyboard, press the appropriate characters from the *Key* column of the preceding list.

Calculator always begins with the memory cleared. When the memory contains any nonzero value, a small M is displayed in the window of the top row.

As an example, you could use the memory feature of the Calculator to balance your checkbook. Enter the opening checkbook balance and click **MS**. To enter a deposit, enter the amount of deposit and click **M+**. To enter a withdrawal, enter a withdrawal amount, click **+/−** to reverse the sign, and click **M+**. The final checkbook balance can be viewed by clicking **MR**. If you make a mistake, click **MC** and start again.

Using the Clipboard with Calculator

The Calculator's Edit menu can be used to transfer the Calculator's results to another Windows application program. Or it can be used to transfer data from another Windows application program to the Calculator as part of a calculation. Both operations make use of Windows Clipboard. The Clipboard is a temporary storage area for editing within or between programs.

Notice that the Calculator Edit menu contains two commands: **Copy** and **Paste**. The **Copy** command copies data from Calculator's display window to the Clipboard. The **Paste** command copies data from the Clipboard to Calculator's display window. The **Paste** command is initially grayed, since the Clipboard is empty.

Note: With most applications, the **Copy** command is initially grayed, since the text or graphic to copy must be selected first. With this application, the copy is from the display window (it is always selected), and the command is always active.

The **Copy** command is used to copy Calculator results in the display window to the Clipboard for pasting to another program. For example, suppose that you wish to copy a Calculator result to an Excel worksheet. With the result in Calculator's display window, select **Copy** from the Edit menu. Make the Excel window active and select the desired cell for pasting the result. Select **Paste** from the Excel Edit menu, and the Calculator result will be pasted to that cell. Notice that the contents of the display window in Calculator are not altered. In the same way, you can copy a Calculator result to any application, such as a Windows Write document. For example, you could copy calculated results to the Clipboard and then from the Clipboard to the desired location in a Microsoft Write document.

The **Paste** command is used to transfer data from another Windows application to Calculator. For example, to copy data from a spreadsheet cell to Calculator, you would first make the Excel window active. Click the desired cell in the spreadsheet and select **Copy** from the Edit menu of Excel. Make the Calculator window active and then select **Paste** from the Calculator Edit menu. The contents of the spreadsheet cell are now displayed in Calculator's display window.

Both the **Copy** and the **Paste** commands have shortcuts that can be initiated from the keyboard without a mouse. Use Ctrl + Ins for the **Copy** command and Shift + Ins for the **Paste** command. These shortcuts are common to all Windows programs.

Note: When pasting text to Calculator, you should generally paste only numeric text. Several alphabetic characters can be interpreted as commands and may initiate actions. For example, a *q* will clear the Calculator.

Using the Scientific Calculator

If you are a programmer or businessperson, you may wish to use Calculator in an advanced mode, or as a Scientific Calculator. In this mode, you can convert values between number systems, use mathematical functions (such as the trigonometric functions), and do statistical calculations.

To switch to the Scientific Calculator, select **Scientific** from the View menu. To switch back, select **Standard** from this same menu. Calculator remembers its last mode, so if you restart Calculator later it will return to the last mode used.

Switching modes does not affect a displayed value. The Scientific mode always starts in Decimal mode with the same displayed value of the Standard mode.

When the Scientific mode is selected, the Calculator keyboard will change and more buttons will be available (see Figure 6.3). The Standard mode buttons are in the approximate center of the calculator. The top row contains buttons for altering the number system and selecting the angle measurement system. To the left and right are an array of new functions.

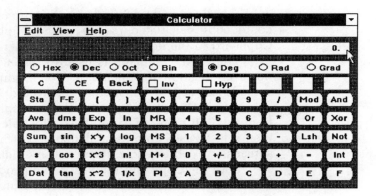

Figure 6.3 The Scientific Calculator.

Changing the Number System

Programmers will find Calculator to be an essential tool for converting values between number systems. From the Scientific mode, enter or paste to the display window the value you wish to convert; then click the number system to which you wish to convert in the upper left. You can convert numbers between hexadecimal, decimal, octal, and binary systems.

For example, enter 34 in the default Decimal mode. Then click **Hex** in the upper left to convert the displayed value to hexadecimal. The display changes to 22. Table 6.2 shows the keys used to change number bases from the keyboard.

Table 6.2 Using the Keyboard to Change Number Bases

Base	Button	Key
Decimal	**Dec**	F6
Hexadecimal	**Hex**	F5
Octal	**Oct**	F7
Binary	**Bin**	F8

When you are using hexadecimal, octal, or binary modes, the right side of the top row changes from the angle measurement selection to the type of value display: Dword (F2), Word (F3), or Byte (F4). You can change this with the mouse or keyboard.

Note: When converting decimal values to other number systems, Calculator truncates the number to an integer before conversion. When converting back to decimal, you will get an integer.

When using the displayed value for copying or moving with the Clipboard, Windows assumes that the displayed value is a text string. You can copy from, or paste to, the display window as with the Standard mode.

Using Statistical Functions

You can also use the Scientific Calculator for statistical calculations. Here is an example:

1. Click the **Sta** button in the upper left of the calculator or press Ctrl + S. A dialog box is displayed (see Figure 6.4). Move the box and the Calculator as necessary to access any buttons you wish to use.

2. Enter the first value. With a mouse, you can click the value. From the keyboard, you must select **RET** first or press Alt + F6 to make the Calculator window active.

3. Click **Dat** or press Ins. The value appears in the Statistics box.

4. Enter additional values in the same way.

5. Click the button for the desired statistical function:

Function	Button	Key
Average	**Ave**	Ctrl + A
Sum	**Sum**	Ctrl + T
Standard Deviation	**s**	Ctrl + D

The result is displayed in Calculator's display window.

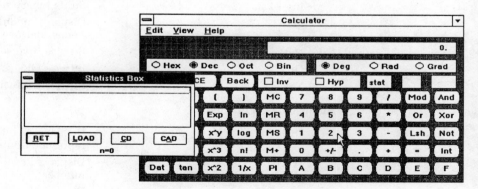

Figure 6.4 Initiating a statistical analysis.

The buttons in the Statistics box have the following functions:

Button	Action
RET	Switch to Calculator window
LOAD	Copy highlighted statistics value to display window
CD	Clear selected entry from Statistics box
CAD	Clear Statistics box

To close the Statistics box, double-click its Control-box menu or select **Close** on its Control menu or press Alt + F4 with the Statistics box window active.

Advanced Calculator Functions

The functions on the Scientific Calculator can be initiated from the buttons or the keyboard. Table 6.3 summarizes the special buttons on this keyboard.

Table 6.3 Advanced Calculator Functions

Button	Key	Action
Operators		
(*or*)	(*or*)	Nests an expression
And	&	Calculates a bitwise AND
Int	;	Truncates decimal value
Lsh	<	Shifts binary left
Inv + Lsh	i + <	Shifts binary right
Mod	%	Displays modulus (remainder of x/y)
Not	~	Bitwise Inverse
Or	|	Bitwise OR
Xor	^	Bitwise Exclusive OR
Number Base Functions		
Dword	F2	Displays 32-bit representation of number
Word	F3	Displays lower 16 bits of number
Byte	F4	Displays lower 8 bits of current number

Table 6.3 (cont.)

Button	Key	Action
Hex	F5	Displays hexadecimal value
Dec	F6	Displays decimal value
Oct	F7	Displays octal value
Bin	F8	Displays binary value
Statistical Functions		
Ave	Ctrl + A	Calculates and displays mean
Inv + Ave	i + Ctrl + A	Calculates and displays mean of squares
Dat	Ins	Enters displayed number to Statistics box
s	Ctrl + D	Calculates and displays standard deviation with population parameter $n-1$
Inv + s	i + Ctrl + D	Calculates and displays standard deviation with population parameter n
Sta	Ctrl + S	Activates Statistics box
Sum	Ctrl + T	Calculates and displays sum
Inv + Sum	i + Ctrl + T	Calculates and displays sum of squares
Trigonometric Functions		
cos	o	Calculates and displays cosine of displayed number
Inv + cos	i + o	Calculates and displays arc cosine of displayed number
Inv + hyp + cos	i + h + o	Calculates and displays hyperbolic cosine of displayed number
sin	s	Calculates and displays sine of displayed number
Inv + sin	i + s	Calculates and displays arc sine of displayed number
Inv + hyp + sin	i + h + s	Calculates and displays hyperbolic sine of displayed number

Table 6.3 (cont.)

Button	Key	Action
tan	t	Calculates and displays tangent of displayed number
Inv + tan	i + t	Calculates and displays arc tangent of displayed number
Inv + hyp + tan	i + h + s	Calculates and displays hyperbolic tangent of displayed number
dms	m	Converts displayed number to degrees-minute-second format
Inv + dms	i + m	Converts displayed number to degrees
Grad	F4	Sets input for gradients if decimal mode
Rad	F3	Sets input for radians if decimal mode

Mathematical Functions

Button	Key	Action
Exp	x	Switches input to scientific notation; to enter 1.15e + 102, enter **1.15**, then **Exp**, then **102**
F – E	v	Toggles display to scientific notation
ln	n	Calculates and displays natural base (base e) logarithm
Inv + ln	i + n	Calculates and displays e to power currently in the display
log	l	Calculates and displays common base (base 10) logarithm
Inv + log	i + l	Calculates and displays 10 to power currently in the display
n!	!	Calculates and displays factorial
PI	p	Returns value of pi
Inv + PI	i + p	Returns value of 2*pi

Table 6.3 (cont.)

Button	Key	Action
x^y	y	Returns x to yth power; enter x, click **x^y**, and then enter y and click =
x^2	@	Returns square of displayed number
Inv + x^2	i + @	Returns square root of displayed number
x^3	#	Returns cube of displayed number
Inv + x^2	i + #	Returns cube root of displayed number

Summary

This chapter has introduced the Calculator application. Calculator is a useful on-screen calculator for quick calculations. It can be used in either a simplified Standard mode or a Scientific mode.

Using Windows Cardfile

Windows Cardfile works much like a Rolodex filing system, permitting you to put items on cards and sort them in a selected order. You can use Cardfile to store addresses and telephone numbers, but its applications are far more extensive than this. For example, you can put graphics or text on the cards and then use the cards as a clip art library. You could also put on the cards all the various tasks that you are working on and sort the tasks in a priority order. Unlike a manual filing system, you can use Cardfile to automatically dial the telephone numbers that are on the cards.

Starting Cardfile

The easiest way to start Cardfile is to double-click the **Cardfile** icon on the Program Manager's Accessories group window. Cardfile then starts and displays an application window with the image of a small card in the work area (see Figure 7.1).

The card is divided by a double line into two parts. The smaller, top portion is called the *index line*, and the text entered to this line is used for sorting the cards in alphabetical order. The portion below the double line is known as the *body* of the card and is used to store information, in either text or graphics form. The body of the card is 40 characters wide and 11 characters high.

For example, to store addresses, you would put the name on the index line in a last name, first name order. The body of the card

Title bar

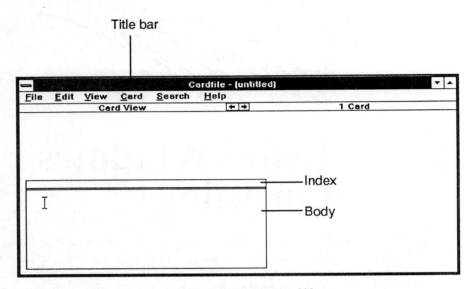

Figure 7.1 Starting Cardfile.

would contain the address and telephone number. This method permits Cardfile to keep the cards in alphabetical order by name. A collection of cards is kept in a file. Files can be opened and saved, just as the schedules in Calendar or the documents in Notepad can. The current window contains the program name and the word (untitled) in the title bar, which indicates that no file is currently open or active. Notice that the insertion point is at the beginning of the first line in the body portion of the card.

Basic Cardfile Operations

To enter data to the first card (which is displayed), use the **Index** option of the Edit menu or press F6. This displays a dialog box for the index line (see Figure 7.2). Enter the index line for the first card in the dialog box and select **OK** or press Enter. Now enter the body of the card in the application window. You can use tabs or spaces to place the text at any location on the card you wish. Cardfile works in a *wordwrap* mode. That is, if you enter more text than will fit into a line, the text will wrap to the next line.

Figure 7.2 Entering the index line.

To enter subsequent cards, select **Add** from the Card menu or press F7. Cardfile will then prompt you for the first line of the card body. Select **OK**. Enter the text for the card body, allowing the text to wrap automatically at the end of each line (see Figure 7.3).

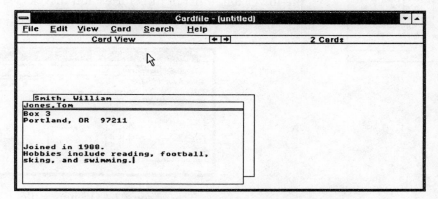

Figure 7.3 Entering the text for the card body.

Using the Cardfile Menus

The Cardfile menu bar contains six menu options: File, Edit, View, Card, Search, and Help. The following sections will discuss each menu option in turn.

File Management—The File Menu

The File menu contains ten commands for managing your card files. When Cardfile is started, the title bar shows the word (untitled) and no file is active. You can then create a collection of cards and save the collection by using the **Save As** command of the File menu.

If you wish to edit the cards later, you can open the file with the **Open** option.

Use the **New** option for creating a new file of cards. Using this option will return Cardfile to the same state as when it was started. That is, Cardfile returns to a blank single card for entry and it closes all open files. This action is most useful if you have been working with one file and wish to start a new file. Using the **New** command will cause Cardfile to query you whether to save the old file if it has not been saved.

Use the **Open** command to open an existing file for editing. You will see a dialog box with a text box in the upper left, a list of files in the lower left, a list of directories and drives (see Figure 7.4), and two buttons—**OK** and **Cancel**.

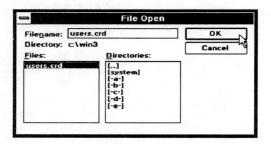

Figure 7.4 Opening a file.

To open a file, you can use either the mouse or the keyboard.

To select a file with the mouse, you can either double-click the filename in the list box or click the filename once and then choose **OK** or press Enter. To change drives, double-click the desired drive designator in the right list box. To change subdirectories, double-click the desired subdirectory. To switch a parent path directory, double-click the double periods.

You can also select files from the keyboard. Use the Tab key to move the indicator to the files list box. Use the direction keys to select a file and press Enter to open the desired file. You can change directories or drives by tabbing to that list box and selecting the new directory or drive. Then press Enter.

Cardfile supports two commands for saving a collection of cards as a file: **Save** and **Save As**. The first time you save a file you should use the **Save As** command. A dialog box will prompt for the filename (see Figure 7.5). Enter the filename with its extension. If you do not enter an extension name, the default extension assumed is .CRD. Use the **Save** command for subsequent saves. The **Save** command

assumes that a file is already active, and the filename is displayed in the title bar. If you try to save a collection of cards with the **Save** command and you haven't named a file yet, the **Save** command is intelligent enough to prompt you for a filename. This is not true of all Windows applications, however. It is best to get in the habit of using **Save As** for saving your data the first time, and **Save** for subsequent saves.

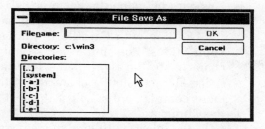

Figure 7.5 Saving a file.

The File menu also has two print commands: **Print** and **Print All**. Use the **Print** command to print the top card in the current card set. Use the **Print All** command to print the entire collection of cards.

The **Page Setup** and **Printer Setup** commands work identically to those of Calendar (Chapter 5). Use **Page Setup** to define headers, footers, and margins. Use **Printer Setup** to change printers and select cartridges or orientation when you are using a laser printer.

The **Merge** command is useful for merging a second file into a currently active file. The two card sets are combined and sorted in alphabetical order. As an example, suppose you have a Cardfile active and open with the filename displayed in the title bar. To merge a second file into it, select the **Merge** command from the File menu. You will see a dialog box displayed that is identical to the one for the **Open** command. Select the file to merge. Cardfile now contains the cards from both files. You can then use the **Save** command to save the combined file under the filename of the file that was active, or you can use the **Save As** command to save the combined file under a new filename.

To terminate Cardfile, use the **Exit** command. Using **Exit** is identical to double-clicking the Control-menu icon or selecting **Close** from the Control menu.

There is no Delete command on the File menu. If you wish to delete a file, use the Windows File Manager program or the MS-DOS command DEL.

Editing Cards — The Edit Menu

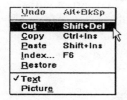

Use the Edit menu to edit the top card of the Cardfile stack. Only this top card can be edited. If you wish to edit a card that is not currently the top card, you must shuffle the deck until the card to edit is on top. Then you can edit it. You can shuffle with the mouse by using the double arrows at the top of the window. You can shuffle from the keyboard by using the PgUp or PgDn keys. You can also use the **Goto** or **Find** commands of the Search menu to get to a particular card.

Editing with Cardfile is similar to editing with other Windows applications. For simple edits, you can use the Del key to delete a character to the right of the insertion point. You can use the Backspace key to delete a character to the left of the insertion point. For more complex edits, select the text and perform the operation using the Clipboard.

To select with the mouse, drag the insertion point over the desired text.

To select with the keyboard, place the insertion point at the beginning of the selected text. Hold down the Shift key and use the direction keys to select the text range.

The Del key removes the selected text without putting it in the Clipboard. The **Cut** command (Shift + Del) removes the selected text from the current card and places it on the Clipboard. The **Copy** command (Ctrl + Ins) places a copy of the selected text on the Clipboard. The **Paste** command (Shift + Ins) places a copy of the Clipboard at the current location of the insertion point. The **Cut**, **Copy**, and **Paste** commands have the standard shortcuts.

The **Undo** command permits you to reverse your edit operation. For example, if you accidentally delete some text from a card and then realize your mistake, you can easily replace it with **Udo**. Simply select **Undo** from the Edit menu. The **Undo** command will reverse only the last edit operation. As a shortcut from the keyboard, you can use Alt + Backspace.

Use the **Index** command to enter the top index line to a card. It displays a dialog box and permits the entry of the text for the line. As a shortcut, you can use the F6 key.

Use the **Restore** command to reverse all edits on the top card of the stack. It can be used only on the top card, and only if the cards have not been shuffled since the edits were made.

Use the **Text** and **Picture** commands for switching the Edit mode. Cardfile is normally in a default Text mode. This permits the editing of any text on the card. If you wish to import a graphic to a card, you must first use the Edit menu to switch Cardfile to the Picture mode. Then you can paste the graphic from the Clipboard to the card. The dual modes permit the separate editing of text and graphics on a card. Text can overlay graphics, and you can select the proper item to edit by using these Edit options and then selecting the text or the graphic.

Tip: When editing, you can use the Home key to move the insertion point to the beginning of a line and the End key to move the insertion point to the end of a line. Ctrl + Home moves the first card to the top of the stack; Ctrl + End shuffles the deck so that the last card is on top.

Controlling the View—The View Menu

The View menu permits you to show the cards in either of two ways: as a card stack or as a list. The **Card** command is the default option, and it displays the full contents of the top card. The cards are in alphabetical order.

The **List** command displays only the index lines of the cards as a list. The list is in alphabetical order. Figure 7.6 shows an example. In the List view, you can edit a particular line by double-clicking the line. This will display the index dialog box from which you can edit the line. From the keyboard, you can use F6 to edit an index line in the List view.

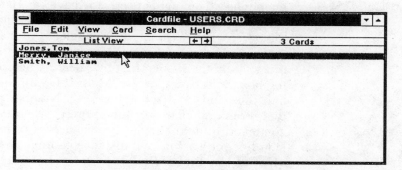

Figure 7.6 A List view.

Managing the Cards—The Card Menu

The Card menu has four commands for managing cards: **Add**, **Delete**, **Duplicate**, and **Autodial**. Use the **Add** command to add cards to the current card stack. You can use F7 as a shortcut key. This command displays a dialog box (see Figure 7.3 earlier) from which the index line can be entered. A new card is displayed at the top of the stack with the new index line. You can then enter the body of the card.

Remember, when creating a new card stack, you cannot use the **Add** command to create the first card. When Cardfile is started or the **New** command is issued from the Edit menu, Cardfile is started with a single blank card. If you try to use **Add** to put data into this blank card, you will instead add a second card to the stack on top of the blank card. You must first use the **Index** command of the Edit menu (or F6) for the first card. Subsequent adds can be done with the Card menu's **Add** command or with F7.

Use the **Delete** command to delete the card that is currently at the top of the stack. The **Delete** command cannot be reversed or undone, so use caution before initiating the command. It has no shortcut.

Use the **Duplicate** command when you need to create a duplicate of the card that is currently at the top of the stack. Use this command for creating several cards that have similar data. Start by using the **Duplicate** command to create a stack of cards with duplicate data on each card. You can then go back and edit the cards, putting in the data that is unique to each card.

The **Autodial** command (F5) automatically dials the telephone number that is on the top card and then prompts you to pick up the telephone. You will need to have a Hayes-compatible modem installed to use this command. The **Autodial** command displays a dialog box from which you can select the dialing option (see Figure 7.7). The dialog box permits you to select the number to dial. You must set up the system first by selecting **Setup** from the Autodial dialog box. Select the port (COM1 or COM2), the dial type (pulse/tone), and the baud rate (see Figure 7.8). **Number** refers to the number to dial. **Prefix** refers to a common prefix when used for dialing. Use this command to define long distance access codes, a code to get an outside line, or a 1 for long distance calling. The prefix is toggled on or off with **Use Prefix**. **Dial Type** refers to the type of telephone—touch tone or rotary pulse. **Port** refers to the serial port to which your modem is currently installed. **Baud Rate** refers to the speed of the modem.

Cardfile automatically selects and displays in the text box the first number on the top card that has four or more digits. Cardfile ignores hyphens that are in the number, but you should avoid using parentheses or spaces in the telephone number. If you have two telephone numbers on the card, move the insertion point so that the dialog box indicates the proper number before initiating the command.

Select **Autodial** from the Card menu (or press F5), and then click **OK** or press Enter. The computer will dial the number and prompt you to pick up the phone.

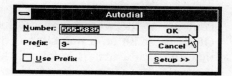

Figure 7.7 Starting an automatic dial.

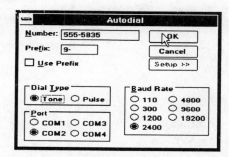

Figure 7.8 Setting the modem dialing parameters.

Searching for Cards—The Search Menu

The Search menu provides three command options: **Go To**, **Find**, and **Find Next**. Use the **Go To** command when you need to find a particular card and you know the index line or a portion of the index line. The shortcut key is F4. Selecting the command or pressing F4 displays a dialog box (see Figure 7.9). You can enter a portion of an index line or the entire index line in the text box for searching. Case is ignored in the search. If no match is found, a message box is displayed to indicate this fact. If a match is found, the card stack is displayed with the card at the top of the stack. If there is more than one card that matches the search pattern, searching again with the same pattern will find the next match.

Figure 7.9 Going to a particular card.

Use the **Find** command when you need to search the body of a card stack. In this case you are looking for a particular card, assuming that you know a portion of it based on a word or phrase in the body of the card. **Find** can be used only in the Card view. As with the **Go To** command, a dialog box is displayed (see Figure 7.10). Type the contents of the word or phrase for which you wish to search. Click **OK** or press Enter. If no match is found, a message box is displayed to this effect. If a match is found, the selected card is displayed at the top of the set with the selected text highlighted.

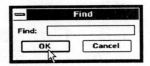

Figure 7.10 Finding a particular card.

You can find subsequent occurrences of text selected with the **Find** command by using the **Find Next** command or, as a shortcut, the F3 key.

One useful application of the **Find** and **Find Next** commands is the creation of a tickler file. The cards can contain the names of your clients or prospects. Each card can have a date for contacting the person again. You can then use the **Find** command to locate the first card containing today's date and use the **Autodial** feature of the Card menu to dial the client or prospect. Then you can use the **Find Next** command to locate the next person to contact.

Tip: If you have too much information for one card, use two cards. Type a -1 at the end of the index line of the first card and a -2 after the index line on the second card. Now, when the cards are sorted, the two cards will always stay together in the proper order.

Getting Help—The Help Menu

Like the other Windows applications, Cardfile has a Help menu from which you can get help on any desired command or procedure (Chapter 2).

Exploring Cardfile

If you haven't already done so, create a small file of at least four cards. Use some familiar addresses and add telephone numbers for each card. The number of cards in the file is displayed under the menu bar. Notice how the cards always stay in alphabetical order. Practice shuffling the cards to get the desired card on top. Practice editing text on both the index line and the body of the card.

If you have a graphics program that runs under Microsoft Windows, practice pasting graphics from that program to a card in Cardfile. See Chapter 4 for an example of this technique.

You can use almost any graphics program that runs under Windows 3. Select the graphic in the graphics program and copy it to the Windows Clipboard from its Edit menu. Open Cardfile and select **Picture** from the Edit menu to put Cardfile in a graphics mode. Then use the Edit menu and paste the graphic from Clipboard to a card.

There are many graphic formats, and Cardfile will recognize only a few of them. If Cardfile will not recognize a graphic format, the **Paste** command of the Edit menu will not be highlighted even though a graphic is in the Clipboard and **Picture** is selected on the Edit menu.

All Cardfile graphics are of relatively low quality, and are bit-mapped images at the screen resolution. Typically, this is only about 75 dpi (dots per inch). This means that Cardfile is not a useful tool for pasting clip art to publications, but it does make a useful tool for managing your clip art libraries. You can keep track of everything in the libraries and where each graphic is stored.

Summary

Cardfile is a useful application for creating an electronic Rolodex file, for maintaining a tickler file or phone book, or for creating clip art libraries.

Using Windows Notepad

Windows Notepad is a useful utility for a wide range of editing applications. You can use it to edit files such as WIN.INI (Chapter 18), to create batch files, or to modify the AUTOEXEC.BAT file. With Notepad, you can build a scrapbook of text that can be pasted to a variety of applications. You can even do simple word processing with it. Finally, you can use Notepad as a log to keep track of your time or projects.

Starting Notepad

To start Notepad, select the **Notepad** program item icon from the Program Manager's Accessories group window. Alternatively, you can start Notepad with an open file from File Manager by clicking or selecting any .TXT or .INI file in a directory. From the DOS prompt, you can start Notepad by entering `WIN NOTEPAD`.

Notepad will then load and display a work area that looks much like a sheet of paper (see Figure 8.1). The cursor, which is called the *insertion point*, is shown as a flashing vertical line in the upper left of the work area. A menu bar is at the top of the work area, and scroll bars are to the right and bottom of the work area.

Menu bar

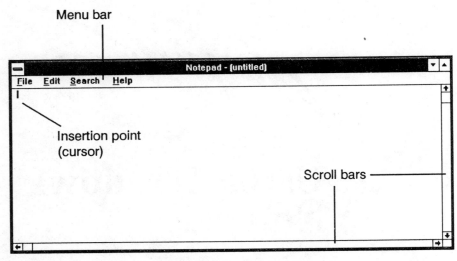

Insertion point
(cursor)

Scroll bars

Figure 8.1 Starting Notepad.

Basic Operations with Notepad

To use Notepad, you simply type the desired text, pressing Enter at the end of each line. Text is entered at the current insertion point. Tabs are converted into eight spaces with Notepad. Once you have finished your entry, you can save your file with any desired name by using the **Save As** option of the File menu.

To use Notepad as a word processor, you must switch Notepad to a wordwrap mode by selecting **Word Wrap** on the Edit menu. Text will then automatically wrap, or drop to the next line, when it reaches the right edge of the window. With wordwrap on, you do not have to press Enter until the end of the paragraph.

Note: Unlike Windows Write and most other word processors, the length of the line with wordwrap on is determined by the width of the window. Resize the window to get the desired width.

For simple edits, you can use the Del key to delete the character to the right of the insertion point or the Backspace key to delete the character to the left of the insertion point. For more complex edits, you can use either the mouse or the keyboard.

To edit with the mouse, first move the insertion point to the beginning of the text to be edited by clicking the mouse at that point. Drag the mouse until the text to be edited is highlighted. Now enter the replacement text from the keyboard. It will overwrite the highlighted text.

 To edit with the keyboard, use the direction keys to move the insertion point to the beginning of the text to be edited. Press and hold down the Shift key while using the direction keys to highlight the text to be edited. Enter the replacement text from the keyboard.

Tip: To edit large blocks of text with the mouse, first click the beginning of the block to move the insertion point there. Then press and hold the Shift key and click the mouse at the end of the block. With the keyboard, you can use Shift+Home to select to the beginning of the line and Shift+End to select text to the end of the line.

As with most Windows application programs, you can use the Edit menu with the Clipboard to cut and copy within a Notepad document or between Notepad and other applications.

Notepad is limited to file documents requiring no more than 16K of space. Although Notepad has no paging feature, this memory space length is approximately 50,000 characters. You can use the **About Notepad** option of the Help menu to track the amount of space that you are using.

Tip: If you find yourself running out of space in Notepad, break the file into two files or import the file to Windows Write.

Using the Notepad Menu

The Notepad menu bar has four options: File, Edit, Search, and Help. The following sections will discuss each of these in turn.

File Management—The File Menu

The File menu is used to manage the files that you create with Notepad. The File menu has eight command options: **New**, **Open**, **Save**, **Save As**, **Print**, **Page Setup**, **Printer Setup**, and **Exit**. These options are identical to those of Calendar or Cardfile and work the same. When Notepad is first opened, the title bar will show the program name and the word (untitled), indicating that no file is in use.

After you have created a document, use **Save As** to save the file the first time. This permits you to specify a filename when saving the document. Subsequent saves can be made with the **Save** command.

Use the **New** command when you are working on one document and wish to start a new document. Notepad queries you whether to save the current document and then resets to start a new document. The title bar will again read (untitled).

Use the **Open** command to open an existing file for editing. As with **New**, Notepad will prompt you about saving any existing file and then will display the dialog box of Figure 8.2. The dialog box contains a list box on the left that displays all files on the current directory matching the template shown in the upper left of the dialog box. The default template for Notepad shows files with the extension .TXT. You can edit the template for working with other files, such as WIN.INI. This dialog box is identical to that of Cardfile (Chapter 7) or Calendar (Chapter 5). Refer to these chapters for more extensive information on using the mouse or keyboard with this box and for explanations of how to change disk drives or directories by using **Open**.

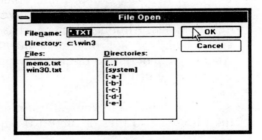

Figure 8.2 Opening a file.

Notice that Windows contains several sample .TXT files. The README files have information that has been updated since the time the manuals were printed. These files should not be altered, but you can print and save them. You can practice using Notepad by creating your own files.

To open any desired file with the mouse, double-click the filename or click **OK**.

To open a file from the keyboard, use the Tab key to tab to the **Files** list box or press Alt + F to select that option. Then use the direction keys to select the file. Press Enter.

After you have saved a file once with the **Save As** command, use the **Save** command for subsequent saves. Notepad will use the filename displayed in the title bar for saving the file. If you have not named the file, the **Save** command will prompt for a filename.

Use the **Save As** command to save a file the first time it is saved or to save an old file under a new name. Notepad will prompt for the filename (see Figure 8.3). If no file extension is entered, Notepad assumes the .TXT extension as a default.

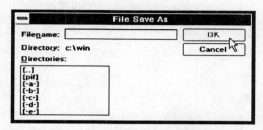

Figure 8.3 Prompting for a filename when saving.

Use the **Print** command to print documents. The command prints the entire contents of the current Notepad document in memory. If you wish to print part of a document, first save the entire document. Then edit the document to delete the portions of the document that you do not wish to print. Next use the **Print** command from the File menu. Finally, reload the original document by using the **Open** command.

Use the **Page Setup** command to define headers, footers, and margins (Chapter 5). Use the **Printer Setup** command to change the printer or any aspects of the printer (such as cartridge, orientation, paper size, etc.).

To terminate Notepad, use the **Exit** command. This command is the same as double-clicking the Control-menu icon, using **Close** from the Control menu, or pressing Alt + F4.

Note: Unlike many word processors, Notepad does not create an automatic backup of the original file when it saves a file. If you might need the original file again, save the new version of the document under a different name.

Notepad provides no command for deleting files from the disk. If you need to delete a file, use the File Manager or return to the DOS prompt and delete the file.

Editing Your Document—The Edit Menu

Use the Edit menu to make changes to a document. Notepad supports the Clipboard for editing. The **Cut**, **Copy**, and **Paste** commands work identically to those of the Calendar, Calculator, and Cardfile Edit menus described in the last chapters. **Cut** deletes the selected text from the Notepad document and places it in the Clipboard. **Copy** creates a copy of selected text in the Clipboard. **Paste** copies the Clipboard contents to the current cursor location. The shortcut keys are identical to those of Calendar, Calculator, and Cardfile.

The **Undo** command is common to many Windows application programs. It permits you to reverse the last edit that you made. For example, suppose you delete a block of text and suddenly realize that you deleted it by mistake. To recover the text, simply select **Undo** from the Edit menu or press Alt+Backspace. The deleted text will appear as it was before the deletion.

The **Delete** command removes the selected text. The command is the same as pressing the Del key. The **Delete** command is similar to the **Cut** (Shift+Del) command, except that the deleted text is not put in the Clipboard.

The **Select All** command is a quick way of selecting the entire contents of the file. Use it for deleting the entire contents of the Notepad or for copying the entire contents of the Notepad to the Clipboard.

Tip: Be careful not to accidentally hit a key when text is selected because the text will be replaced by the key you have hit.

Use the **Time/Date** command for placing the current time and date at the insertion point in the Notepad document. The shortcut keyboard command is F5. Use the **Time/Date** command for putting a date and time stamp in a document.

Use the **Word Wrap** command to switch the Notepad to a word-wrap mode. In a normal default mode, Notepad functions as an editor and requires a carriage return at the end of each line. The wordwrap mode permits you to enter very long lines, and you can use the horizontal scroll bar to scroll within the line. When wordwrap is turned on, the horizontal scroll bar disappears. Notepad automatically breaks the line at the right edge of the window. The number of characters in a line is determined by the width of the current window. Remember that wordwrap applies to the entire document. Also, once you turn wordwrap on, it applies only to the current Notepad session. If you load Notepad again (even with the same document), the wordwrap will be turned off. The wordwrap mode is useful for writing short letters.

Finding Text—The Search Menu

The Search menu is useful for finding the location of a particular word in a document. When **Find** is selected from the Search menu, the dialog box of Figure 8.4 is displayed. Enter the word for which you wish to search and toggle **Match Upper/Lowercase** if the case should also be matched. **Match Upper/Lowercase** can be toggled with the mouse or from the keyboard by using the Tab key and the Spacebar. You can also select the direction of the search (**Forward** or **Backward**). The default search is forward. Click **OK**.

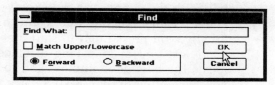

Figure 8.4 Initiating a search.

The search will always start from the insertion point, so set the insertion point before selecting the command. The search will stop on the first match that is found. If you wish a word search, place a space before and after the word in the dialog box. This will work unless the word is the last word of a sentence.

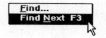

To find the next occurrence of the word set by the **Find** command, use the **Find Next** command. F3 is the shortcut key for **Find Next**.

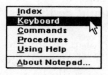

Tip: You can use Ctrl + Home as a shortcut for placing the insertion point at the beginning of the document before a search.

Getting Help—The Help Menu

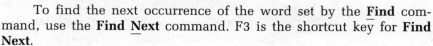

If you need help for a command or procedure, use the Help menu. Chapter 2 describes how to use this menu. You can also use the **About Notepad** option of this menu to find the size of your current file.

Exploring Notepad

Notepad is a useful program for keeping track of your time. For example, suppose that you are a computer consultant and that you are working with several clients. You start Windows, make Notepad active with the file you use for your time log, and then start Windows Write to compose a letter.

Suddenly the phone rings, and it is one of your clients needing some help. You quickly make the Notepad window active and press F5, which drops the date and time into the Notepad document. You talk with the client for a while and then hang up. You then enter the client's name and press F5 again to enter the ending date and time. Finally, you press Enter to start a new line.

Next you make a long distance call. You switch to Cardfile to locate the telephone number and to initiate the telephone call. Once you have hung up, you switch back to Notepad, press F5, and enter a record of the long distance call. The telephone number is copied from Cardfile to the Clipboard and then pasted from the Clipboard to the Notepad document. There is no chance of making an error because the number that is pasted is identical to the one that is called. At the end of the month, you can use your Notepad log for billing clients or for checking your long distance calls.

If you need memory space or wish to keep the screen uncluttered, you can always keep Notepad with the log open as an icon at the bottom of the screen instead of keeping its window open. Double-clicking the icon will quickly make the Notepad active again with your log file.

Special Features

Notepad has several features that are worth mentioning. It provides special support for creating log files, as demonstrated in the last example. To use this feature, the text string .LOG should be the first line of the Notepad file.

To see how this works, let's try it. Open a new Notepad file and put .LOG as the first line of the file (use capital letters). Now save the file under any name. Now open the file again and you will see that Notepad has placed a time/date stamp at the end of the file and has placed the insertion point at the end of the file after the time/date stamp. Enter your notes and save the file again (see Figure 8.5). The time and the date reflect when you opened the file. This information is useful for keeping a running log of a task. For example, suppose you are making changes to a software product. You could create a log file. Each time you make a program edit, bring up the file and enter the type of change at the end after the time/date stamp.

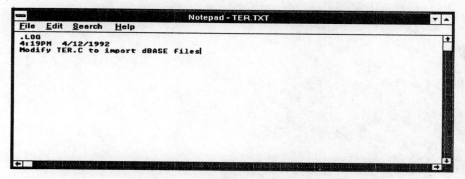

Figure 8.5 Creating a log file.

Notepad also supports the entry of any special characters from the extended ASCII set (Appendix E) to the document. To enter an extended ASCII character, hold down the Alt key and (with the keyboard in numeric mode) press the numeric value for the special character. The special character will appear on the screen. Remember that all printer character sets do not support the extended ASCII set. If a special character appears on the screen, it will not print on the printer unless the printer font set supports the extended ASCII set.

Summary

Notepad is a useful application for keeping a log of your work, editing a batch file, editing the .INI files (Chapter 18), or even writing letters. Like Clock and Calendar, it is often loaded as an icon when starting Windows so that it is easy to make active.

Using Microsoft Terminal

Terminal is a communications program that permits you to use a modem to connect with other computers to exchange information. Using Terminal, you can connect with any of the various information services (such as CompuServe or Genie) or bulletin board systems (BBS) to send or receive electronic mail and do file transfers. You can also use Terminal to transfer information between computers by using the computer's serial ports and a connecting cable.

What You Will Need

Terminal permits you to transfer information between computers in the same room by using a connecting cable or to transfer information between computers on a telephone network by using a modem.

To use Terminal to transfer information between computers in the same room, you need a special type of cable known as a *null modem* cable. This cable is used to connect the serial ports of the two computers. Both computers must have some type of communications software, such as Terminal.

To use Terminal to transfer information between computers on the telephone system, your computer must have a modem. The modem either replaces (if internal) or connects to (if external) a serial port of the computer. The modem is also connected to the telephone system, generally by a telephone cable supplied with the modem.

Terminal works with many types of modems, but the most common are the Hayes-compatible modems sold by many manufacturers.

Note: Hayes-compatible means that the modem uses control codes defined by Hayes Microcomputer Products, Inc. This is not a standard, however, because Hayes is constantly changing the control codes as its products evolve. As a result, all modems marketed as Hayes-compatible are not the same.

To use Terminal, you should also have some knowledge of modems, serial ports, and protocols. If using communications software is new to you, look for some introductory books on this topic. Appendix D provides troubleshooting ideas if you have problems.

Tip: If you are new at computer communications, you might start with local bulletin boards. These are generally free, and you won't run up a bill while you learn. Check with a local user group or a computer store to find the better ones in your area. Some systems stay quite busy. Start with a small BBS to get better access time.

Starting Terminal

Once your modem is installed, start Terminal by selecting the **Terminal** program icon in the Program Manager's Accessories group window. This will load Terminal, start it, and display Terminal's application window (see Figure 9.1).

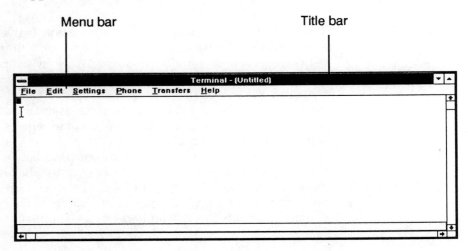

Figure 9.1 Starting Terminal.

Notice that the opening screen has six menu options: File, Edit, Settings, Phone, Transfers, and Help. The first two of these, File and Edit, are familiar from other Windows applications. In this case, the File menu controls various Terminal files for accessing each remote service that you use. Notice in Figure 9.1 that no file is selected and that the title bar shows the word (Untitled).

Exploring Terminal

For your first session, try to call a remote system and download a file. Here is the basic procedure to follow:

1. Obtain the remote computer's basic settings (see the discussion immediately following the list).
2. Start Terminal.
3. Set up the modem, communications, and phone parameters from the Settings menu.
4. Save the settings using **Save As** on the File menu.
5. Dial the number by using the **Dial** option of the Phone menu.
6. Enter identification and password information to the remote computer.
7. Use the remote system for the desired tasks.
8. Log off the remote system.
9. Hang up the modem by using **Hangup** on the Phone menu.
10. Exit Terminal.

To call a remote system, you will need to get the basic information on the remote computer: its telephone number, baud rate, data bits, stop bits, parity, type of flow control, and protocols supported. If you don't have all this information, you can make some assumptions and probably get your system to work. You will need, of course, the remote system's telephone number.

Start Terminal and get the initial screen.

Tip: If you had Terminal files (.TRM files) that you used with other versions of Windows, these will also work with Terminal in Windows 3.0. Transfer these to your Windows directory, since you may wish to open one for dialing.

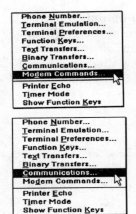

Now define the settings for your system by using the Settings menu. First, define the modem and modem command set. The default settings are for a Hayes-compatible modem. If you are using another type of modem, select **Modem Commands** and set the parameters for your modem.

Now set the communications parameters. Select **Communications** from the Settings menu and define the communications parameters for your system (see Figure 9.2). Set **Connector** to the correct serial port. Set the others to the correct value for the particular remote system that you are accessing. If you don't know the values for the remote system, set the parameters as follows:

Parameter	*Setting*
Baud Rate	Highest supported by your modem, generally 1200 or 2400
Data Bits	8
Parity	None
Stop Bits	1
Flow Control	Xon/Xoff

All of these parameters are the default values except for the baud rate, which has a default of 1200.

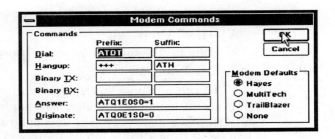

Figure 9.2 Setting the communications parameters.

Finally, set the telephone number by using **Phone Number** on the Settings menu (see Figure 9.3). Enter any prefixes necessary, such as a 9 for an outside line or a 1 for long distance services.

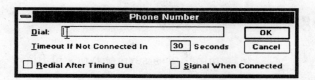

Figure 9.3 Setting the phone number.

At this point, you should save your settings in a file. Select **Save As** from the File menu. Enter the name you wish to use for the file and select **OK**.

Now initiate the dialing by selecting **Dial** from the Phone menu. The computer will dial the number and make the connection to the remote system. You should then follow the procedures of the remote system. For a BBS, this generally means entering your name and password. If you are a new user, you can usually define your own password.

If you are calling an information service (CompuServe, Genie, etc.), you generally access the remote system through an intermediate service with a local telephone number. When you sign up for one of these information services, they provide complete directions. Use Terminal to dial the local access number (which is also a computer) and then give the code for accessing the remote system.

When you have finished your work on the remote system, you enter a *signoff* command. This is normally the letter *G* or the word *bye* or *logoff*. Select **Hangup** from the Phone menu to disconnect from the phone line.

Note: It is important that you log off the remote system properly before disconnecting at your end. This forces the remote system to hang up the phone. If you fail to log off properly, the remote system may remain on the line for a while after you disconnect. If this happens, many data services will continue to bill time to your account for a few minutes.

Finally, if you have changed any parameters since you last saved the settings, select **Save** or **Save As** from the File menu and save the settings.

You can exit Terminal in any of several ways: double-clicking its Control-menu icon, selecting **Close** from the Control menu, choosing **Exit** from the File menu, or using Alt + F4.

Note: If you have trouble getting this short tutorial to work, first read the section "Setting Up Terminal for a Session." One or more of your parameters may be incorrect. If the tutorial still fails to work, read Appendix D for more troubleshooting information.

Managing Your Files

Terminal uses several types of files:

- *Text files* are useful for preparing letters ahead of time and for saving incoming text. These files are usually sent and received from the **Transfers** menu. You can create or edit text files with Notepad.

- You can send and receive *binary files* by using the binary file options of the **Transfers** menu. Binary files include programs and files in special formats.

- You can also create *parameter files* that contain the setup options for various services. Parameter files enable you to dial a service quickly without having to enter all the parameters. You can use the File menu for retrieving or saving parameter files. For example, if you dial CompuServe regularly, you could store the telephone number, baud rate, and other specifics for this data service as a single file. You could then open that file and dial the service.

The commands on the File menu are similar to those of other Windows applications. **New** permits you to create a new parameter file for a particular telephone number or service. **Open** permits you to open a parameter file. The techniques for using this dialog box have been described in previous chapters. The **Save** command permits you to save an edited configuration file. The **Save As** command permits you to save a parameter file under a specified name. The default extension is .TRM. The filename for the current parameters is displayed in the title bar. The **Exit** command terminates Terminal and is similar to using Alt + F4 or double-clicking the Control-menu icon.

Notice that there is no printing command on the File menu. Printing of a session is initiated from the Settings menu. You can, however, use the File menu to select the printer to use, just as you do with other Windows applications that have been discussed.

Setting Up Terminal for a Session

Use this section for more help in setting up Terminal if the default settings used in the short tutorial don't seem to work. Different remote systems have different setup parameters for their system. Once you've found the correct ones for a particular remote system, use the File menu to save them to a file with an appropriate name.

The settings for a particular remote system are defined from the Settings menu. Let's look at each type.

The Modem Settings

Use the **Modem Commands** option of the Settings menu to define the modem you are using and its control codes. The command displays a dialog box from which you can choose a modem or the modem commands (see Figure 9.4). This defaults to a Hayes-compatible modem. You use **Modem Defaults** to select a modem, which then places the normal control codes for that modem in the Commands area. You can then edit the command codes for that modem. For example, if you use pulse dialing, you can modify the Hayes settings for dialing from ATDT to ATDP. Select **OK** to save the settings.

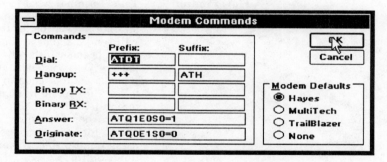

Figure 9.4 Defining the modem commands.

Communications Settings

Use the **Communications** command of the Settings menu to change the communications setting. A dialog box will be displayed (see Figure 9.5) from which you can define the communications parameters. Table 9.1 defines the options.

Table 9.1 Connection Settings

Option	Action
Baud Rate	Defines the communications data transfer rate. This rate is normally set to the highest speed supported by your modem. For a 2400-type modem, the baud rate would be 2400. Use a lower rate if you are accessing a remote system that cannot support your data transfer rate.
Data Bits	Defines the number of bits transferred at a time—normally 7 or 8 bits.
Parity	Selects the type of parity. If you are using 8 bits, select **None**. If using parity (normally with 7 bits), select either **Odd** or **Even**. If **Odd**, the 8*th* bit is always set so that the sum of the bits is odd. If **Even**, the sum is always even. **Mark** forces the 8*th* bit to always be on; **Space** forces it always off.
Flow Control	Tells Terminal what to do if the incoming buffer becomes full. **Xon/Xoff** is the default and normal setting. In this mode, Terminal will send a signal to the remote system if the buffer becomes full. The remote system then pauses. Once the local system has caught up, it sends another code to the remote system to tell the remote to continue. The **Hardware** option tells Terminal to use hardware to signal when the buffer is full. Use this option for local transfers between computers using a null cable. If **None** is selected, no flow control is used.
Parity Check	When toggled on, gives visual indications of a byte if an error occurs.
Carrier Detect	When toggled on, tells Terminal to use the modem's control codes to determine when a connection has occurred. If you have trouble connecting, try turning this option off. This will allow Terminal to use its own method to determine when a connection is made.
Connector	Defines the modem port, normally COM1 or COM2. If no connector is used, select **None**.
Stop Bits	Defines the time between characters. For most applications, select **1**.

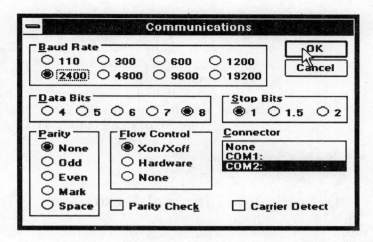

Figure 9.5 Defining the communications parameters.

Defining the Phone Parameters

To define the number to be called and to define related parameters, use the **Phone Number** command of the Settings menu. A dialog box will be displayed in which you can enter the phone number (see Figure 9.6).

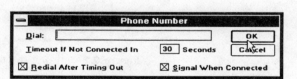

Figure 9.6 Setting the phone parameters.

You can use parentheses or dashes when entering a phone number, but they are ignored by Terminal. You can uses commas to force a delay, with each comma providing a 2-second delay. For example, to get a 4-second delay after obtaining an outside line, you could dial: 9,,555-1234. This technique is handy when you need to dial 9 for an outside line and wait for another dial tone before dialing the number.

With this same dialog box, you can use the **Timeout If Not Connected In** parameter to define how long Terminal should wait for the remote system to answer the phone. The default is 30 seconds. This value depends on the number of rings for which the remote system will wait before answering.

If you are dialing a very busy BBS, you may find it hard to get in. For an automatic redial when the remote system is busy, toggle on the **Redial After Timing Out** option. The **Signal When Connected** toggle will force the computer to beep when the connection is established.

Defining the Terminal Emulation

Remote systems may send control signals to provide some level of screen control, such as clearing the screen, cursor movement, or color support. The remote system assumes that your system can recognize these control signals and act on them. Use the **Terminal Emulation** command of the Settings menu to specify how these screen control codes are defined. This command displays a dialog box for setting the emulation (see Figure 9.7). For most bulletin board systems, the default ASCII (DEC VT-100) is the proper selection. For information services, you will need to select the proper emulation to match their settings.

Figure 9.7 Defining the terminal emulation.

Defining the Terminal Preferences

If the incoming text is double-spaced, is not spaced at all (lines on top of each other), or produces no characters or double-characters when you type, use the **Terminal Preferences** command of the Settings menu to change the terminal preferences.

Figure 9.8 shows the dialog box that is displayed. Table 9.2 defines the options.

Table 9.2 The Terminal Preferences Options

Option	Action
Line Wrap	Automatically wraps lines at the end of the line.
Local Echo	Displays keystrokes from the keyboard. Toggle this option on if what you type is not visible on the screen.
Sound	Turns on the system bell for the remote system.
Columns	Defines the column width for received text.
Terminal Font	Defines the font used by Terminal.
Show Scroll Bars	Displays scroll bars to scroll over buffer.
CR→CR/LF	Toggle on if lines are displayed on top of each other. Toggle off if display is double-spaced. You can set this option for transmissions to the remote computer (**Outbound**) or transmissions from the remote computer (**Inbound**).
Cursor	Defines the cursor type.
Translation	Defines the character set of international transmissions.
Buffer Lines	Defines the buffer size.

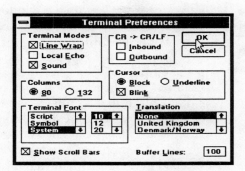

Figure 9.8 Setting the terminal preferences.

Working with Text

As you use Terminal, incoming data is saved to a buffer. You can use the commands, view the menus, or even use another program while transfers are in process. The work area displays a small portion of this buffer, and you can use the vertical scroll bar at the right to scroll the window over the buffer area.

Using the Buffer

The buffer size is defined by the **Buffer Lines** option of the **Terminal Preferences** command. The application window workspace is a window to this buffer. When you use the **Pause** command of the Transfers menu, the screen becomes stationary and is easier to read. When you are ready again, you can select the **Resume** command of the Transfers menu. While you are paused, data continues to flow into the buffer, waiting until you can read it later. If the buffer is too small, it will eventually overflow and (if the **Xon/Xoff** protocol is selected on the **Communications** dialog box) the remote system will stop sending until you've had time to catch up.

Keeping the **Buffer Lines** value high ensures that you can pause often and work with the text in the buffer. You can also scroll back over text you have previously received. A high value also means that a lot of memory is tied up and unavailable to other programs. If you need memory, keep the buffer small. If you like to pause or scroll back, keep the buffer large.

You can use the Edit menu, as with other applications, to move data to or from Terminal's window with the Clipboard. Note one difference, however. There is no **Cut** command, and a new **Send** command is on the Edit menu.

Use the **Copy** command, as with other applications, to copy text to the Clipboard. You can then use **Paste** in another application (or Terminal) to position the text in that application's window or in another place in Terminal's window.

If you paste from the Clipboard to Terminal, it is the same as entering text from the keyboard. The result is that the pasted text is sent to the remote system. For example, you could compose a letter in Notepad and then copy it to the Clipboard in Notepad. You could dial your remote system and prepare to send. Then you could select **Paste** from Terminal's Edit menu. This will send the letter to the remote system.

The **Send** command is equivalent to a **Copy** and **Paste** from Terminal's window. Use it to send text in Terminal's window to the remote system. It has the shortcut Ctrl + Shift + Ins.

Use **Select All** to select all text in the window and scroll buffer. Use **Clear Buffer** if you need to clear the buffer or free some memory.

To print text, you can use one of three methods:

- The first method is to print incoming text directly. You can toggle the printer on or off by selecting **Printer Echo** from the Settings menu. When the printer echo is toggled on, all incoming text is printed.

- The second method is to select what you wish to print and copy it to the Clipboard by using the **Copy** command of the Edit menu. Then paste it to Notepad or Microsoft Write and print it from that program.

- A final method is to capture text as a text file by using the Transfers menu. You can then print this file from another program.

Transferring Text Files

Terminal supports the transfer of text files. Text files are those created with a text editor or word processor and saved in an unformatted form. For example, you could compose a letter with Notepad and save it as a file. You could then dial the remote system. When you are ready to transmit, you could initiate the transfer of the text file. The remote system would receive it as though it were typed at the keyboard. There is very little check or verification of the transferred files. If accuracy is important, transfer a text file by using a binary transfer (see "Binary File Transfers").

Setting Text Transfer Parameters

Before transferring text, you should set the text transfer parameters. Select **Text Transfers** from the Settings menu. On the dialog box (see Figure 9.9), set the transfer parameters.

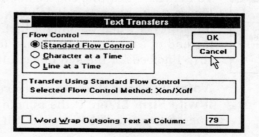

Figure 9.9 Setting the text transfer parameters.

The default transfer method is standard flow control, which uses the method defined on the Communications dialog box, normally **Xon/Xoff**. If you choose **Character at a Time** or **Line at a Time**, the dialog box changes to permit setting the options for either.

If you choose **Character at a Time**, you can set these values:

Delay Between Characters   Slows the transmission of characters to the specified value.

Wait for Character Echo   Sends a character, waits for echo, and then compares the transmitted and received characters. If the received character is correct, the next character is sent.

Avoid these types of transfer if possible because they are very slow.

If you choose **Line at a Time**, you will see these options:

Delay Between Lines   Slows the transmission of lines to the specified value.

Wait for Prompt String   Sends a line and waits for a returned code. You can specify the code. The default code is ^M, which is a carriage return.

Word Wrap Outgoing Text at Column   Specifies the column for automatic wordwrap.

Once you have selected your options, choose **OK**.

Transmitting Text Files

To transfer a text file, choose **Send Text File** from the Transfers menu. Figure 9.10 shows the dialog box that is displayed. Select the file to transmit (as when opening a file). If you wish to attach a linefeed at the end of each transmitted line, toggle **Append LF** on. If you wish to strip linefeeds at the end of each line, toggle **Strip LF** on. Choose **OK**.

Note: If the remote system receives your file double-spaced, transmit it with **Strip LF** on. If the remote system receives your file with one line on top of another, transmit it with **Append LF** on.

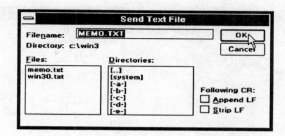

Figure 9.10 Sending a text file.

To control the transmission, you can use the **Pause**, **Resume**, or **Stop** commands of the Transfers menu or you can use the same control buttons at the bottom of the window. **Pause** temporarily halts transmission, **Resume** continues from a **Pause**, and **Stop** terminates the file transmission.

Receiving Text Files

Receiving text files is a type of capture that permits you to save incoming text. To receive a text file, select **Receive Text File** on the Transfers menu. Figure 9.11 shows the dialog box that is displayed. If this is a new file, enter the name that you wish to assign to the incoming file. If you wish to append to or overwrite an existing file, select the directory and filename of this file. Select the desired options as follows:

Append File   Adds new text to the end of the specified file.

Save Controls   Saves any formatting or control codes in the incoming text.

Table Format   The incoming text is assumed to be tabular. Converts two or more sequential spaces in the incoming text to tabs.

After you have chosen the desired options, select **OK**.

As an example, the first time you dial into a BBS you may wish to get a list of the files on the system. You can initiate the listing and then capture the incoming text to a text file (see Figure 9.12).

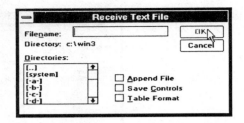

Figure 9.11 Setting up to receive a text file.

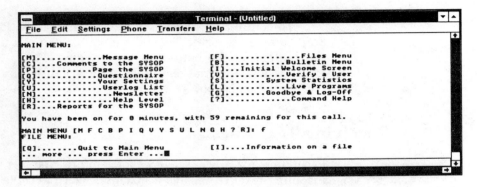

Figure 9.12 Capturing a text file.

The **Pause**, **Resume**, and **Stop** commands on the Transfers menu (or the same buttons at the bottom of the screen) can be used to control the transmission in the same way they are used for transmitting text.

Viewing Text Files

To view a text file before sending it or after it has been received, select **View Text File** from the Transfers menu. As with transmitting text, the dialog box (see Figure 9.13) permits you to append linefeeds or strip them. If the text lines are on top of each other when viewing, choose **Append LF**. If the text is double-spaced, choose **Strip LF**. Select **OK**. The **Pause**, **Resume**, and **Stop** commands work the same as when transmitting or receiving text.

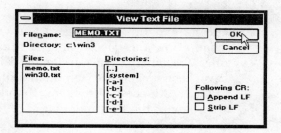

Figure 9.13 Viewing a text file.

Note: Use text transfers only for text files, such as .TXT files. Unlike binary transfers (see the next section), text transfers have no check to verify the transmission accuracy. For this reason you should not use text transfers for critical text data, such as financial information.

Binary File Transfers

Binary file transfers are used to transfer program files or other nontext files. You can also use them to transfer text files when accuracy is important.

Protocol Selection

To transfer binary files accurately, some common rules must be used by both the transmitting and the receiving systems. The basic concept is simple:

■ The transmitting system sends part of the file (a block). A byte or bytes are attached to this file, defining a mathematical value that is calculated from the bits in the block.

■ The receiving system receives the block and extra bytes and then calculates its own check value of the received bits by using the same formula.

■ The receiving system compares the two values and, if they match, sends an acknowledgment to the transmitting system that the block was received correctly. The transmitting system then sends the next block. If there is no match, the receiving system notifies the transmitting system, which transmits the block again.

The transfer process is a two-way process, and both the transmitting and the receiving systems must use the same rules (block length, how the check value is calculated, etc.). A particular set of rules for binary transmission is called a *protocol*. Many protocols have been developed for binary file transfers. Xmodem, Xmodem/CRC, 1K Xmodem, Ymodem, Zmodem, CompuServe-B, and Kermit are a few of the most popular.

Terminal supports two protocols: Xmodem/CRC and Kermit. To initiate a binary transfer, the transmitting system must support one of these protocols. Xmodem/CRC is popular with bulletin board systems. Kermit is popular with main and mini computer transfers.

To select the protocol you wish to use, select **Binary Transfers** from the Settings menu. Then select **Xmodem/CRC** or **Kermit** on the dialog box (see Figure 9.14). Then select **OK**. For **Xmodem/CRC**, the **Communications** settings should be 8 bits with parity set to **None**. For **Kermit**, you can use 7 or 8 bits and parity can be specified. When sending text files using the extended ASCII character set, select 8 bits and no parity.

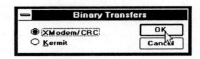

Figure 9.14 Selecting the protocol.

Note: The transmitting system must support the same protocol. Terminal supports a very limited selection. **Xmodem/CRC**, for example, doesn't work well with packet-switched lines to information systems, such as CompuServe. You should use the CompuServe-B protocol for these lines. Terminal doesn't support CompuServe-B.

Transmitting a Binary File

To transmit a binary file to a remote system, first select the proper protocol on your system. Then prepare the remote system to receive your file. For most systems, this means telling the remote system that you wish to upload the file and specifying the protocol you will use. Once this is done, the remote system goes into a waiting mode until you start. Select **Send Binary File** from the Transfers menu. On the dialog box (see Figure 9.15), select the file to transmit. Choose **OK**. Transmission will be initiated.

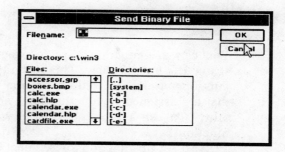

Figure 9.15 Transmitting a binary file.

If you wish to terminate the transfer, choose **Stop** from the Transfers menu or click the **Stop** button. You cannot pause a binary transfer.

Receiving Binary Files

To receive a binary file from a remote system, select the proper protocol on your system. Then tell the remote system to transmit the file. For most systems, this means telling the remote system that you wish to download a file and specifying the filename on the remote system and the remote system's protocol.

Once the remote system is ready, select **Receive Binary File** from the Transfers menu. On the dialog box (see Figure 9.16), enter the name you wish to assign to the incoming file. Choose **OK**. Terminal then sends an acknowledgment that it is ready, and the remote system will start transmitting.

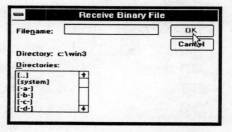

Figure 9.16 Starting to receive a binary file.

Using Function Keys

You can use function keys to execute commands or assign a text string to a function key. This technique can be used to automate various operations and reduce on-line costs. The command sequences that are assigned to function keys are a limited type of macro capability. To use a function key, press Alt + Ctrl + Fn, where n is the function key.

To set up function keys, select **Function Keys** from the Settings menu. Figure 9.17 shows the dialog box. Notice that you can assign a name and command sequence for each of eight function keys. To the right is a box labeled **Key Level** with four option buttons. Using it, you can select any of four function key levels. At each level, all eight function keys have unique names and command sequences. This means that you really have 32 function key assignments available.

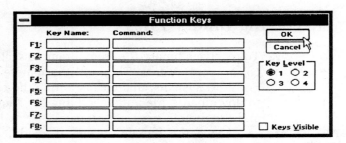

Figure 9.17 Assigning the function keys.

In making the command assignments, you have available the following controls:

Control Code	Action
^A – ^Z	Send ^A to ^Z to remote system
^$D<*nn*>	Delay *nn* seconds
^$B	Transmit 117-millisecond break
^$C	Initiate a dial
^$H	Initiate a hangup
^$L1 – ^$L*n*	Change to function key level *n*

You can also assign a text string to a function key. The text string could be your name, an ID code, a password, or any other useful text. For example, you could assign the following to a function key:

```
^$C^$DO4^M$DO2Joe^MCobb^M^$DO3or^M
```

To use the preceding command sequence, remember to press Alt + Ctrl + F*n*, where *n* is the function key to which the text string is assigned. This particular string dials a number, delays, sends a carriage return to synchronize baud rates, waits, sends the first and last names with carriage returns, delays, and sends a password.

If you want the keys at the bottom of the window to be visible, toggle **Keys Visible** on. Then select the **Show/Hide Function Keys** command of the Settings menu.

When you save a file from the File menu, the function key settings are saved with the other settings. You can have different function key setups for different services.

On-line Tips

Terminal is somewhat limited in comparison to many communications products on the market. Although greatly improved from its Windows 2 version, it still has a limited number of protocols and limited modem control, and it needs a script feature. If you do much communications, you should invest in a communications application product, such as Crosstalk for Windows (see Appendix G).

Here are a few tips for using Terminal:

- Using information services, such as CompuServe, can be expensive. Plan your sessions before dialing and have specific objectives.

- The first time you dial into a new system, find a files list and download it as a capture. Then sign off and scan the list at leisure to find files you wish to download. Then dial in again for the files.

- Prepare electronic mail ahead of time that you wish to send. Then transmit it by pasting from the Clipboard or as a text file.

- Set up function keys for access to the remote systems you use. This will speed up access and, with systems that charge, reduce on-line costs.

- Monitor your on-line time. If you select **Show Function Keys** from the Settings menu, the time is displayed in the lower right of the window. If you then select **Timer Mode** from the Settings menu, the on-line time is displayed instead.

■ On **Terminal Preferences** setting, keep the local echo off unless necessary. This ensures that the text on your screen is echoed from the remote system, and you can see what you send as the remote system received it, i.e., better accuracy. On most services, you can choose if you wish the remote system to echo. That's the better alternative.

Summary

Terminal is a valuable communications program for transferring data between computers. Terminal supports text file transfers, binary file transfers with either of two protocols (Xmodem/CRC or Kermit), and a limited macro capability.

Playing Games: Reversi and Solitaire

Microsoft Windows provides two games for entertainment: Reversi and Solitaire. Playing these games is a fun way to learn to use Windows applications.

The Reversi Game

Reversi is a computer game that is provided with Windows. It is somewhat similar to the Japanese GO game. Although deceptively simple, Reversi is actually quite complex and can keep you busy for hours.

Starting Reversi

To start Reversi, select the **Reversi** program item icon on Program Manager's Games group window. From the DOS prompt, you can start the game by entering **WIN REVERSI**. The game will start and will display the board and four playing pieces (see Figure 10.1).

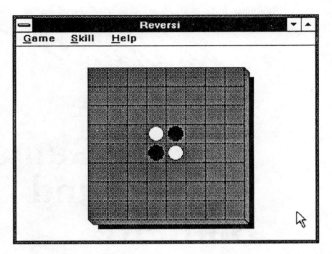

Figure 10.1 Starting Reversi.

Playing Reversi

The white (monochrome monitor) or red (color monitor) circles are your playing pieces. The black (monochrome monitor) or blue (color monitor) circles are the computer's pieces. The basic rules are quite simple:

1. Turn the black pieces (circles) to white by trapping them between white circles. You can trap pieces horizontally, vertically, or diagonally in straight lines.
2. Play until the board is filled.
3. If you can't move (and only if you can't move), select **Pass** from the Game menu.

The basic goal is to capture as many pieces as possible. When the board is filled, the person with the most pieces wins. The best way to learn is to play a few games. You will soon get the hang of the basic rules. When you drag the mouse, the cursor changes to a plus in the squares where you can make legal moves. You can use the mouse or the keyboard to make your moves:

■ To make a move with the mouse, point and click the selected square.

■ To make a move with the keyboard, use direction keys to select the square and press the Spacebar.

The game is not as easy as it looks, since the ownership of the squares changes as the game progresses. Capturing a location doesn't mean you can hold it.

Tip: Press and hold the Tab key to see all of the available moves.

Once you have mastered the default beginner level, you can make the game harder by changing the skill level. To change the skill level, select the desired level from the Skill menu. On more advanced levels, the computer will take longer to make moves and an hourglass will be displayed while it is "thinking."

If you want a better chance at winning, you can take a hint by using the **Hint** command of the Game menu. On your first few games, you may wish to use the **Hint** command at each move to get an idea of how the computer makes its decision.

To start a new game at any time, select **New** from the Game menu. To exit Reversi, use Alt+F4 or double-click the Control-box icon. There is also an **Exit** command on the Game menu.

Here are a few tips for winning:

1. Short-term strategies will generally lead to defeat. Use long-term strategies and think several moves ahead.

2. Avoid placing markers in row 2, column 2, the next to the last column, or the next to the last row if at all possible.

3. Try to capture the corners.

Terminating Reversi

To terminate the game, select **Exit** from the Game menu, double-click the Control-menu icon, choose **Close** from the Control menu, or press Alt+F4.

Solitaire

Windows also includes a version of a one-deck Solitaire game that is challenging and fun and contains good graphics. The version of Solitaire that is used is a variation of the Klondike version, also known as Canfield in England. It is fast, and winning depends on both luck and skill.

Note: The rules involve the use of color, so it's hard to play Solitaire on a monochrome monitor.

Starting Solitaire

At start-up (or if **Deal** is selected from the Game menu), the cards are dealt in a row of seven cards, with the first card on the left face up. Another row of six cards is dealt on top, with the first card face up.

Five more rows are dealt in the same way—each with one fewer card, and each with the first card face up. These are the *row stacks*. The rest of the deck is placed on the table face down. At the upper right are the four foundations on which cards are played (see Figure 10.2). These are the *suit stacks*.

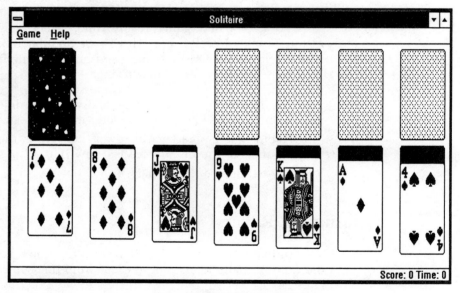

Figure 10.2 Starting Solitaire.

Objective

The basic objective is to build the four suits on each of the foundations in ascending order, starting with the Aces as soon as they are available.

Rules of Play

The face-down cards of the deck are turned face up one at a time by clicking the top card or by using the direction keys to select the deck and pressing the Spacebar. You can play onto the foundations (suit stacks) from this face-up card or from any top card in the row stacks below it. If the face-up card is not playable, it is placed face down in a waste heap.

You can also add the face-up deck card to any column in the row columns in descending alternate-color order (regardless of suit). The top card of each column is always available to play onto a foundation card or another column. Whenever a face-up card is removed (from the waste heap or the row columns), any underlying card is available for play and can be turned up.

As you play, you can also transfer any sequence of cards from one row to another, but only the face-up cards can be transferred. Empty columns can be filled only by Kings. Kings can be taken from the waste heap if on top or can be taken from any column. If taken from a column, they bring the cards on top of the King with them.

The Ace ranks the lowest (and is always the first card on a foundation). The next cards in sequence are two through ten. These are followed by the Joker, the Queen, and then the King. If you win a game, you will be rewarded by a very nice animation.

Tip: Since the right side of the tableau has more face-down cards, the left columns will give out first while you still have plenty of face-down cards on the right. To win, you will need to move sequences from the right columns leftward as opportunities arise. Always try to move cards from the stacks with the most face-down cards to other stacks.

Scoring

Solitaire supports either of two scoring systems: standard or Vegas. You can choose from either by selecting **Options** on the **G**ame menu.

With standard scoring:

- ■ You get 10 points for each card moved to the suit stacks.
- ■ You get five points for each card moved from the deck to the row stacks.
- ■ You lose 15 points each time you move a card from the suit stacks to the row stacks.

■ With Draw One, you lose 100 points for each pass through the deck after the first. With Draw Three, you lose 20 points for each pass through the deck after the third. You can choose to draw one or three from the **Options** command on the Game menu.

■ You also earn points based on how fast you play, and you earn a bonus when completing a timed game.

When using Vegas scoring, you start $52 in the hole—the amount you spend to play. You get $5 for each card placed on the suit stacks, but you have only a single pass through the deck. In the **Options** dialog box, if you turn on **Keep Scoring**, Solitaire keeps a running total of your winnings.

Options

You can add some variety to the game by using the Game menu. Use the **Deal** command when you wish to start a new game and redeal. Use the **Undo** command to undo the last play. Use the **Deck** option to change the pattern and colors on the backs of the cards. The **Options** command provides several game variations (see Figure 10.3). You can deal one or three cards at a time, use standard or Vegas scoring, turn the timer on or off, turn the status bar on or off, and toggle **Outline dragging** on or off.

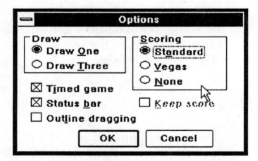

Figure 10.3 Selecting the options.

Tip: If you toggle **Outline dragging** on, moving the cards gives you an indication of all viable moves.

Use the Help menu if you need more information on how to play the game.

Terminating the Game

To terminate the game, select **Exit** from the Game menu, double-click the Control-menu icon, choose **Close** from the Control menu, or press Alt + F4.

Summary

Reversi and Solitaire are games that can provide a fun challenge during your work breaks. Reversi is a skill game based on the Japanese GO game. Solitaire is a card game that requires skill and luck. Both are a good way to learn how to use Windows applications.

Using Windows Write

Windows Write is a simple word processor that is included with Microsoft Windows. Although easy to use, Write has many of the advanced features that the more competitive commercial products do. Such features include wordwrap, justification, margin control, block moves and copies, and search and replace. Even if you already use products like WordPerfect or Microsoft Word for most of your word processing, Windows Write offers some unique features that make it worth your while to learn it for some applications. Besides being easy to use, Windows Write supports graphics, the Windows Clipboard, and all the fonts you have installed as part of your Windows system. It also serves as a good introduction for using Microsoft's more formidable Windows-based word processor, Word for Windows.

Starting Windows Write

The easiest way to start Windows Write is to select the **Write** icon from the Program Manager's Accessories group (double-click it or highlight it with the direction keys and press Enter). You can also start Write from the DOS prompt by entering `WIN WRITE`. Windows Write will load and display the application window shown in Figure 11.1. Notice that the window looks much like Notepad's window, except for the title and menu bars.

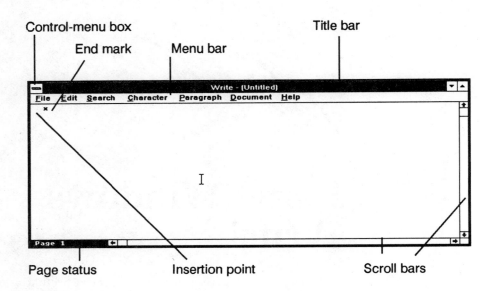

Figure 11.1 The initial screen for Windows Write.

In the upper left of the work area, you will see a flashing vertical bar which is the *insertion point*, or the location where text will be entered if you type on the keyboard. To the right of the insertion point is a funny-looking box known as an *end mark*. This box is used to mark the end of the document. At the right of the screen is a vertical scroll bar with which you can scroll through a long document by using the mouse. At the bottom of the screen is a horizontal scroll bar that permits you to scroll horizontally in the document with the mouse. At the lower left is the *page status*, which currently displays Page 1. The page status always displays the current working page. The title bar displays the name of the application program, Write, and the word Untitled in parentheses. The Untitled indicates that there is currently no file active. If you open an existing file or save your work as a file, the title bar changes to reflect the name of this file.

Exploring Write

Before getting too far in this chapter, take a few minutes to explore Write on your own. Enter a few lines of text from the keyboard. You should use the Enter key only at the end of a paragraph. Windows

Write automatically wraps text at the end of the line. Use the Back-space key to correct your typing if you make a mistake as you enter the text.

You will probably find that Windows Write is easy to use. Just as with other Windows applications, you can use the **Save As** command to save your document when you finish. You can use the Edit menu to make corrections in your text. Using the Search menu, you can find any word or phrase in your text. The next three menus —Character, Paragraph, and Document—are used to format your work. Take a look at all the menus, explore the scroll bars, and print your document from the File menu by using the **Print** command.

Using the Write Menus

The menu bar of Write includes seven menu options: File, Edit, Search, Character, Paragraph, Document, and Help. We will examine each of these in turn.

File Management—The File Menu

The first six commands of the File menu are **New, Open, Save, Save As, Print**, and **Printer Setup**. These commands are similar to those of other Windows applications. However, when you use these commands, you will notice that some of the dialog boxes have more options than in the other Windows applications.

As with other applications, use the **New** command to restart the program. More specifically, use it for clearing the screen and starting a new document when you have been working on another. If the old document has not been saved, Write will query you whether you wish to save the old document. The screen will then clear, and the title bar will again display the word (Untitled). This is much like putting a clean piece of paper on your desk and getting ready to write on it. The insertion point is a flashing vertical bar in the upper left, and the end mark follows the insertion point. The page status indicates page 1.

Use the **Open** command when you are opening files that you have already created for editing. When this command is initiated, the Open dialog box is displayed, as shown in Figure 11.2. At the left is a list of files that match the template in the upper left. The right list box gives available directories. The default template in the list box shows the .WRI extension, which is the extension used by all Windows Write files. You can edit this template to show other files. For example, if you wish to edit a Microsoft Word file, you would edit this template for the .DOC extension and then click **OK** or press Enter. If you wish to change disk drives, you can either double-click the disk drive in the list box or click the disk drive once and click **OK** or press Enter. If you wish to move down a subdirectory, you can double-click the subdirectory name in the list box or click it once and click **OK**. If you wish to move up to a parent directory, double-click the two periods in the right list box. In this way you can easily move around between disk drives, directories, and subdirectories when you need to locate files to open.

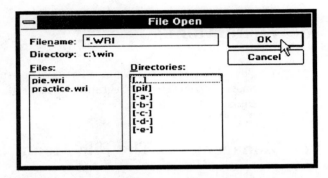

Figure 11.2 The dialog box for the **Open** command.

If you try to open a Microsoft Word document, first change the template in the Open dialog box to select the .DOC files. When you select the file you want and choose **OK**, a dialog box will appear, asking if you wish to convert the document to Microsoft Write. Choose the **Convert** option. If you try to read an ASCII formatted file, such as a Notepad .TXT file, you will also be prompted for conversion to Microsoft Write. Select **No Conversion**. If you make a mistake on this dialog box, select to open the file again, but don't save the first file before opening.

Note: Back up a file before converting it to the Write format.

Use the **Save** command for saving your work to a disk once you have used **Save As** to save it the first time. If you forget and try to save your file the first time with **Save**, Windows Write will recognize that you have not defined a filename. Write then prompts you for the filename just as if you were using the **Save As** command. This is a bad practice, however, because not all Windows applications will prompt you. For better security of your files, use the **Save As** command to save a file the first time and **Save** on subsequent saves.

Use the **Save As** command to save your document the first time, since a filename has not yet been defined. Write prompts you with a dialog box (see Figure 11.3). Enter the filename in this dialog box. The default extension, if you do not define one, is .WRI for Windows Write files. Notice also the additional options at the bottom of the dialog box.

Make Backup forces Write to make an automatic backup of the previous file each time you save your work. This file will have a .BKP extension. The **Text Only** option permits you to save only the text of your file, omitting graphics. The **Microsoft Word Format** option permits you to save your file in the Microsoft Word format with the .DOC extension. This option also creates a backup with a .BAK extension. Graphics will be lost if you save your file in a Microsoft Word format. This option is useful for spell checking because Windows Write does not have a spelling checker. You can simply import the text to Microsoft Word and do your spell checking there.

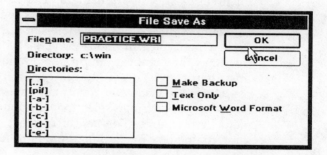

Figure 11.3 Saving the document.

Use the **Print** option to print your document on the current printer device. Selecting this command displays a dialog box from which you can choose your print options (see Figure 11.4). The first option defines the number of copies to print. **Draft Quality** is useful for printing your documents quickly at a lower resolution, if your printer supports a draft mode. **Pages** is useful for defining the page range of the document to print. Use this option if a page jams in the printer and you need to reprint only that one page. Printing is initiated by clicking **OK** or pressing Enter.

After a document is printed, Write places on the screen, as part of the document view, a small double-right arrow to indicate page breaks. The marks are not *dynamic;* that is, the page break marks will

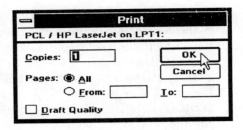

Figure 11.4 Printing the document.

not change as you edit your document. If you make edits in your document and wish to see where the new page breaks will occur without printing the document, use the **Repaginate** command on the File menu.

Use the **Printer Setup** command to change the active printer. This command displays a dialog box from which you can select the desired printer (see Figure 11.5). The command also has another useful function. If you are using a laser printer, it selects the active cartridge to use and the orientation. When you select the laser printer and click **Setup**, a second dialog box is displayed (see Figure 11.6) from which you can choose several printer options. You can set the cartridge, the print resolution, the orientation, and other features from this dialog box. This feature is very important because the fonts displayed by the Character menu are determined by the printer. As you change your cartridge selection, the fonts displayed in the Character menu will change. You can also select or install soft fonts from this same dialog box by clicking **Fonts** on the dialog box.

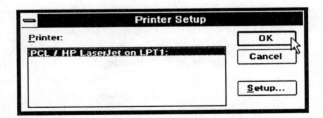

Figure 11.5 Changing the printer.

Use the **Repaginate** command to mark page breaks in the document without printing the document. This command is useful for seeing where the page breaks occur before you print the document at the printer. When you select this option, a dialog box is displayed (see Figure 11.7). The box has one option: **Confirm Page Breaks**. This

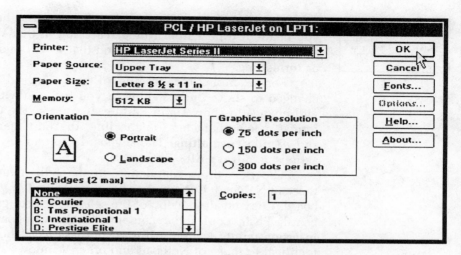

Figure 11.6 The second dialog box.

option forces Write to prompt you for confirmation of each page break. In most cases, you should select this option, since without it Write will make its own decision as to where page breaks should occur. These may not be where you want them. The page breaks will be marked in the screen view of the document with a double-right arrow.

Figure 11.7 Repaginating a document.

The **Exit** command permits you to terminate Windows Write and return to the Program Manager.

Editing Your Document—The Edit Menu

The Edit menu is much like the Edit menu in other Windows applications and has many of the same options.

Note: On starting, no options on the Edit menu will be active, since there is no text to edit. To explore the options, you must first enter some text and then select the text.

The **Undo** command permits you to undo the last change that you made. It differs from Notepad's **Undo** in that Write's **Undo** command will display the type of action that it will undo: typing, editing, or formatting.

For example, type a line of text. The Edit menu has now changed to show **Undo Typing**. If you try to edit the line, the menu will change to show **Undo Editing**. If you use the Character menu to format a few characters on the line, the Edit menu will change to show **Undo Formatting**. The keyboard shortcut keys for undoing any action are always Alt+Backspace.

The next three commands on the Edit menu are identical to those of Notepad. **Cut** removes the selected text or graphic to the Clipboard. **Copy** creates a copy of the selected text or graphic in the Clipboard. **Paste** copies the contents of the Clipboard to the current insertion-point location. All three of these have shortcut keys that are identical to those of Notepad and other Windows applications: **Cut** is Shift+Del, **Copy** is Ctrl+Ins, and **Paste** is Shift+Ins.

The next two commands are unique to Windows Write. Use **Move Picture** to move a graphic horizontally in the document. Use **Size Picture** to change the size of a graphic. The next chapter will show you examples of both commands, but for now we will simply review the basic commands.

To move a picture with the mouse, use the following procedure:

1. Select the graphic to move.

2. Select the **Move Picture** command from the Edit menu. The graphic will be marked with a rectangle. A small icon will appear in the rectangle.

3. Move the rectangle horizontally with the mouse to place the graphic in the new position.

4. Click the mouse at the new position. The graphic will move to the new position.

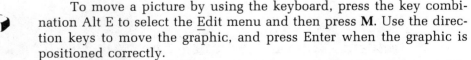

To move a picture by using the keyboard, press the key combination Alt E to select the Edit menu and then press **M**. Use the direction keys to move the graphic, and press Enter when the graphic is positioned correctly.

The **Size Picture** command works similarly. Select the graphic and then the command. The graphic is marked with a rectangle, and contains an icon. Move the icon to the lower right and resize the graphic with the mouse. Click the desired size. You can also resize from the keyboard with the direction keys and Enter.

Locating Text—The Search Menu

Use the Search menu for locating or replacing text. The Search menu has four commands: **Find**, **Repeat Last Find**, **Change**, and **Go To Page**.

Use the **Find** command to find specified text. When the **Find** command is selected, a window is displayed in which you can specify the text for which to search (see Figure 11.8). Notice that this window is different from the dialog boxes displayed by other commands you have used. There is no Cancel button. To abort a **Find** command, you can double-click the icon in the upper left to close the window or use Alt + F4 if the Find window is active. To switch between the Find window and the document window, you can click either window to make it active or you can use Alt + F6.

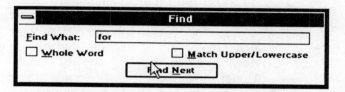

Figure 11.8 Initiating a **Find** command.

The text for which you wish to search is entered in the text box of the Find window. You can also specify the options **Whole Word** and **Match Upper/Lowercase**. If **Whole Word** is checked, the **Find** command will succeed only if Write can find the specified characters as a whole word. For example, suppose you have the words *for* and *form* in your text. In the default mode, if you put *for* in the Find box, Write would stop at both *for* and *form*. If you have **Whole Word** checked, Write would stop only at the word *for*. The **Match Upper/Lowercase** option will locate text only if the case of the letters in the Find window matches the case of the letters in the document. In the default mode, Windows Write ignores case. The search will be initiated for the specified text. If found, the text is highlighted (selected). The search will always begin at the current location of the insertion point. You can use Ctrl + Home to move the insertion point to the beginning of a document so that the search will start at the beginning.

You can initiate a search for the next occurrence by clicking **Find Next** in the Find window. You can also close the window and use the F3 key or the **Repeat Last Find** command of the Search menu to locate the next occurrence in the document. You can use wildcard characters in the Find phrase to specify searches. Table 11.1 shows the wildcard characters that are permitted. For example, *b?b* would match on *bab* or *bob* because *?* represents a wildcard character match.

Table 11.1 Wildcard Characters Permitted in Windows Write

Template	Matches
?	Any character
^w	Any combination of tabs, spaces, page breaks, or paragraph marks
^t	Any tab character
^p	Any paragraph mark
^d	Any page break

Use the **Change** command of the Search menu for search and replace operations. This command is similar to the **Find** command in that a window is displayed containing a title bar and a control-menu icon (see Figure 11.9). The Find phrase can be specified in the window, and you can also specify a match for **Whole Word** or **Match Upper/Lowercase**. The difference is that you also specify a character string to replace the text for which you are looking. Notice that the window contains these options: **Find Next**; **Change, then Find**; **Change**; and **Change Selection/All**.

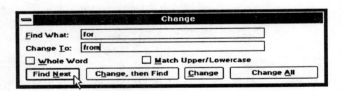

Figure 11.9 Initiating a search and replace.

The last option in the box will be **Change Selection** if you select text and **Change All** if you select no text. Use the **Change Selection/All** option with discretion, since it performs a global replacement without prompting, and some of these replacements may not be where you expect them. The replacement begins from the current location of the insertion point. As with **Find**, you can use Alt + F6 to switch between windows. If the Change window is active, you can use Esc, Alt + F4, or a double-click of the Change control-menu icon to abort the replacement.

Formatting Characters—The Character Menu

Before discussing the Character menu, let's look briefly at how the menu bar is organized. The next three menus are Character, Paragraph, and Document. The order of the menus refers to the hierarchy of the document organization, from the smallest unit to the largest. The Character menu is used for formatting characters in the document. The Paragraph menu is used for formatting paragraphs in the menu. The Document menu is used for formatting the entire document. The program doesn't adhere strictly to this rule, but keeping this in mind will help you understand the role of each menu.

The Character menu, then, is useful for controlling the formatting of characters on the screen. Once a command is issued, it will affect whatever characters are selected on the screen. You could select a single character, a word, a sentence, a paragraph, or the entire document. Simply select the characters you wish to format (see "Editing Your Document," Chapter 12) and then select the command.

Notice that the Character menu is divided into four sections. The first two sections act together to control the attributes of the character. Using the attributes sections, you can create bold, italic, or underlined text. You can also create superscripts and subscripts. Use the **Normal** command for resetting the attributes to *normal*, that is, without any special attributes. Notice there are four shortcut keys for setting the attributes. Ctrl+B will set the attributes to bold, Ctrl+I will set the attributes to italics, and Ctrl+U will set the attributes to underline. The F5 key resets the attributes to a normal mode. The attributes in the second section can be mixed. You can select both **Bold** and **Italic**, for example. Check marks will appear next to the attributes that are selected.

Selecting **Superscript** places the characters slightly above their normal position and in a slightly smaller size. This is useful for entering footnotes, mathematical equations, and chemical formulas. The **Subscript** attribute places characters slightly below the normal position and slightly smaller. This is useful for chemical formulas.

The third section of the Character menu is useful for selecting any of three fonts. *Font* refers to the individual design or styling of the character. The particular fonts that appear on the menu depend on the printer selected. This menu displays a maximum of three fonts. If your printer supports more fonts, you can select additional fonts by using the **Fonts** command in the fourth section.

It should be emphasized that the Character menu is a *dynamic* menu. The fonts section will change with the printer selected. If you have a laser printer, it also will change with the cartridge selected. If you need a font that is not on this menu and if your printer supports it, use the **Printer Setup** command from the File menu to select the desired printer and cartridge. The dialog box of the **Fonts** command should then change to reflect the new fonts available. The fonts section may also change.

The fourth section is used to control the size of the font. Clicking **Reduce Font** reduces the character size by two points. Clicking **Enlarge Font** increases the character size by two points. Again, the sizes available are affected by the current printer. If your printer does not support a larger size in a particular font, clicking **Enlarge Font** will change neither the display nor what is printed. If your printer supports a wider range of font sizes and these commands don't seem to work, check the dialog box of the **Fonts** command to see which sizes are available. Then use the **Printer Setup** command on the File menu as necessary to change the printer or cartridge.

Use the **Fonts** command for selecting any of the fonts available on your printer as well as for choosing font sizes. The fonts dialog box (see Figure 11.10) shows all the fonts that are available with the current printer and all the font sizes available for each font. As you select different fonts in the list box, the sizes displayed in the size box will change to reflect the sizes available for that particular font. Both the font list box and the size list box have scroll bars.

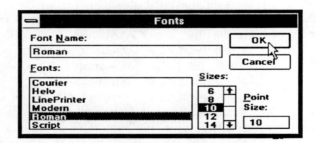

Figure 11.10 Changing the font.

The **Fonts** command dialog box has another useful function: it permits you to set up a document for a printer on another system. Suppose, for example, you have a Postscript printer at your work place. At home you have Windows Write, but only a dot-matrix printer. There are two ways you can create a document at home that will print on the Postscript printer at work, assuming you also have Windows Write at work:

■ *Method One.* When you are creating the document at home, select the **Fonts** command and type the name of the font and the size you want, even though these are not displayed in the fonts list box. The program will accept your selections, even though the screen will not show the new font or size.

■ *Method Two.* Install the print driver for your at-work printer into your home Windows program, even if you don't have a PostScript printer. Then you can select that printer from the **Printer Setup** command, set up the cartridge and other features for the printer, and select the font and font size that you need in the program. The display will change to reflect the printed image, even though you can't print it at home on your dot-matrix printer. You can switch back and forth between the two printers with the **Printer Setup** command or with Control Panel (Chapter 17).

If you wish, you can even install Windows to two directories. In one directory, you could install Windows for the printer that you have at home, and in the second you could install it for the printer at work. This is the preferred alternative if you do much with both printers because each version of Windows will then start with the proper default printer. (This will, however, use a lot of disk space.)

Tip: Font sizes are measured in points. A *point* is equal to 1/72 of an inch. The font size is measured from the top of the highest letter to the bottom of the lowest descender of the character set. Since capital letters have no descenders, you cannot get the character height by measuring a capital letter. A 12-point font, for example, would measure 1/6 of an inch from the top of the highest letter to the bottom of the lowest.

Choosing a Font

The font that you choose is an important part of your message. Over a thousand fonts are available to publishers today. For most purposes, you will need only a few fonts on your computer. The most popular fonts are probably Courier, Line Printer, Times Roman, and Helvetica.

The Courier font is common to most typewriters and is almost always a single 12-point size. The Line Printer font is normally an 8-point size. Both of these are *fixed-width* fonts; that is, each character in the character set has the same horizontal width. An *i* takes up just as much horizontal space as a *w*.

Times Roman and Helvetica, in contrast, are *proportional* fonts; that is, the characters are of varying widths. An *i* would take much less space than a *w*. Times Roman is a *serif* font. In serif fonts, the main strokes of the letters have small horizontal lines at the top or bottom of the stroke. These *serifs* help to guide the eye along the printed line. Times Roman is popular for lengthy text, such as newspapers, magazines, and books, because it is easy for the eye to read.

Helvetica is a *sans serif* typeface (no serifs on the letter strokes) that is frequently used in headlines and section headings. It is also easily readable, however, and can be used in business correspondence, brochures, and proposals.

Avoid the use of too many fonts in one document. Using too many fonts distracts from the message and makes the text hard to read.

Tip: If the entire selected region is the same font, style, and size, the Character menu will have a check mark by the font name, and the Fonts dialog box will indicate the font size.

Formatting Paragraphs—The Paragraph Menu

Use the Paragraph menu to format paragraphs in a document. The Paragraph menu has four sections. The first section restores the settings to a normal, or default, mode. The second section sets the alignment. The third section sets the spacing. The fourth section sets the indents.

Remember that anything you set from this menu applies only to the currently selected paragraphs (the paragraph in which the insertion point is located) and to subsequent paragraphs you enter. If you want a command to apply to the entire document, you must select the entire document first (see "Editing Your Document," Chapter 12) and then initiate the command.

The first section of the Paragraph menu has a single **Normal** command. Selecting this command restores the selected paragraph to the normal alignment, spacing, and indents; that is, left-aligned, single-spaced, and no indent.

The second section permits you to set the alignment. The *alignment* is the positioning of the text within the line. The default **Left** alignment places the text flush left with the left margin, and the text is ragged at the right margin. This alignment is often used for correspondence and even some newsletters. **Centered** alignment places the text centered within the current margins. This is useful for headlines, headings, and other design elements. **Right** alignment places the text flush with the right margin. You might use this alignment for a date at the top of a letter. **Justified** alignment places the text in the paragraph flush with both left and right margins, adding spaces between words as necessary to justify the text. **Justified** alignment is used in books and in some newspapers and magazines.

The next section of the Paragraph menu is used to define the spacing of the paragraph. You can select from **Single Space**, **1 1/2 Space**, and **Double Space**. The text spacing in the document is automatically adjusted for different font sizes.

The final section is used to set the indents of the paragraph. The **Indents** command displays a dialog box from which you can set the left indent, the first line indent, and the right indent (see Figure 11.11). For example, for a quotation you might wish to set a left indent and a right indent for the paragraph.

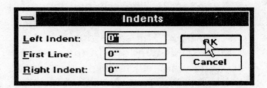

Figure 11.11 Setting the paragraph indents.

By controlling the indent of the first line, you can create normal indents or hanging indents. In a hanging indent, the first line extends further to the left than the rest of the paragraph. This kind of indent is often used with numbered lists or bulleted text. For a hanging indent, the **First Line** value is negative.

Indents are measured from the current margins. The margins are set from the **Page Layout** command of the Document menu. Set the margins first and then the indents.

Windows Write places a hidden character, or *paragraph mark*, at the end of each paragraph. This mark contains the formatting information for the paragraph and is not displayed on the screen. You must be careful not to erase this paragraph mark when you are editing. Erasing it is easy to do when you are merging or breaking paragraphs. If you accidentally erase a paragraph mark, the formatting information for that paragraph will be lost and the paragraph must be reformatted. You can select, delete, copy, and move a paragraph mark just as you can any other character. When moving or copying paragraphs, be sure to include the paragraph mark at the end of the paragraph so that the format will be retained.

Formatting the Document—The Document Menu

Use the Document menu to set headers, footers, the ruling line, tabs, and the page layout. This menu, like the Character and Paragraph menus, is divided into sections. The first section sets any headers and footers, the second sets the ruler and tabs, and the third section controls the page layout.

The **Header** command defines a line or lines that will print at the top of every page. When you issue the command, you will see a Page Header dialog box overlaying a new HEADER window (see Figure 11.12). The original document window is no longer visible. This new HEADER window is displayed with the title bar showing HEADER. The same document window menu bar is displayed in the HEADER window. In the work area of the HEADER window, you can type whatever text you wish for the header. You may use one or more lines. The Page Header dialog box defines the distance of the header from the top of the page and whether it will print on the first page. You can switch between the two windows that are displayed by clicking the window you wish to make active or by using the Alt + F6 key.

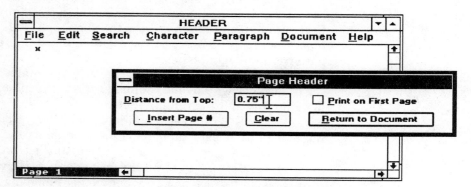

Figure 11.12 Entering a header.

Once the header is entered, you can return to the document window by using the **Return to Document** button on the Page Header dialog box. The header will not be shown in the document window. If you want to clear the header later, select **Heading** from the Document menu and click the **Clear** button of the Page Header window. Editing a header is much like editing a document. Display the heading by using the **Header** command and use the Edit menu or the editing methods explained in "Editing your Document" (Chapter 12). Once a header is defined, it will print on every page of your document.

Tip: When you are defining the header location, be careful to specify a sufficient distance from the top in the Page Header dialog box. The header is printed within the margins of the document. Some printers, including laser printers, will not print text if it is too close to the edge of the page. Be sure that the value specified in the Page Header window is within the printing area of the page as defined for your printer.

The **Footer** command works similarly to the **Header** command, except that it places the text at the bottom of the page. The original document window disappears, and instead a Page Footer dialog box is displayed on top of a new work area having the title bar FOOTER. In the FOOTER window, you enter the text that you want to appear at the foot of each page. The Page Footer dialog box permits you to control the distance from the bottom of the page and whether the footer will print on the first page. You can switch between the two windows by clicking the window to make it active or by using Alt + F6. Once the footer is entered, clicking **Return to Document** will restore you to the original document. The footer will not be displayed in the document window.

You can insert page numbers either in a header or in a footer. Both the header and footer windows have small buttons that indicate **Insert Page #**. Clicking this button inserts the current page number at the insertion point. The page number will be indicated by the word *page* with parentheses around it. You can include text as well as the page number. For example, you could have the word *Page* or *page* before the page number, e.g., *Page 21*.

The **Ruler On** command displays a ruler line at the top of the document page and shows small icons that are useful with a mouse for setting tabs, spacing, and alignment (see Figure 11.13). Notice that the icons are in three groups. The two icons on the left are used for setting tabs, either normal tabs or decimal tabs. The center three icons are used for setting the spacing, and the icons on the right are used for setting the alignment. The current values are shown as highlighted icons.

The tabs are set by using the two left-most icons. The first one sets a regular tab in the document. Windows Write defaults to automatic tabs at half-inch increments. Setting your own tabs will clear these preset tabs. To set a normal tab, click the icon at the far left to highlight it. Then click the location in the ruler line where you want to set a tab. A small right-angled arrow, shaped like the tab arrow, will appear on the ruler line. The other tab icon is used to set decimal tabs. These tabs are used for placing numbers in columns in which the decimal points must be aligned. To set a decimal tab, click the decimal tab icon and then click the location in the ruler line where

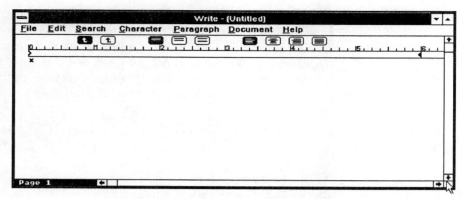

Figure 11.13 Setting tabs, spacing, and alignment.

you want to place the tab. To remove a tab, drag the tab marker down and off the ruler.

At the left and right of the ruler line are two black arrows that indicate the current margins. You can change either margin by dragging the corresponding margin with the mouse. Inside the left margin is a small, white rectangle. This is the indicator for the current indent. You can change the indent by dragging this small rectangle to the desired position on the ruler line.

Note: A decimal tab defines the location of the decimal point.

Use the **Ruler On** command to control the settings of an individual paragraph. These settings are also document controls, however, in the sense that once something is set from this command it will apply to all subsequent text entered to the document. For example, you could set this command before entering any document text, and all text for that document would follow the alignment and spacing that you had specified. You could then use the Paragraph menu commands to change individual paragraphs, such as a quoted paragraph in which you wanted a left and right indent.

Once the ruler is turned on, the menu changes to display **Ruler Off**. Select this command to hide the ruler.

If you have no mouse, you can use the **Tabs** command to set the document tabs from the keyboard. This command displays a window (see Figure 11.14) from which you can set either regular or decimal tabs.

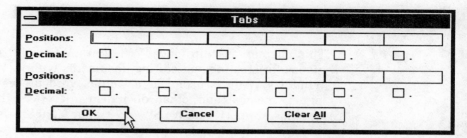

Figure 11.14 Setting the tabs.

The **Page Layout** command is used to set the starting page number, margins, and the unit of measurement. The **Start Page Numbers At** command defaults to 1, and is used for automatic page numbering in headers or footers.

Windows Write permits you to set four margins: left, right, top, and bottom. The default values are a left and right margin of 1.25 inches and a top and bottom margin of 1 inch. The default measurement unit is an inch. You may change any of these for your document (see Figure 11.15).

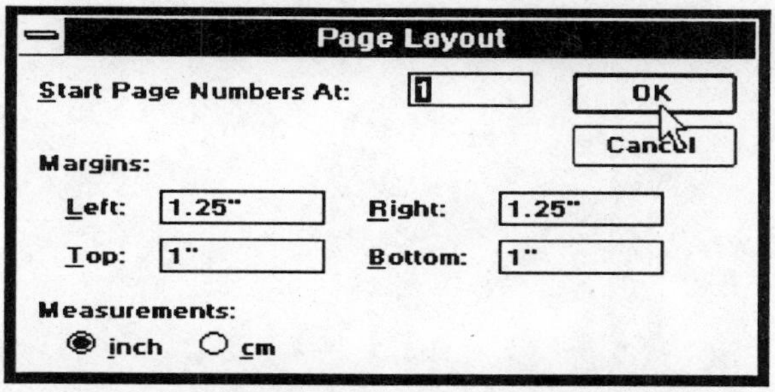

Figure 11.15. Setting the margins.

In formatting your document, you can force page breaks at specific points in your document. The general strategy for long documents is to use the **Repaginate** command of the File menu to mark the page breaks in your document without printing it. The page breaks will be indicated by a double-right arrow. You can then adjust them either by editing (adding and deleting text) or by using the Ctrl+Enter keys to force a page break at a specific location. The forced page break will be indicated by a dotted line across the page.

Summary

This chapter has introduced Windows Write and some basic techniques for creating and editing documents with it. You will find that Windows Write is useful as a simple word processor for preparing letters, memos, and other documents. It offers the advantages of graphics support and WYSIWYG (What You See Is What You Get) display—features not supported by many other word processors. Before leaving this chapter, practice using Write with a few simple documents. Then turn to Chapter 12 for more advanced techniques that you can use with Windows Write.

Applying Windows Write

Now that you've learned the basic Write commands, let's apply them. This chapter will describe editing techniques, including hyphenation, and then guide you through an editing example.

Editing Your Document

Windows Write provides an extensive array of editing features for a document. Some of these are unique to the Windows Write application and are not supported by Notepad or other Windows applications.

As with Notepad, text that you type from the keyboard is entered at the insertion point or as a replacement for selected text. The insertion point is a flashing vertical line. You can edit with the mouse or with the keyboard.

Editing with a Mouse

Editing is generally simpler with the mouse, but it depends on the user's personal preference. The *mouse cursor* is a solid vertical line with small arrows at each end. As you move the mouse about, the mouse cursor follows the movements of the mouse. When you move the mouse slightly to the left of the text area, the mouse cursor changes to a small arrow that points upward. This far left edge of the window is the *selection bar area*. The mouse behaves differently when the cursor is in the selection bar than when it is in the text. If you click the mouse in the text area, the insertion point moves to the location where you click the mouse. If you double-click a word, the entire word is selected and any text entered from the keyboard will replace that word. Holding down Ctrl and clicking the mouse will select the entire sentence.

When the mouse cursor is in the selection bar, clicking the mouse selects the entire line to the right of the mouse cursor. Double-clicking the mouse selects the entire paragraph. Holding down Ctrl and clicking the mouse will select the entire document. Table 12.1 shows the mouse selection options.

Table 12.1 Options for Mouse Selections

To Select	Mouse Action
Character	Click character.
One word	Double-click on word.
Several words or text string	Drag from beginning to end.
Block of text	Click at beginning; then hold down Shift and click at end.
Line	Click at left of line in selection bar.
Several lines	Drag in selection bar.
Paragraph	Double-click in selection bar at left of paragraph.
Sentence	Hold down Ctrl and click in sentence.
Entire document	Press Ctrl and click in selection bar.

Tip: Selecting the entire document is useful when a format must be applied to the entire document.

To select a block of text, first click the mouse at the beginning of the block to move the insertion point to that location. Then hold down the Shift key and click the mouse at the end of the block. The entire block will be selected and highlighted.

Once you have selected the text, you can delete it with the keyboard by choosing the **Cut** command of the Edit menu, or you can create a copy in the Clipboard by using the **Copy** command of the Edit menu. Selecting the **Paste** command from the Edit menu will replace any selected text in the document with the contents of the

Clipboard. When any text is selected, whatever is entered from the keyboard or pasted from the Clipboard always replaces the current text of the document. If no text is selected, text entered from the keyboard or pasted from the Clipboard will be inserted at the current insertion point.

If no text is selected and there is only an insertion point, Windows Write acts in an *insert mode*. Whatever text you enter is entered at the insertion point. Text to the right of the insertion point is moved to permit space for the new text. When one or more characters are selected, Windows Write is in a *replace mode* (or *overwrite mode*). Whatever characters are entered from the keyboard or whatever characters are pasted from the Clipboard will replace the selected characters.

Editing with the Keyboard

You can also do extensive editing directly from the keyboard without a mouse. This is useful for working with a laptop computer when there is no space for a mouse. You will also find that some types of edits are faster and easier from the keyboard than from the mouse, for example, selecting a word or a sentence. In general, you should also use the keyboard instead of the mouse when recording a macro (Chapter 15).

As with the mouse, text typed from the keyboard will be entered at the current insertion point. You can use the Left and Right Arrow keys to move the insertion point one character at a time. You can use the Up and Down Arrows to move the insertion point up or down a line. Holding down the Ctrl key and using the Right and Left Arrows will move the insertion point a word at a time. The Home key moves the insertion point to the start of a line, and the End key moves it to the end of a line.

For moving larger distances, you can think of the **5** key on the keypad as a *goto key*. Table 12.2 shows how you can use this **5** key with the direction keys to move the insertion point over larger distances. For example, pressing **5** plus the Down Arrow moves the insertion point down one paragraph. Pressing **5** plus Home moves the insertion point to the beginning of the document, and **5** plus End moves the insertion point to the end of the document. You can also use PgDn to move one screen down in the document and to move the insertion point to the next screen. PgUp moves you up in the document, placing the insertion point in the new page. Ctrl+PgUp moves the insertion point to the top of the current page, and Ctrl+PgDn moves the insertion point to the bottom of the current page.

Table 12.2 Using the Keyboard to Move the Insertion Point

To Move	Action
One character	Use ← or →
One word	Ctrl + ← or Ctrl + →
One line	Use ↑ or ↓
Start of line	Home
End of line	End
One sentence	5 + ← or 5 + →
One paragraph	5 + ↑ or 5 + ↓
Top or bottom of window	Ctrl + PgUp or Ctrl + PgDn
Top or bottom of document	5 + Home or 5 + End
Scrolling Movement	
One screen	PgDn or PgUp
Start of document	Ctrl + Home
End of document	Ctrl + End
One page	5 + PgDn or 5 + PgUp

To select a block of text, first place the insertion point at the beginning of the block. Hold down the Shift key and move the cursor point to the end of the block. For example, to select to the end of the line from the current insertion point, hold down the Shift key and press End. To select from the insertion point to the end of the paragraph, press Shift + 5 + ↓ .

There are a few keyboard shortcuts that you should remember. These are so useful that you might want to use them even with the mouse. Shift + → or Shift + ← selects the current character. Ctrl + Shift + ← or Ctrl + Shift + → selects the current word. Shift + ↑ or Shift + ↓ selects the current line. Table 12.3 shows the keyboard selection keys.

Table 12.3 Keyboard Selection Keys

To Select	Action
Character	Shift + ← or Shift + →
Word	Shift + Ctrl + ← or Shift + Ctrl + →
Line	Shift + ↑ or Shift + ↓

Note: As a general rule, hold down the Shift key and press the corresponding keys for moving the insertion point.

Remember that all the editing commands of the Edit menu have shortcuts. To cut the currently selected text and place it in the Clipboard, use Shift + Del. To create a copy of a selected text in the Clipboard, use Ctrl + Ins. To paste the contents of the Clipboard at the current insertion point, use Shift + Ins. You can also use the Del key to delete the selected text without putting it in the Clipboard.

Using Hyphens

Hyphenation is useful for improving the image of justified text in small columns. When you are using Windows Write with justified text, Write justifies the text (makes the right margin straight) by placing extra space between the words. If the columns are fairly narrow, this extra space can be objectionable (see Figure 12.1). To minimize this extra space, you should hyphenate words that occur at the end of a line (see Figure 12.2). Windows Write does not hyphenate automatically, but it does support manual hyphenation.

When   using justification   in narrow columns, it is often necessary to use hyphens to improve readability and eliminate white space.

Figure 12.1 Justifying a narrow column.

To understand the use of hyphens, you must understand the difference between a hard hyphen and a soft hyphen. A *hard hyphen* is a hyphen that is entered from the keyboard by using the hyphen key. A hard hyphen remains in the document regardless of the line breaks. Hard hyphens often occur in hyphenated words, such as in the phrase *time-dependent variable*. A *soft hyphen* is a hyphen that is used only at the end of a line. If subsequent edits change the line so that the word is no longer hyphenated, the hyphen will disappear. To insert a soft hyphen, use Shift + Ctrl + −. Remember that placing a soft

**When using justi-
fication in narrow
columns, it is often
necessary to use
hyphens to im-
prove readability
and eliminate white
space.**

Figure 12.2 Using hyphenation to improve the document.

hyphen in your text will not cause the hyphen to show on the screen unless it is at the end of a line. When editing, you can tell where the soft hyphen occurs because the insertion point requires an extra character space to move over it; that is, you must press the left or right arrow twice to move the insertion point to the next character.

Use soft hyphens when you are placing justified text in narrow columns. Sometimes you may wish to edit the text or make other changes to minimize the extra space.

Using Windows Write Productively

As an example of using Windows Write, let's see how it can be used to compose a letter with graphics by using the features we have already discussed. This example assumes that you have a PostScript printer and Microsoft Excel for Windows 3.

If you don't have a PostScript printer, read Chapter 17 and install the PostScript driver. You will enjoy seeing the results on the screen, even without the printer. When you are ready to print, switch the printer and the fonts to a font that you can support and print the letter. If you don't have Microsoft Excel, Chapter 14 will show you how to draw the same graph with Windows Paintbrush.

There are two basic methods of entering text and formatting: formatting as you go or formatting after the text is entered. Formatting as you go implies that you first set the initial format. As you enter each paragraph, you set the character and format options that you wish to use for that paragraph. This is generally a disadvantage, however, because it is hard to concentrate on the text that you are entering. You will usually find it easier to enter the text without worrying about formatting, concentrating on the message and the words you are using. Then you can go back and format it. If you have a single format that will apply to a large body of your document, it is a good idea to set this format first.

For this example, let's enter a simple letter and format it later. We will also include some graphics. Type the following text for your letter:

```
ABC Marketing
408 Etna Street
Portland, OR 97212

(555-1234)

June 12, 1992

ACME Publishing
103 Best Street
Portland, OR 97212


Dear Ms. Smith:

  Enclosed are the regional sales statistics for the
first half of the year. The total is up 9% over last
year, but some regions are doing better than others. In
particular, it looks like the new sales plan we imple-
mented in the Western region is working well. Let me
know if we should implement the Western region plan in
any of the other three regions.

Sincerely,


George Baker
```

Now let's have some fun. Use the first five lines (including the telephone number) to create a letterhead. Select the first line and use the Character menu to set the font to Palatino. Use the Size menu to set the size to 26 points. Use the Style menu to set the attributes to bold and italic.

Note: The fonts and sizes available will vary with the printer installed. You may wish to install a PostScript printer for the exercise even if you don't have the hardware.

Now select the rest of the address lines. Set these to Palatino, 12 points, bold, and italic. Then select all three address lines and the telephone number and use the Paragraph menu to set the alignment to **Centered**.

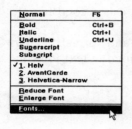

Select the rest of the letter and use the Character menu to set the font to Helvetica, 12 points, and normal attributes. Now select the date line, and from the Paragraph menu select **Right Alignment**. Finally, on the last two lines for the salutation and the name, use some tabs to move the salutation and name as far right as you wish.

The chart that we want to insert in the letter is based on a spreadsheet. The chart can be set up in Microsoft Excel or with Windows Paintbrush. If you have Microsoft Excel, use it to set up the chart. Figure 12.3 shows the spreadsheet, and Figure 12.4 the resulting chart. Use a stroked font (such as Modern) at 6 points to simplify resizing.

Within Excel, select the chart by using **Select Chart** on the Chart menu. Then select **Paste** from Excel's Edit menu to place the chart in the Clipboard. Return to Windows Write and place the insertion point where you want the chart to be. Then use the Edit menu to **Paste** it to the letter. It won't be the right size and will be too large, but you can use the Edit menu to resize and move it.

To resize, select the chart and then choose **Size** from the Edit menu. Grab the left edge of the chart and move it right to reduce the horizontal to 70 percent. You can use the indicator at the lower left to monitor this. Repeat with another sizing to move up the lower edge to reduce the vertical to 70 percent. Then select the chart and select **Center** on the Paragraph menu to center it. Add the chart title if it is not in the letter.

Note: Sizing is very tricky, as this exercise will show. Select the command. The pointer changes to a small box. The area selected is now outlined by a dotted line. Move the mouse cursor within the selection area to the edge you wish to move without using the mouse button. The edging line will then move with the mouse. Watch the indicator in the lower left and click the left mouse button when the size is correct. If the sizing doesn't work, press Esc to clear the command and start again. If things get really bad, delete the chart (select it and press Del); then paste it from the Clipboard and try again.

Chapter 14 will show you how to create the chart with Windows Paintbrush. As with Excel, you then copy the chart to the Clipboard and paste it to the letter.

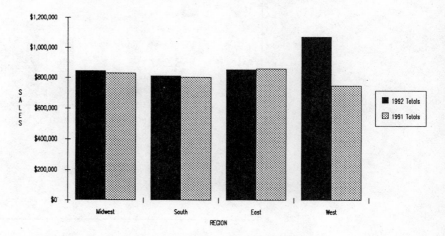

	A	B	C	D	E	F
1	*1992 Regional Sales - Jan-Jun*					
2						
3		Midwest	South	East	West	Totals
4	January	$93,000	$113,000	$132,000	$131,000	$469,000
5	February	$128,000	$125,000	$110,000	$135,000	$498,000
6	March	$150,000	$130,000	$148,000	$152,000	$580,000
7	April	$160,000	$150,000	$154,000	$205,000	$669,000
8	May	$155,000	$155,000	$160,000	$210,000	$680,000
9	June	$158,000	$140,000	$150,000	$240,000	$688,000
10	1992 Totals	$844,000	$813,000	$854,000	$1,073,000	$3,584,000
11	1991 Totals	$830,000	$805,000	$860,000	$750,000	$3,245,000

Figure 12.3 The Excel spreadsheet.

Figure 12.4 The chart.

Before printing, save the letter by using Write's **Save As** command from the File menu. Then print the final letter by using the **Print** command from the File menu (see Figure 12.5).

Tip: Always save your work before printing. This ensures that your letter is saved if the computer should hang up during the print operation.

Tip: You can use Windows Write to create simple letterheads. For example, you could create a stationery form with a letterhead by deleting the entire text of the letter and saving the page with only the return address. You could use Paintbrush or other drawing tools to create a logo and paste this to the letterhead.

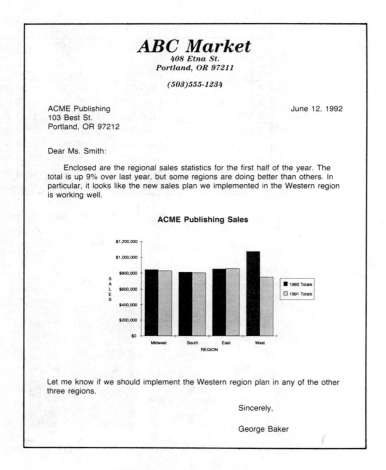

Figure 12.5 The final letter.

Now let us look at some of the features of the letter we have just created. Unlike Notepad, the wordwrap occurs at the page margins. Changing the width of the window does not change where the line ends. You can adjust the width of the text lines by adjusting the margins from the document menu.

This kind of display is known as *WYSIWYG*; that is, what you see on the screen is what you get. The image that is shown on the screen matches the image of the letter that will be printed. If you were using a different printer that did not support the Palatino font (non-PostScript), you would find that this font was not available for selection or display. The character sizes for the fonts you do have limit what you can create on the screen. In other words, the screen image you see is what will be printed.

Tip: When you are creating documents, save your work frequently. The document that you see on the screen is saved only in computer memory, and is not saved on disk. If a power glitch occurs or someone steps on the power cord and disconnects it, your work will be lost unless you have saved it. A good rule of thumb is to save your work every 15 to 20 minutes.

Tip: Another editing trick is to use two windows. Windows Write supports only a single window, but you can open two copies of Windows Write, each with its own window. You can load a copy of your document to each window and then make moves or copies between the windows. This eliminates the need for a lot of scrolling if you are making several copies from one area of the document to another.

Tip: Keep your files short. If you are working with a long document, you will probably find it helpful to break the document into several files.

Summary

As you can see from this chapter, it's easy to do word processing and some level of desktop publishing from Windows Write. Windows Write, however, is no competitor for the more advanced word processors. Windows Write does not support footnoting, multicolumns, spell checking, or outlining. For any of these more advanced features, you will have to go to a better word processor, such as Microsoft Word, Word for Windows, or WordPerfect.

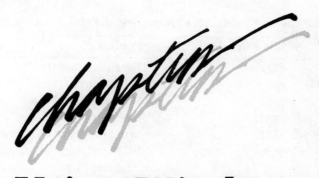

Using Windows Paintbrush

Windows Paintbrush is a Windows application that permits you to create freehand sketches and charts. These can be pasted into Windows Write documents or desktop publishing programs (such as Page-Maker), or they can be printed directly from Windows Paintbrush.

What Is a Paint Program?

Graphics application programs generally fall into one of two classes: paint programs or drawing programs. *Paint programs* are used to create *bit-mapped graphics*; that is, the graphic is displayed, printed, and stored as a collection of pixels (bits). You edit the picture by turning the bits on and off. The graphic is often called a *raster image*. When you print the graphic, you print the graphic image as a bit map. If you examine the image closely, you will see that the graphic objects have jagged edges and often have poor resolution. They also cannot be resized easily. The advantages are that raster-image graphics are fast, make the best use of color, and are easy to edit. Table 13.1 lists some popular paint (raster-image) programs.

Table 13.1 Examples of Paint Program Products

File Extension	Product
CUT	Dr. Halo, Halo DPE
GEM	GEM Paint
IMG	GEM Paint, Halo DPE
MAC	MacPaint
MSP	Windows Paint (Windows 2.0)
PCX	PC Paintbrush, Windows Paintbrush
PIC	PC Paint Plus
PIX	HiJaak
TIF	(scanner programs)
BMP	Windows Paintbrush, Clipboard

Drawing programs, in contrast, represent objects as mathematical entities. The graphics are often called *vector graphics*. As such, the resolution of a graphic created with a drawing program is limited only by the output device. Commands are sent to the printer as drawing commands rather than as pixels. Vector graphic-image files take less disk space than raster files and the images are easy to resize, but the graphics are clumsy to edit and graphic displays are slow. Table 13.2 lists some popular drawing programs.

Table 13.2 Examples of Drawing Program Products

File Extension	Product
DIF	AutoCad and CAD programs
GEM	GEM Artline
GMF	Lotus Freelance Plus
PCT	MAC PICT format, used by Ventura Publisher
PIC	Windows Draw!, Lotus 1-2-3
PGL	Hewlett-Packard plotter file
WPM	Windows metafile (Excel, etc.)

Windows Paintbrush is a painting program; that is, it uses bit-mapped graphics. Graphics can be created only in the screen resolution: approximately 75 dpi (dots per inch). This doesn't mean that you can't create high-resolution print images. Figure 13.1 shows a graphic printed from Paintbrush at a 300-dpi resolution. The drawing was originally created in Windows Draw! and printed on a laser printer at 300 dpi. The printed drawing was then scanned and saved as a bit-mapped TIF image. The TIF file was converted to PCX format and loaded to Paintbrush. Printing it at the screen 75 dpi would have taken six pages. Instead, it was printed with the command **Use Printer Resolution** on Paintbrush's Print dialog box. This technique reduced it to one page and 300 dpi.

Figure 13.1 A high-resolution graphic from Paintbrush
(courtesy of Micrographix).

Both paint and drawing programs have advantages and disadvantages, as shown in Table 13.3. Paint programs are useful for freehand sketches and other graphics where objects cannot be easily defined by mathematical expressions. Drawing programs are better for detailed graphic work of high resolution, such as computer-aided design.

Table 13.3 Comparison of Graphic Program Types

Paint Programs	Drawing Programs
Raster image	Vector image
Difficult to resize	Easy to resize
Resolution often poor	Resolution limited only by output device
Easy to edit	Difficult to edit
Large files	Moderate size files

Note: Paintbrush is considerably different from the Paint program supplied with Windows 2.0. One difference is the file format. Paint saves files in an MSP format. Paintbrush uses both PCX and bit-mapped (BMP) formats. It can also read the older MSP formats.

Starting Windows Paintbrush

The best way to try out Windows Paintbrush is to do some sketching. Even if you are not an artist, with a little experience you'll find that you really surprise yourself.

Start Windows Paintbrush by double-clicking the **Paintbrush** icon on the Program Manager's Accessories group window. You can also start Paintbrush from the DOS prompt by entering WIN PBRUSH. Another alternative is to start Paintbrush from a previously created graphics file by clicking the graphics filename from File Manager. Paintbrush then loads along with the data file.

Notice that Paintbrush has a title bar and menu bar like other Windows programs (see Figure 13.2). The eighteen icons to the left in two rows are known as the *toolbox*. They represent various tools that can be used for painting. At the lower left is a small *Linesize box* for selecting the width of a drawing line or width of borders. At the bottom is a *Palette* for selecting colors (on a color monitor) or patterns (on a monochrome monitor). Between the Palette and Linesize box is a small box showing the current foreground and background colors and patterns. Notice from Figure 13.2 that the default tool is the brush, the current paint pattern is a solid fill, the line width is narrow, and the drawing colors are black foreground on a white background. Paintbrush, unlike the older Windows Paint, supports color.

Image Attributes...
Brush Shapes...
Edit Colors...
Get Colors...
Save Colors...

Note: With a color monitor, Windows defaults to a palette for selecting colors. To change the display to select patterns, select **Image Attributes** from the Options menu and select **Black and White** in the **Colors** area. Then reset the display by selecting **New** from the File menu. On a monochrome monitor, Paintbrush defaults to a patterns palette.

To the right of the toolbox is the *canvas*, or drawing area. The canvas is the white part of the work area. The window shows only a small part of the total canvas. To see the larger area, you can select **Zoom Out** from the View menu.

In almost all cases when using Paintbrush, you will want to maximize the window before starting. Do this now by clicking the

Toolbox   Menu bar   Title bar

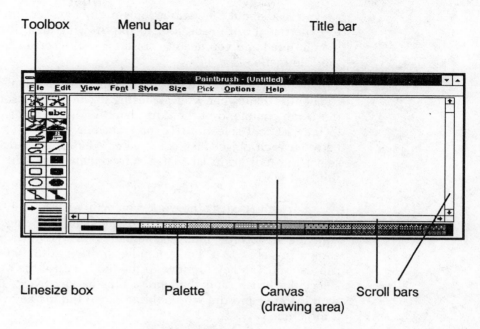

Linesize box   Palette   Canvas   Scroll bars
                                             (drawing area)

Figure 13.2 The Paintbrush window.

small up arrow in the upper right of the window. Chapter 18 shows how to set up Windows so that it automatically maximizes on loading.

Before examining the tools closely, you may wish to doodle a bit with Paintbrush on your own and experiment with the tools. To select a tool, click the appropriate tool in the toolbox. The tool you are currently using is highlighted in the toolbox. To select a foreground painting color or pattern, click the color or pattern with the left button of the mouse. To select a background color or pattern, click it with the right button.

To create a drawing, first set the painting pattern and color, line width, and brush width for a particular object. (The brush width is selected from the Options menu.) Then select the tool you wish to use by clicking the tool with the mouse in the toolbox. The mouse cursor icon changes to indicate the type of tool being used.

Next, move the tool to the canvas area. Drag the tool over the canvas where you wish to paint. Release the mouse button to move the tool (mouse) without drawing. Notice that dragging the mouse is like putting the tool down and moving it.

Some tools have special functions. These will be described shortly. For example, the scissors-like tool in the upper right of the toolbox is used to select a portion of a graphic for copying or moving.

As you read about the various tools in the next section, you may wish to experiment with each tool in the drawing area. If the screen gets too cluttered and you need to erase the entire screen, select **New** from the File menu.

Tip: When you are drawing, save your work frequently—much more frequently than when you are using a word processor. You can use the **Undo** command of the Edit menu to clear a mistake. It will undo to the last tool selection. To protect your work, click the same tool between each object that you create. When the result is satisfactory, select the tool again so that a subsequent paste will not clear your finished work.

For almost all paint work, you will wish to use the mouse. The mouse gives you better control of freehand drawing. The keyboard equivalents for the mouse commands in Windows Paintbrush are shown in Table 13.4. For example, to draw a line with a brush, you can use the Tab key to move to the toolbox, use the direction keys to select the brush, and then press the Ins key. Next, tab over to the working area and draw by holding down the Ins key while you press a direction key.

Table 13.4 Equivalent Keyboard Commands for Paintbrush

Mouse Action	Keyboard Equivalent
Click (left button)	Insert
Press right button	Del
Double-click	F9 + Ins
Double-click right button	F9 + Del

The Tools

Paintbrush supports eighteen tools that you will find very helpful for drawing. Figure 13.3 shows the tools available in the toolbox.

Pick

Use the *pick* to select a portion of a painting for copying, moving, or deleting. Define the selection area by selecting the tool and clicking the tool at the upper left of the area you wish to define. Then drag the tool to create a dotted rectangle that defines the area (see Figure 13.4). The dotted rectangle will remain on the screen unless you make another selection or select another tool. Only one area can be selected at a time.

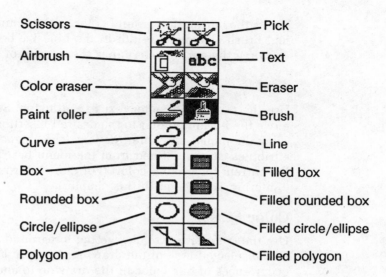

Figure 13.3 The Paintbrush tools.

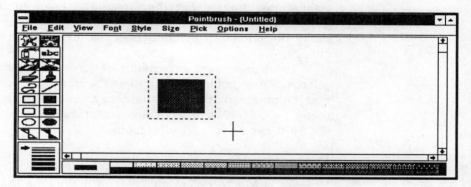

Figure 13.4 Using the pick tool.

Scissors

Use the *scissors* to select nonrectangular portions of a drawing for copying, moving, or deleting. After selecting the scissors, use the tool to draw a net around the object to be selected. The scissors is useful for selecting nonrectangular shapes.

Airbrush

Use the *airbrush* for filling nonenclosed spaces. (If the space is enclosed, the paint roller is probably a better choice.) The airbrush paints the current foreground color, pattern, and width, using the current brush shape and width in the Linesize box. The speed at which you drag the cursor determines the density of the spray.

Text

Use the *text* tool to enter text to a drawing. Select the tool and then move the I-beam pointer to the desired insertion point in the drawing. Click the mouse and enter the text. The character size, font, and style attributes can be defined from the menu bar. The color of the text is the current foreground color. (For more information on using text, see "Entering Text" later in this chapter).

Color Eraser

Use the *color eraser* to change the foreground and background colors in the selected area of the drawing. You can also use it to change all occurrences of one color in the drawing to another.

To change an area of color in the drawing, first set the background color (or pattern) to the new color (or pattern) by using the right mouse button. Set the foreground color to the current foreground color. Set the width of the eraser from the Linewidth box. Move the cursor to the drawing area and drag it over the area to change.

To change every occurrence of a color (or pattern) to another, select the new color (or pattern) as the foreground color and the current color (or pattern) as the background. Double-click the color eraser tool. To erase a straight horizontal or vertical line, hold down the Shift key as you drag the mouse.

Eraser

Use the *eraser* to delete any part of a drawing that you no longer need. You can double-click this icon to erase the entire drawing. More specifically, it changes all foreground color that it touches to the current background color (see "Erasing Objects" later in the chapter).

Tip: Don't use the eraser on corners or tight spots. It is too easy to erase something you don't want to erase. Instead, zoom in and work at the pixel level. Alternatively, you can use the filled box tool to create a rectangle that has a white fill. You can then move this white-filled rectangle over the area you wish to erase.

Paint Roller

Use the *paint roller* to fill an enclosed space with the current foreground pattern and color.

Tip: When you are using the paint roller, be sure that the space is really enclosed. If the shape has even a single pixel open, the fill will leak out and cover the entire workspace. Click the paint roller after each fill to make undoing easier. If you experience problems in creating a fill, immediately click **Undo** from the Edit menu and then zoom in to see where the hole is in the enclosed shape.

Brush

Use the *brush* to sketch. The brush always draws a line in the current foreground color and in the width defined by the Linewidth box, using the current brush shape. The brush is the default tool when Paintbrush is started. You can change the brush shape by using the **Brush Shapes** command of the Options menu. To draw a straight horizontal or vertical line, hold down the Shift key as you drag the mouse.

Curve

Use the *curve* tool to create a curved line in the foreground color and in a width defined by the Linewidth box. Simply select the tool and draw a line; then grab the line with the mouse where you wish the apex of the curve and pull. The line will bend to form a curve with the mouse selection point as the apex. To complete the curve, click the end point of the line you drew.

If you need a second apex, draw the line as before and drag a point on the line to create the first apex. Then drag a second point for the second apex (see Figure 13.5). To clear a curved line and restart, click the right button of the mouse.

Line

Use the *line* tool for drawing straight lines in the foreground color and pattern. The lines can be vertical, horizontal, or angled. The line width is defined by the Linewidth box. To draw straight vertical or horizontal lines, hold down the Shift key as you draw the line. The minimum line width in normal mode is 2 pixels. To draw a 1-pixel line, zoom in and draw.

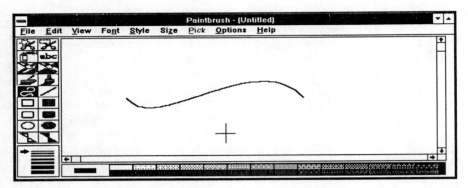

Figure 13.5 Using the curve tool.

Box and Filled Box

The next eight icons are used to draw shapes in the drawing area. As shown in Figure 13.3, the four tools on the left create a hollow shape and the four tools on the right create the same shape filled with the current pattern.

Use the *box* tool to draw rectangular shapes in the drawing area. The box is drawn with a border defined by the Linewidth box and in the foreground color and pattern. Selecting the tool and clicking in the drawing area defines one corner of the rectangle. You can then drag the mouse to complete the rectangle. If the *filled box* tool is selected, the rectangle will be filled with the current background color and pattern.

Tip: To make a borderless rectangle, make the foreground and background colors (and patterns) the same.

Tip: To draw a square or filled square, hold down the Shift key while drawing.

Rounded Box and Filled Box

Use the *rounded box* tool to draw a round-cornered rectangle with the current line width and foreground color/pattern. Click at one corner of the rounded rectangle and then drag the pointer to create the desired rectangle. Release the mouse button. If you select the *filled rounded box* tool, the rectangle will be filled with the current background color and pattern.

Tip: To make a borderless rounded rectangle, make the foreground and background colors (and patterns) the same.

Tip: To draw a rounded square or filled rounded square, hold down the Shift key while drawing.

Circle/Ellipse and Filled Circle/Ellipse

Use the *circle/ellipse* tool to draw ellipses and circles in the drawing area. The ellipse (or circle) is drawn with a border defined by the Linewidth box and in the foreground color and pattern. Click the mouse on the tool. Then move to the drawing area and click at the center of the desired circle. Drag the tool to create the ellipse. The ellipse will be drawn with the current line width. If the *filled circle/ellipse* tool is selected, the ellipse will be filled with the current background color and pattern.

Tip: To make a borderless circle or ellipse, make the foreground and background colors (and patterns) the same.

Tip: To draw a circle or filled circle, hold down the Shift key while drawing.

Polygon and Filled Polygon

Use the *polygon* tool to draw polygons with the current line width. This tool works differently from the others in that you initially click the mouse where you wish the first corner of the polygon. Then draw one edge of the polygon by dragging the mouse. Next, click the mouse at the remaining corners of the polygon, double-clicking the last corner. Paintbrush will draw lines to connect the corners, using the current line width and foreground color and pattern. If the *filled polygon* tool is selected, the polygon will be filled with the current background color and pattern.

Tip: To draw straight horizontal or vertical edges, hold down the Shift key when drawing.

Tip: Although there is no tool for drawing wedges, you can use the circle/ellipse and line tools to create a wedge. First, mark the circle center with a small dot. Then use the circle/ellipse tool to define the outer circle. From the center of the circle, draw lines to define the straight edges of the wedge. Finally, use the eraser tool to erase the unneeded portions of the circle.

Setup

Before starting a drawing, set up the canvas by using the **Image Attributes** command of the Options menu (see Figure 13.6). Define the page size, the units of measure for the size, and the **Colors** (**Black and White** or **Color**). Click **OK**.

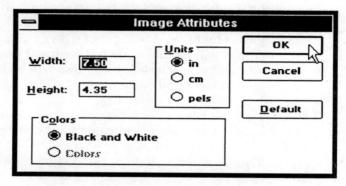

Figure 13.6 Setting up the canvas.

File Management

The drawings that you create with Windows Paintbrush are saved in files. Paintbrush supports (exports and imports) two basic file formats: .PCX and Windows bit-mapped (.BMP). The Windows bit-mapped format supports monochrome, 16-color, 256-color, or 24-bit formats. Paintbrush also imports files in the older Paint (MSP) format.

The Windows (.BMP) format is the preferred format, particularly if you are porting graphics between Windows programs. This is also the preferred format for porting graphics to or from other machines, for example, to a Macintosh.

Use the .PCX format when the Windows format is not supported. For example, the Hijaak product from Inset Systems (Appendix G) converts between the .PCX format and over two dozen others (including PostScript).

The File menu is used to manage files. The File menu works identically to that of other programs and has eight options: **New**, **Open**, **Save**, **Save As**, **Page Setup**, **Print**, **Printer Setup**, and **Exit**. If any file is open, the current filename is displayed in the title bar. When the program is first started, the title bar displays the word (Untitled), indicating that no file is open. The options on the File menu dialog boxes, however, are slightly different.

Use the **New** command (Ctrl + N) to clear the canvas and restore the title bar to its initial (Untitled) display. Use the **Open** command to open an existing file for editing or printing (see Figure 13.7). The default extension for Paintbrush files is .BMP. To change the type of file saved, select the type of file to open in the **Open From** box and then select the file to open. Select **OK**. If you need more information on a file, select the file and **Info**.

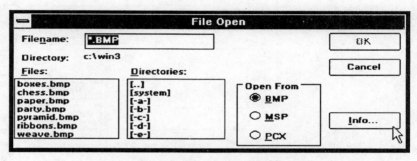

Figure 13.7 Opening a file.

When you initiate this command, you'll probably find several files in the Windows directory having the .BMP extension. These files are various backgrounds for the desktop and can be selected with the Control Panel program on the Main group window. Notice, however, that you can edit them from Paintbrush or create new ones for the desktop.

Use the **Save** command (Ctrl + S) to save to disk a document for which the filename has already been defined. Use the **Save As** command to save the document the first time (see Figure 13.8). The default extension is .BMP. Enter the filename and select **OK**. If you need to save your drawing in a different format, select **Options** (see Figure 13.9). Select the format for saving and **OK**. You can use **Info** to get information on any Paintbrush file. Select the filename and **Info**.

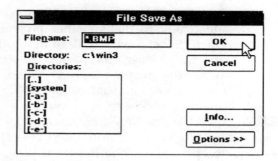

Figure 13.8 Saving a file.

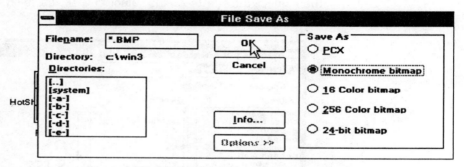

Figure 13.9 Using the save options.

Printing the Drawing

Use the **Print** command to print the current drawing (see Figure 13.10). The options on this menu are defined in Table 13.5.

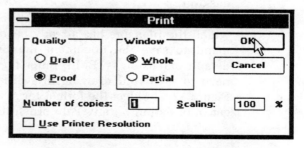

Figure 13.10 Printing a drawing.

Table 13.5 Print Options for Windows Paintbrush

Option	Action
Number of Copies	Defines the number of copies to print.
Draft/Proof	Defines the quality of the output image if the printer supports multiple speeds.
Whole/Partial	Prints the entire drawing area or a part (see the text discussion).
Scaling	Defines the print image scaling. The default scaling is 100%. Printing an image at 200% will make it more ragged. A 75-dpi, 1-inch line at 100% will be 75 dots in two inches at 200%.
Use Printer Resolution	Print at the printer resolution. This changes the size of the image as necessary to get the printer resolution. A 75-dpi, 1-inch line printed with this option will be ¼ inch long on a 300-dpi laser printer.

To print part of a drawing, select **Partial** from the Print dialog box. The entire drawing will be displayed. Use the cursor to draw a selection box around the portion to print. Paintbrush will then print that part of the drawing.

Use **Page Setup** to define the page layout (Chapter 5) and **Printer Setup** to change printers or printer options (Chapter 5).

The **Exit** command terminates the program and is the same as double-clicking the Control-menu icon or pressing Alt+F4.

Controlling the View

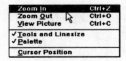

Paintbrush supports graphic zooming to permit you to zoom in or out on your drawing. There are three basic viewing modes: normal, detail, and the entire canvas. When the **Zoom In** command from the View menu is selected, Paintbrush displays a small rectangle. Move the rectangle over the area to zoom and click the mouse. The area will be shown enlarged with a pixel grid. In this mode (see Figure 13.11), you can do detailed drawing by turning pixels on and off. Click the left button to turn a pixel on, the right button to turn it off. You can also scroll while zoomed in. You cannot do cuts, copies, or pastes while zoomed in. Almost all menu commands are turned off except the **Undo** command.

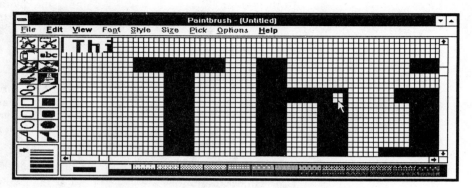

Figure 13.11 Working in a zoomed-in mode.

Tip: When you are using the mouse to draw lines and shapes, do not draw too fast. If you draw too fast, all the proper bits will not be turned on. This is particularly true in the zoomed-in mode. For better control, drag the mouse slowly.

When **Zoom Out** is selected from the normal mode, the entire canvas is displayed. In the zoomed-out mode, you can do some level of editing. Cutting, copying, and pasting are supported, and the selection tool works for this mode. For example, if you wish to create a logo for some stationery, you could zoom out and move the rectangle to the center top portion of the canvas. You could then zoom in and edit the logo in this area.

To view the entire picture without the window, select **View Picture** (Ctrl + C) from the View menu. The screen then shows the entire canvas area zoomed to fill the screen. You can also use this menu to selectively turn off the Tool and Linesize boxes or the Palette. Use Esc to return the screen to a normal viewing mode.

With some painting, you may wish to display the cursor position for detailed positioning (as you will see in the next chapter). To display the cursor position, choose **Cursor Position** on the View menu.

Basic Object Editing

Most of your graphic editing will be done from the Edit menu or with the eraser tools. The following sections will explain how to select objects for editing and then how to move, copy, and erase them.

Basic Rules

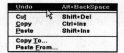

The **Undo** command of the Edit menu is one of the most valuable commands of this menu. If you're drawing something and suddenly realize you have made a drawing mistake, you can quickly get back the original drawing by selecting the **Undo** command. If the latest object you drew is not exactly what you expected, simply undo the object and try again. The command always undoes from the last tool selection. Thus, when you use the same tool to create several objects, a basic rule is to reselect the tool each time you start a new object.

A second basic rule is to save often. Whereas with word processing you might save every 15 to 20 minutes, with Paintbrush you should save after every few objects, sometimes as often as every object.

Selecting Objects

To edit a drawing, you must first select something on the drawing to edit by using either the scissors or the pick tool. The pick tool in the upper right of the toolbox selects rectangular areas. Use the pick tool for most selections. For complex shapes that cannot be selected with the pick tool, use the scissors in the upper left. Then the options of the Edit and Pick menus become active and can be applied to the selected area.

Moving and Copying Objects with the Clipboard

Many of the Edit menu functions are identical to the corresponding commands in other Windows applications. The menu commands are identical and have the same shortcuts. The Edit menu has the same Clipboard commands—**Cut**, **Copy**, and **Paste**. In Paintbrush (as in other programs), these commands apply to a selected area. The **Cut** command removes a selected area from the drawing and places it in the Clipboard. The **Copy** command creates a copy of the selected area and places it in the Clipboard. The **Paste** command copies the contents of the Clipboard to the drawing at the current position or, if you wish, to another drawing.

For example, to copy a drawing that you have created into a Windows Write document, first use the selection tool to select the portion of the drawing you need. Next, use the **Copy** command to place it in the Clipboard. Then make Windows Write active and move the insertion point to where you wish to paste the drawing. Finally, paste the drawing by using the **Paste** command of the Windows Write Edit menu.

Note: In the zoomed-out view, you can only paste opaquely. In other words, the pasted object will cover any object below it.

The **Paste** command is active only if a graphic is in the Clipboard with a format that Paintbrush recognizes. If you use Windows Draw! to place a vector image in the Clipboard (.PIC format), the **Paste** command will not be active because Paintbrush doesn't recognize the .PIC format.

Moving and Copying Objects without the Clipboard

You can move or copy objects directly on the canvas without using the Clipboard. To move an object, select the object and drag it to the new location. Using the left button to drag moves it transparently. In a *transparent move*, the lower object will still be visible when the first object is moved over it. Using the right mouse button to drag moves the object opaquely. In an *opaque move*, the moved object will cover any object below it (see Figure 13.12).

To copy an object, select the object and hold down the Shift key while dragging the copy to its location. Using the left button copies transparently, the right button opaquely.

Note: To paste transparently, the background of the object cutout and the current background color must be the same.

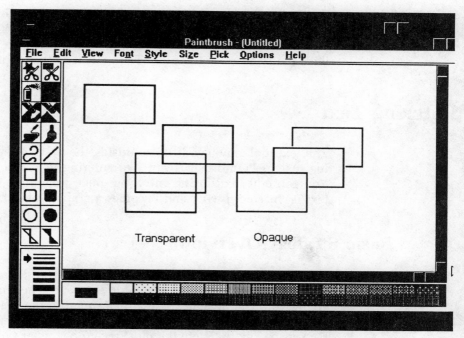

Figure 13.12 Transparent and opaque moves.

Erasing Objects

You can erase objects by using an eraser tool or by cutting a selected area. The eraser tool is used like a pencil eraser. By moving the eraser tool over parts of the drawing, you change all the foreground color under the eraser to the specified background color. You can control the width of the eraser from the Linesize box. By double-clicking the eraser tool, you can erase the entire drawing.

You can use the color eraser to change an area of color. For more information, see the previous description of these tools.

The eraser tool is not easy to use in tight quarters. Your best option in this case is to zoom in on the part of the drawing that you need to edit. Then toggle the pixels one at a time by using the mouse (see "Controlling the View" earlier in the chapter).

For example, you can use a scanner to scan some clip art for a company logo. The result will probably be a .TIF file, which can be converted to .PCX with a conversion tool, such as Hijaak. Now import this file to Paintbrush, zoom it, and clean it up by turning bits on and off. Finally, save the graphic as a bit-mapped file.

If you are erasing an object, it's often easier to select the object with the scissors or the pick. Then cut it to the Clipboard.

Entering Text

The text tool may be a little confusing the first time you use it. Entering text in Paintbrush is not like entering text in a word processor. You can edit text during entry, but once something else is done, the text is "pasted down" and becomes a graphic object.

Basic Strategy Overview

Before entering text in Paintbrush, select the character color, size, font, and style that you want for the text. Then click the pointer where you wish to start the text placement in the drawing. Now enter the characters from the keyboard to the pointer. You can use the Backspace key to delete the most recent character typed. You can use the menus to change the style, font, or attributes of the characters you just entered. Press Enter to start a new line. You can edit as you enter, as long as you don't do any of the following:

- Select another tool
- Use the scroll bar
- Click the mouse
- Reposition the text cursor
- Resize the window

Once you do any of these, the text is "pasted" to the drawing; that is, the entire text entry becomes a graphic object. After this point, the text can be edited only as a graphic object. You can't change the font or style now, but you can cut, paste, and do a variety of special effects (Chapter 14). For example, once text is pasted, you can select and copy a letter of the text string to the Clipboard and then paste it somewhere else. You can use the Pick menu to flip it, redo it in inverse, or do other graphic operations.

Selecting the Font

The Character menu is used to specify the font for the text inserted with the text tool. A font is a particular character design (Chapter 11). Painting and drawing programs can use one or more of three kinds of fonts: bit-mapped, stroked, and system. Many graphics programs use one or more types of these fonts. With *bit-mapped fonts*, the characters are stored as bit-mapped images much like other objects in a painting program. *Stroked fonts* (or vector fonts) are composed of lines, and are really mathematical objects. *System fonts* are the internal fonts that are installed as part of the program or system, such as the cartridge fonts of a laser printer.

Windows Paintbrush uses bit-mapped fonts. This means that the quality of the characters is limited to the resolution of the display. Text is sent to the printer as a graphic bit-mapped image. Adding a cartridge, soft fonts, or PostScript to the printer won't improve the font, size, or style selection. You can't send the output to a plotter, which uses vector graphics. The characters are sent to the printer bit by bit, just as though you were sending a graphic to the printer.

You select the desired font from the Character menu. The current font is checked. Remember that these are bit-mapped fonts supplied by Microsoft with Windows. The fonts available depend on the printer you are using. You cannot change the font of any text that is already pasted down.

You can see the bits of a particular font character by drawing some text on the screen and then using the **Zoom In** command of the View menu to examine the characters closely. Figure 13.13 shows examples of the fonts that are supplied in Windows Paintbrush for a Hewlett-Packard Series II Laserjet.

Terminal

Helv

Courier

Tms Rmn

Modern

System

Σψμβολ

Roman

Script

Figure 13.13 Windows Paintbrush fonts.

Controlling Character Size

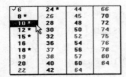

Use the Size menu to define the size of the characters created by the text tool. The size of the characters is measured in points, with one point equal to ½₂ of an inch (Chapter 11). A 36-point character, then, would be one-half inch high. The available sizes depend on the printer installed. If no printer is installed, the sizes are determined by the screen font. Available font sizes are shown in black on the Size menu. Unavailable sizes are gray and cannot be selected. Sizes marked with an asterisk are exact bit-mapped font sizes supplied with Windows. Other sizes in black are scaled from the other fonts. Because bit-mapped images should be scaled only by integral values, the extended size values are integral multiples of the asterisked values supplied.

Since the sizes displayed are printer-dependent, it is possible that a printer font and size are selected that do not have a corresponding display font. If you are trying to display a larger printer font than is available for the display, Windows will scale one of its smaller screen sizes upward to the best of its ability. If you are trying to display a smaller printer font than is available, Paintbrush will substitute a font that supports that smaller size. Using cartridges or PostScript won't give you more sizes. Paintbrush characters are all bit-mapped.

Controlling the Style

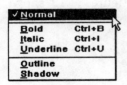

Use the Style menu to control the character attributes, the alignment, and the relationship with text to overlaying or underlaying graphics. The first sections of the Style menu control the attributes of the character. Notice that the menu supports six attributes: **Normal**, **Bold**, **Italic**, **Underline**, **Outline**, and **Shadow**. The ones you will probably use the most have shortcut keys. **Bold** is Ctrl+B, **Italic** is Ctrl+I, and **Underline** is Ctrl+U.

You can also select an **Outline** or a **Shadow** style (see Figure 13.14). These styles create characters in the foreground color, using the background as shadow or fill.

Except for the default **Normal**, you can mix the other attributes to create a wide variety of styles, such as italic outline.

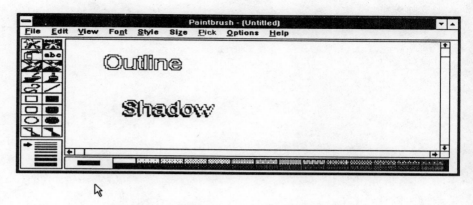

Figure 13.14 Outline and shadow styles.

Summary

This chapter introduced you to Windows Paintbrush—its screen, tools, and menus. It explained the difference between a painting and a drawing program and the basics of using a painting program. Paintbrush is useful for creating bit-mapped graphics or for editing graphics created with other programs. It supports color and provides eighteen graphics tools.

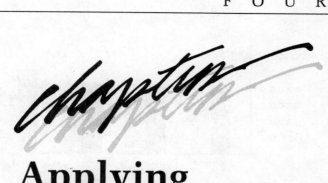

Applying Windows Paintbrush

Now that you have learned the basics of Windows Paintbrush in Chapter 13, you're ready to apply your knowledge. This chapter will show you how to create a bar chart with Paintbrush, how to edit graphics, and how to use text.

Exploring Paintbrush

Tip: When you are creating a drawing, it is important to save your work often. Mistakes are easy to make, and you may find yourself unable to return to your starting point. To eliminate this type of problem, save your work after creating every few objects. As you work with the examples in this chapter, save often.

In Chapter 12 you created a Windows Write document that included an Excel bar chart. But what if you don't have Excel? With Windows Paintbrush you can create a bar chart that looks very similar to the Excel chart of Chapter 12. You can then paste your chart to your Microsoft Write document. Figure 14.1 shows the final graph.

Start Paintbrush and maximize the window. If you have a color monitor, use the **Image Attributes** command of the Options menu to set **Colors** to **Black and White**. You will need to see the cursor position as you draw the chart. Use the **Cursor Position** command of the View menu to turn on the cursor position display.

Next, use the text tool to place the values for the *y* axis (see Figure 14.2). Use the Modern 8-point size (a vector, or stroked, font). Put two carriage returns between each value.

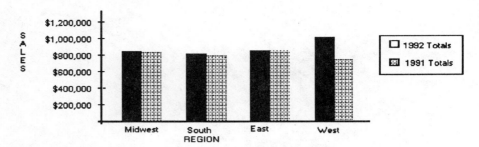

Figure 14.1 A bar chart created with Windows Paintbrush.

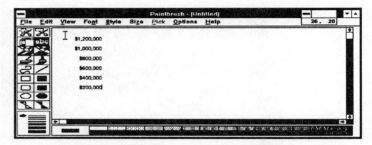

Figure 14.2 Entering the *y* axis values.

Tip: For precise work in drawing lines, hold down the Shift key and use the line tool.

Now draw the *y* axis by using the line tool with the minimum line width. Add the tick marks for the values by using the same tool. Draw the horizontal *x* axis (see Figure 14.3).

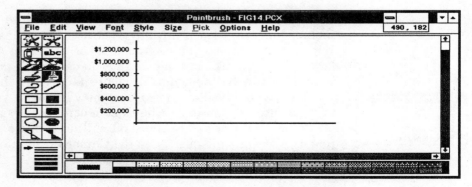

Figure 14.3 Adding the axis.

Tip: Don't forget to save your work frequently.

Now draw the bars with the box fill tool. The bars are placed at 25-pixel widths. Each bar is 25 pixels wide, and the pairs are separated by 25 pixels. Use the solid pattern for 1992 and another pattern for 1991. To correct any details on each bar, use the **Zoom In** from the View window. To simplify setting the bar heights, draw some horizontal grid lines by using the line tool while holding down the Shift key. Use a third pattern for these lines so that they can be easily erased later (see Figure 14.4).

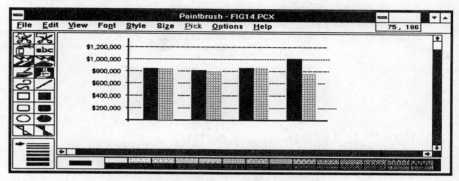

Figure 14.4 Drawing the bars.

Tip: Don't forget to turn off any pattern (return to solid foreground) before zooming in for editing.

Once you've drawn the bars, be sure that you have saved the graph and then use the color eraser to remove the grid lines. Zoom in one last time and clean up the bars where you've erased the grid lines. Now add the region labels and the axis labels by using the text tool.

Finally, add a legend to the right of the chart. First, use the box tool to draw the legend box. Then use the box tool to draw a small box for the first year. Select it and use the right mouse button with the Shift key to copy a second box in the legend. Use the paint roller tool to fill the second box with the right pattern. Add the titles with the text tool (see Figure 14.5).

Once you have finished your chart, save it as a file by using the **Save** command of the File menu. Using the pick tool, select the entire chart and copy it to the Clipboard by using the **Copy** command of the Edit menu. Start Windows Write, and use the Edit menu of that program to paste the chart into the document at the proper point. Now you can use the **Move Picture** and **Size Picture** commands of the Windows Write Edit menu to position and size the chart correctly.

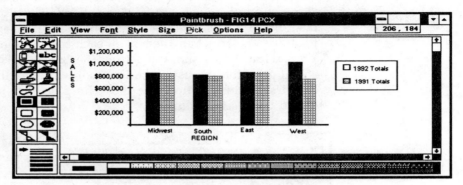

Figure 14.5 The finished chart.

Advanced Graphics Editing

In Chapter 13 you learned the basics of editing:

- Erase by using the eraser tools, by cutting, or by zooming in for detail pixel changes.
- Move by dragging with a mouse. Use the left button for transparent moves and the right button for opaque moves.
- Copy by dragging with the mouse while holding down the Shift key. Like moves, copies can be transparent or opaque.
- You can also use the Clipboard for moves or copies.

Creating Special Effects

You can create some interesting effects in Paintbrush: sweeping, flipping, inverting, tilting, shrinking, and enlarging. *Sweeping* is the process of creating a trail of copies of an object, such as a trail of smoke clouds from a locomotive engine. Sweeping gives the illusion of motion. To sweep, select a portion of your drawing with a selection tool. Then hold down the Ctrl key and drag the object quickly across the drawing. Use the left mouse button for transparent sweeping, the right mouse button for opaque sweeping. To paste down the object, click outside of the object. This will create multiple copies of the selected area in the path that you drag. You can control the number of copies and how close together they are by the speed at which you drag the mouse.

Flipping is another special effect. To flip an object horizontally (side-to-side), select the object and then select **Flip Horizontal** from the Pick menu. To flip an object vertically (top-to-bottom), select **Flip Vertical** from the Pick menu. Selecting another tool pastes the flipped drawing to the canvas.

With *reversing*, you can create reversed text to add impact to a drawing. To invert the colors of an area, select the area and then choose **Inverse** on the Pick menu. On a black and white area, this will change the black to white and the white to black. With colors, the colors are inverted (blue becomes yellow). Click the mouse outside of the area to paste the reversed object to the drawing.

Tilting an object enables you to convert a rectangle to a trapezoid. You can define the angle of the tilt. To tilt an object, select the object and choose **Tilt** from the Pick menu. Now move the cursor to where you want the upper left corner of the new object to be. Click the mouse and drag the object to the desired angle. You can tilt multiple copies of the same object. When you have finished, select another tool to paste the tilted objects to the drawing.

Note: Tilting tilts a copy of the original object anywhere in the drawing, leaving the original object unchanged. If you want the original object cleared on tilting, choose **Clear** on the Pick menu before tilting.

Shrinking or *enlarging* changes the size of an object while keeping its shape the same. You can also use these effects to change the aspect ratio of an object. Select the object and then choose **Shrink + Grow** on the Pick menu. Move the mouse to where you want the upper left corner to be and drag the mouse to define an area for the new object. If you want to maintain the same aspect ratio in resizing, hold down the Shift key while moving the mouse.

Note: Shrinking or enlarging resizes a copy of the original object anywhere in the drawing, leaving the original object unchanged. If you want the original object cleared on resizing, choose **Clear** on the Pick menu before resizing.

Using the Clipboard

Like other Windows programs, Paintbrush lets you use the Clipboard from the Edit menu for moves and copies between files in Paintbrush or between Paintbrush and other programs. You can use the Clipboard only with graphic formats supported by Paintbrush.

In addition to the normal Clipboard commands, Paintbrush also supports the use of a type of disk-based Clipboard with the **Copy To** and **Paste From** commands of the Edit menu. Use these commands if you need to save Clipboard images between sessions. For example, if you have a company logo as a Paintbrush file and use it frequently in many publications, save it to the disk by using the **Copy To** command in the Edit menu. When you need it in a design, use the **Paste From** command to retrieve it. For file saving and retrieving, you can use the .BMP or .PCX formats, just as you do elsewhere in Paintbrush.

You can also use the Clipboard for creating symmetrical shapes. To draw a heart, for example, first use the curve tool to draw the left side of the heart (see Figure 14.6). Create a copy of this partial drawing in the Clipboard by using the **Copy** command from the Edit menu. To create the right side of the heart, flip the heart horizontally in the drawing by using the **Flip Horizontal** option of the Pick menu. Then paste the left side back to the heart from the Clipboard by using the **Paste** command (see Figure 14.7). This technique can be used to create a wide variety of object shapes when they must be symmetrical about a horizontal or vertical axis.

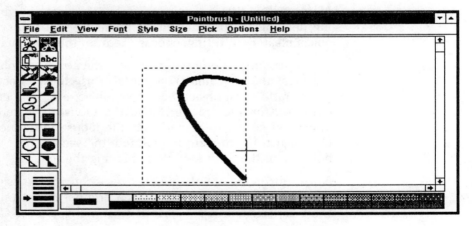

Figure 14.6 Starting to draw a heart.

Tip: Create a graphics library of the objects you use frequently. Use it as your own clip art library, keeping all the objects in a single document. To use this clip art, open two copies of Paintbrush. With one copy of Paintbrush, open your library file. The other copy of Paintbrush contains your working document. When you need an object from the library, select it and copy it to the Clipboard. Then paste it

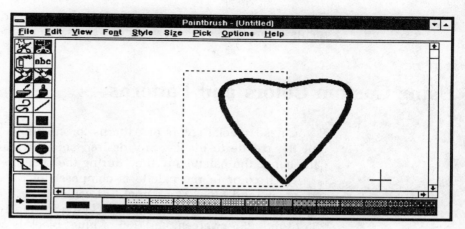

Figure 14.7 The final heart.

from the Clipboard to your working document. Another alternative is to create a clip art library by using Cardfile.

Working with Text

Once text is pasted in a drawing, it can be flipped, inversed, resized, or tilted just as any other object can. You can also select portions of a text string and do special effects with the selected portion.

Tip: If you need to flip text that is close to other objects, you may not be able to use the pick tool to select it. In addition, you can't use the scissors to flip text. The solution is to select the text with the scissors and then move it to another location in the drawing. Flip it with the Pick menu and then move it back to its normal position.

You can do many creative things with text. For example, start by creating the text on a rectangular background. Then select the background and text and invert them with the **Inverse** command. To create reversed text on a patterned background, select **Outline** from the Style menu and enter the text. Draw a box around the text and choose the fill pattern you need. Then use the paint roller tool to add the pattern. On some letters, such as *a* and *o*, you may need to fill the interiors.

Tip: Don't try the outline style and fancy letters for headlines in newsletters or for any lengthy text passages that someone must read.

Fancy letters are hard on the eyes. Use them primarily for announcements or brochures where you need short, attention-getting text.

Using Custom Colors and Patterns

If you need special colors or patterns for creating a graphic, you can edit the palette to display any desired color or many patterns. You can change the palette any time during the creation of a drawing.

Each color in the palette is composed of a varying amount of red, green, and blue. The amount of each of these is expressed as a digital value from 0 to 255, with 255 being the most intense. White is 255 of red, 255 of green, and 255 of blue. Black is zero of each.

To change a color on the palette, click the color and choose **Edit Colors** from the Options menu (see Figure 14.8). On the displayed dialog box, use the scroll boxes to alter the amount of each primary color or enter the new values in the boxes to the right. The sample in the dialog box shows the new color as you work with the colors. Moving the scroll box to the right for a color makes it more intense. When you have finished your design, select **OK**. Selecting **Cancel** aborts your edit without changing the colors. **Reset** changes the colors to the original values as they were when you entered Paintbrush.

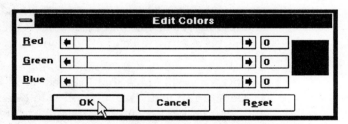

Figure 14.8 Editing the colors.

Tip: For quick access to the **Edit Colors** dialog box, double-click the color or pattern to change.

Tip: As you experiment, you will notice that you can also use the scroll bars in the dialog box to alter patterns.

If you create a new palette that you would like to save and use in subsequent sessions, choose **Save Colors** from the Options menu and enter the filename for the palette. The default extension is .PAL. To retrieve the palette at a later time, select **Get Colors** from the Options menu and enter the filename.

Applications

Windows Paintbrush has many useful applications. Use it for creating logos on brochures or letterheads or to create your own clip art for newsletters, church bulletins, or personal letters. Create your own Christmas cards, birthday cards, or thank you notes. Use Paintbrush to create presentation charts and diagrams.

Tip: You can find a lot of clip art on bulletin boards and CompuServe. These may not be in .PCX or .BMP formats, but you can use utility programs to convert the format to the .PCX format of Paintbrush. You can then load the image to Paintbrush and edit it to meet your needs.

Limitations of Paintbrush

Because of Paintbrush's extensive fonts, you might be tempted to use it as a desktop publishing tool for newsletters or posters. Paintbrush has, however, some real limitations for this type of application. Here are a few:

1. You can't paste text (except graphic pastes in Paintbrush's format) to a canvas.
2. You can see only a small part of the page at a time, making alignment difficult.
3. Graphic pages take a lot of disk storage.

For most layout work, you should invest in a good desktop publishing program. Create your graphics with a paint or draw program and create the text with a word processor. Then merge text and graphics with a desktop publisher, doing the layout with it.

Summary

If you have explored the exercises of this chapter, you should have a good start on learning how to apply Paintbrush to meet your needs. From bar graphs to creative images, you will find Paintbrush fun to use.

Using Windows Recorder

Windows Recorder permits you to save a sequence of keyboard or mouse movements and repeat them at a later time by using specified shortcut keys. The resulting sequence is called a *macro*. This chapter shows you how to use Recorder to improve your efficiency and productivity when using Windows. You can also use Recorder to create self-running presentations (demos).

Exploring the Recorder

When using Windows, you will probably find that certain operations are repeated frequently. For example, each day you might start the computer with Windows and check your appointment schedule. If you are a salesperson, you might start Cardfile and look for the first prospect with today's date. Using Recorder, such operations can be stored as a single procedure (a macro) and initiated from two keystrokes. Let's try an example to see how it works.

Let's assume you need a macro to check your appointment schedule each day. First, start Recorder by selecting the **Recorder** icon on the Program Manager's Accessories group window. Make sure that the Program Manager will not be minimized. Recorder starts and displays a work area (see Figure 15.1).

Now place the cursor in the program at the point where you wish to start recording. (Note: This is not the mouse cursor but the keyboard cursor or the insertion point in most programs). In Figure 15.1 no positioning is necessary.

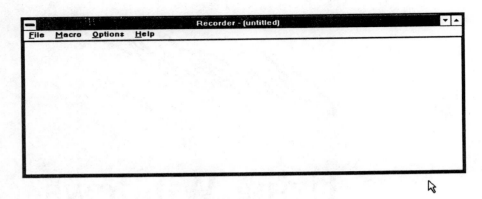

Figure 15.1 Starting Recorder.

Next, make the Recorder window active and choose **Record** from the Macro menu. In the first text box, type the macro name S̄tartup. For the shortcut key, type **z**. Leave Ctrl checked (see Figure 15.2); this will start the sequence with Ctrl + z. In the **Record Mouse** box, select **Ignore Mouse**. Choose **Start** to start the recording. The Recorder program is minimized to a flashing icon (see Figure 15.3).

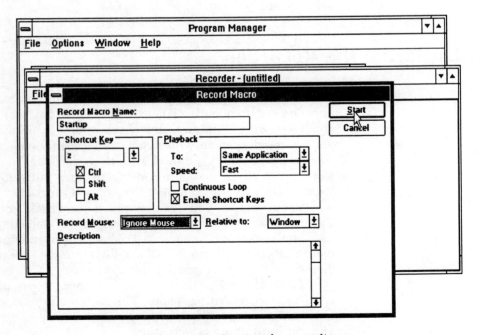

Figure 15.2 Starting the recording.

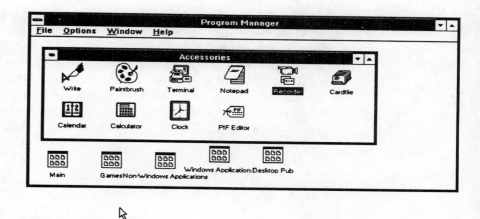

Recorder - (untitled)

Figure 15.3 Recording.

Now initiate the Calendar program without using the mouse. For example, from the Program Manager window, press Alt F R to get the Run dialog box, type `Calendar`, and press Enter. Calendar will start. Open your appointment file by entering Alt F O and typing the file-name. Today's appointments are now displayed (see Figure 15.4).

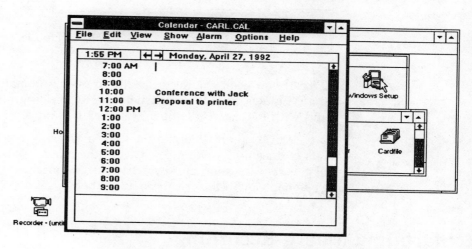

Figure 15.4 Displaying today's appointments.

Now terminate the recording by clicking the **Recorder** icon or by pressing Ctrl + Break. In the Recorder dialog box display, select **Save Macro** and **OK**. The Recorder icon stops flashing.

Now try out your macro. Close Calendar so that the Program Manager is displayed and press Ctrl+z. Calendar should start and display today's schedule.

You have one final task: you must save the macro in a file. If you try to terminate Windows now, it will prompt you that the Recorder file has not been saved. After recording a macro, you should make the Recorder window active again and use the **Save As** command of its File menu to save the macros (see Figure 15.5). A given file can have many macros, so you can keep all of your personal macros in a single file if you wish.

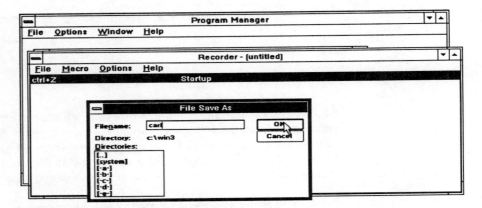

Figure 15.5 Saving the macro file.

Tip: If you want the Recorder file to open automatically upon starting Windows, start Windows with the Recorder minimized as an icon and with the macro file open. Chapter 18 shows how to do this.

At this point you should have a working macro, but probably lots of questions. Why did we avoid the mouse? Why use Ctrl as part of the start-up shortcut keys? How is the macro edited? The rest of this chapter will look at these and other issues.

Starting a Macro Recording

You start a macro by choosing **Record** from the Macro menu. The dialog box (see Figure 15.2 earlier) defines how the macro is to be recorded.

Assigning a Name

Use the **Record Macro Name** box to assign a name for a macro. This is optional when you are using shortcut keys but is required if you are not using them. You can use up to 40 characters. If you need to save more information about the macro (procedures or other documentation), use the **Description** area of the Record Macro box. You can enter almost unlimited text here.

Assigning a Shortcut Key

In most cases, as in this example, you'll want to assign a shortcut key to the macro. Windows supports using Ctrl, Alt, or Shift as a prefix key with almost any keyboard key as a shortcut. For most Windows macros, you should use the Ctrl key. Using Alt could cause conflicts with some Windows commands.

To select the key to use with the prefix key, type the letter or symbol to use or open the scroll box for selecting the key and choose any key on it. Note that shortcut keys can be enabled or disabled from the **Playback** box.

Using the Mouse

If possible, you should avoid using the mouse. The mouse makes the macro dependent on the type of video used (EGA, VGA, etc.) as well as the current screen environment. If you resize a window, the macro may not work. To ignore the mouse, select **Ignore Mouse** in the **Record Mouse** box.

Note: Choosing to use the mouse here and simply not clicking or dragging it Ãwhen recording is not enough to prevent problems. The current mouse cursor may be outside of the application window when the application is run, causing an error condition.

If you do need to use the mouse, use the **Record Mouse** box to define how to record the mouse. Here are the options:

Option	Action
Clicks and drags	Record the mouse click and the drags only. Don't record other mouse movements.
Everything	Record mouse movements, clicks, and drags. Don't use this option unless all mouse

movements must be recorded. (When using this option, always use Ctrl + Break to terminate recording instead of clicking the icon.)

Tip: In using the mouse, you should generally have the application in a zoomed-out window and you should set **Relative To** to **Screen**. Chapter 18 describes how to start an application in a zoomed-out window.

Choosing the Reference

In recording a macro, you can choose whether the actions are relative to the window or to the entire screen. Select the **Relative To** scroll box and define it as **Window** or **Screen**. Use **Screen** when your window is zoomed-out.

Other Record Options

The **To** box permits you to link a macro to an application. If you select **Same Application**, the macro can be played only in the application from which it was recorded. This is the default and normal record mode. If you select **Any Application**, it can be started from any application. Use **Any Application**, for example, to assign a character string to a shortcut key. You could assign your name or company name to a shortcut key. Pressing the key combination enters the text string to any Windows application.

The **Speed** box defines the playback speed. It can be set to record at the **Recorded Speed** or **Fast**. Use the **Continuous Loop** option to define a macro for a demo. This executes the macro in a continuous loop until Ctrl + Break is pressed.

Starting a Macro Playback

Before using a macro, you must first open the file containing the macro from the File menu. Available macros will then be displayed in the application window.

To initiate execution, press the shortcut keys, double-click the macro, or select the macro and choose **Run** from the **M**acro menu.

Editing a Macro's Properties

You cannot edit any command of the macro, but you can edit the *parameters* or *properties* of the macro that are set from the Record Macro dialog box.

To edit a macro's properties, select the macro in the window and then choose **Properties** on the Macro menu (see Figure 15.6). You can then edit the macro as desired. Notice that some properties, such as those relative to the mouse and type of display, cannot be changed.

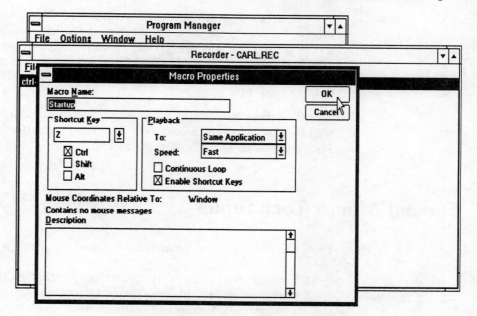

Figure 15.6 Editing a macro's properties.

If you need to edit a command within the macro, you must delete the macro and record it again. You cannot edit the macro file with an editor.

Deleting a Macro

To delete a macro, first open the file with the macro from the File menu. The available macros will be displayed in the window. Then select the macro and choose **Delete** from the Macro menu.

File Management

The macros you create are stored in files that are managed from the File menu. This menu is much like that of other Windows applications: **New** creates a fresh work area, **Open** opens an existing macro file, **Save** saves the current file, and **Save As** saves the macros in a file for which you define the name. The default extension is .REC. These are not text files, and cannot be opened with Notepad. Macro files are limited to a size of 64K. If you need a larger file, try nesting the macros.

You can also merge macros from two files to a single file. To merge, first open the *destination file*, or the file to which you wish to merge additional macros. Delete macros that will be in the file that you will merge into it. Choose **Merge** from the File menu. Select the file to merge and **OK**. Save the new file by using the **Save As** command of the File menu.

Note: If there are duplicate shortcut key assignments, a dialog box will be displayed to inform you. Use the **Properties** command of the Macro menu to redefine these shortcut keys.

Special Macro Techniques

Here are three special techniques for using macros with Windows:

- You can nest macros up to five levels; that is, one macro can start another. In this way you can use macros as procedures in a program. If a series of commands is used in multiple macros, set them up as a separate macro. If you wish to prevent a macro from being used by other macros, turn off the **Enable Shortcut Keys** toggle of the Record Macro dialog box.

- The Recorder window normally minimizes to an icon when you are playing back a macro. If you wish to keep it as a window, toggle off **Minimize on Use** on the Options menu.

- You can define the default parameters on the Record Macro dialog box from the Options menu. To change the defaults, choose **Preferences** on the Options menu (see Figure 15.7).

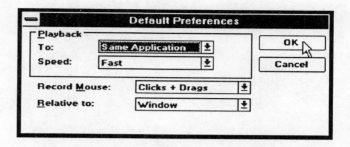

Figure 15.7 Setting the preferences.

Summary

This chapter has explained how to use Windows Recorder to create macros. You can use macros to improve your efficiency and to automate repetitive everyday tasks. Here are a few tips for using macros:

- Plan your macro ahead of time. You may wish to walk through it without recording it first to make sure everything is correct.
- Avoid, if possible, using the mouse in recording. It makes the macro video- and window-dependent.
- If you find yourself frequently repeating a series of operations, record them as a macro.
- Use macros for Windows applications (WinApps) only.

Advanced Techniques

To use Windows productively, you need to know how to customize and tune Windows for your system. Part Three will show you how to do this. You will find important discussions on

- *Managing the printer resources (Chapter 16).*
- *Customizing Windows with Control Panel or an editor (Chapters 17, 18).*
- *Installing printers and soft fonts (Chapter 17).*
- *Getting a screen dump (Chapter 18).*
- *Running non-Windows applications with Windows (Chapters 20, 21).*
- *Transferring data between applications (Chapter 22).*
- *Using Windows with a network (Chapter 22).*

Managing the Printer

This chapter explains how the Windows environment manages the printer or printers in your system. You will learn the basics of printer management and how to use the Windows spooler—Print Manager.

Printing Overview

The method of printing used by an application running under Windows depends on whether the application is a Windows or a non-Windows one. In both types of programs, you must have a printer driver that does the actual printing. The *printer driver* is the software code that directly controls the printer.

Printing from a Non-Windows Application

When printing from a non-Windows program running outside of Windows, you use a printer driver that is part of the program. Ventura, WordPerfect, and Lotus 1-2-3 all have their own printer drivers. Each has a printer driver installed for each printer that is in use.

When you are printing from a non-Windows application running under Windows, printing is identical to printing from that same application without Windows. Each program must have its own printer driver. If you have an HP LaserJet, each program must have a printer driver for the HP LaserJet. As a result, each software product you purchase must include several disks with a collection of printer drivers. Moreover, your hard disk becomes cluttered with large application programs, each including its own printer drivers. Finally, each time you purchase a new printer, every application program must be reinstalled for that printer. For example, each time you install a program such as WordPerfect, Ventura, or Lotus 1-2-3, you must install the printer driver for that program on your disk.

Printing with Windows Applications

Microsoft Windows eliminates this problem by making the printer drivers for your system a part of the Windows environment. You install the drivers for your printers when you install Windows. All drivers are then available for every Windows application that you use. If you purchase a new printer later, you simply add the driver for that printer to the Windows environment by using Control Panel (Chapter 17). Once this is done, the new printer is available to every Windows application. All the fonts that you install for the printer are available for all Windows applications.

When you print from a Windows application, the application sends the printer output as a print file to the Print Manager, another Windows applications program. When you request a print, Print Manager automatically loads as a minimized program; that is, it runs in the background. Print Manager creates a print queue of all print requests sent to it, printing them in order as you continue with other work.

Note: Since Windows and non-Windows programs use different methods of printing, don't try to mix print requests. Avoid multitasking Windows and non-Windows programs when you are printing.

Using Printer Buffers

Printing is a relatively slow process compared with most computer operations. Unless you use a buffer or spooler, you'll find that each time you initiate a print job you must wait until the printing has finished before you can do other computer work. This can take a while, and it's wasted time. In addition, with any type of multitasking environment (and Windows supports multitasking), you will need some type of system management for the print jobs.

A *buffer* is an area of memory or disk that temporarily holds what is to be printed until the printer is ready for it. To print a document, the program's print command quickly dumps the document to this buffer. The document is then printed from the buffer while you continue your work. Buffers can be used with both Windows and non-Windows applications to improve productivity. DOS has a PRINT utility that permits you to use part of conventional memory as a buffer for printing.

There are two types of buffers that you can add to your system: hardware or software. A *hardware buffer* is a small external box that is installed between the computer and the printer. It has some memory and perhaps a small processor. You "print" from the computer very quickly to the memory in this box, after which the computer is free and the box takes over the printing work. Some hardware buffers make it easy to support multiple printers or fast file transfers to other computers. A good example of this type of product is Fifth Generation's The Logical Connection.

A *software buffer* is an area of memory in the computer or on the disk that temporarily holds what is to be printed. It is managed by a program that runs in the background and steals processor clock cycles while you are using another program. This means that (unlike with a hardware buffer) the processor is running slower during a printing cycle, but at least the computer is usable. Print jobs are temporarily kept as a queue in memory or in disk files. The background program prints from this queue, and it is called a *spooler*. Windows contains a Print Manager application program that acts as a spooler for Windows applications. Hardware buffers are more expensive, but they keep the computer at maximum efficiency if you are using only a single task at a time. Software buffers are not as efficient, but they have the potential to support multitasking.

The amount of control that the user has over the printing process varies with various software and hardware buffers. It is nice to be able to pause or terminate a print job. Printing a long document can waste a lot of paper if you find a mistake on the first page after it is printed. If the telephone rings, it's also convenient to be able to pause a noisy printer.

Windows contains a software buffer and printing manager. You can access and control it by using the Print Manager icon on the Program Manager's Main group window. Print Manager lets you pause or terminate print jobs. You can choose also whether you wish to use the Print Manager. Windows defaults to installing the spooler software buffer and its manager. You can turn off the spooler by using the **Printers** option of Control Panel (Chapter 17). Here are some guidelines to help you decide whether to leave the Print Manager on or turn it off:

1. If you experience printing problems (hangups or no printer output), turn off the spooler until the problem is resolved. It's

easier to find the problem with the spooler off. You may find that the problem goes away when the spooler is turned off.

2. Certain applications may not work with the spooler or may work best without it. In this case you may wish to turn off the spooler.

3. If memory space is a premium, purchase more memory or turn off the spooler. Another alternative is to invest in a hardware buffer and print from only a single application at a time.

4. If the computer runs too slowly when it is printing, turn off the spooler. Invest in a hardware buffer and print from only a single application at a time.

5. If you already have a hardware buffer or plan to purchase one, turn off the spooler unless you will be printing from more than one application at a time. This will keep your processor running faster.

6. The spooler is used for Windows applications only. For non-Windows applications running under Windows, you must spool with a hardware buffer or use an external spooler program (which would be a *TSR*, or terminate-and-stay-resident program).

When any type of buffer is used, print jobs are queued to the buffer. The jobs are then printed from the buffer in the order in which they were received. If you reboot the computer during a print job from this queue, the queue contents will be lost. This is not true of a good hardware buffer. With an external hardware buffer, you should expect the printing to continue even if the computer is turned off.

The Windows Print Manager

The Windows Print Manager is a software buffer and print manager that automatically prints in the *background*, that is, while you are doing other work on the computer. You can install Windows to use Print Manager or, alternatively, print directly from your Windows application programs. If the Windows Print Manager is turned on (the default mode), Print Manager is automatically activated when you request your first print. The print request will load the Print Manager program and the Print Manager icon will appear at the bottom of the screen (see Figure 16.1). The Print Manager program then prints "invisibly" in the background (minimized) while you continue with your work, using whichever window is active. The computer will be a little slower.

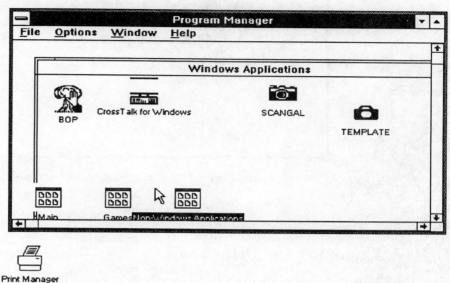

Figure 16.1 Windows screen after spooler loading.

To change print priorities, to pause a print job, or to terminate a print job, make the Print Manager program active by double-clicking the **Print Manager** icon. The Print Manager program will then display an active window (see Figure 16.2). The work area shows each installed printer, its connection, the printer status, any active print jobs in the queue for that printer, and the status of each job. Each print job is identified by the program that initiated the print and the status of the file. Print Manager prints from the top down. The top-most job is the one currently printing. At the top right of the window, a message box displays the current status of the Print Manager. To the left of the message box are three buttons to control the printing. As with most applications, there is also a menu bar with three options: Options, View, and Help.

Note: Terminating Print Manager clears the print queue, eliminating all waiting print jobs. When you are through using Print Manager as an active program, minimize it again unless you wish to clear the queue.

Tip: To load the Print Manager manually, select the Print Manager icon on the Program Manager's Main group window. The Print Manager will immediately become active.

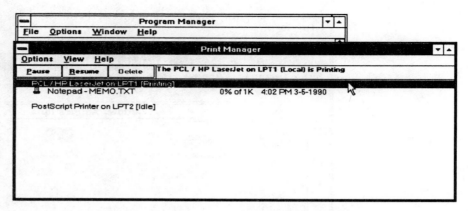

Figure 16.2 Making the spooler program active.

Changing the Print Order

If you want to change the print order of a file in the queue, you can use the mouse or the keyboard:

In the queue, use the mouse to click the file that you wish to change and drag it to the new position in the queue.

From the keyboard, use the direction keys to select the file to change. Then hold down the Ctrl key and move the file to the new position.

Pausing and Resuming Printing

If you need to temporarily pause the printing, make the Print Manager active and choose the **Pause** button or press Alt+P. Use this technique if the phone rings during a noisy print, the printer jams, or you wish to view the first few pages of a printout before continuing.

Note: If you are using an external hardware buffer, pausing the printer will not stop the printer until the external buffer is clear. To resume printing, choose the **Resume** button or press Alt+R.

Tip: You can batch print jobs by selecting the Print Manager on the Main group window and using **Pause** to suspend the printing. Then load the queue. Once you are ready to start the printing, select **Resume** from the Queue menu.

Removing a File from the Queue

To remove a file from the queue, make the Print Manager active and select the file to be deleted by using the direction keys or the mouse. Then choose **Delete** or press Alt+D. A dialog box appears to confirm the deletion. Choose **OK**.

To delete all files in the queue, close the Print Manager. You can close Print Manager in one of several ways: by selecting **Exit** on the Options menu, by double-clicking the Control-menu box icon, by pressing Alt+F4, or by selecting **Close** on the Control menu.

Tip: Graphics are often printed on a laser printer by using a banding process in which only part of the page is sent at a time to the queue. Terminating a graphic print may mean that part of the page is already printed or is in the printer memory. To clear the printer with graphic printing, you may have to eject a page or you may have to turn off the printer and then turn it on again.

Controlling Printing Speed

Print Manager does its printing by stealing clock cycles from other applications. This means that other applications run slower while the printing is in process.

You can use the Options menu of Print Manager to control the printing speed. If you select **Low Priority**, applications run fast but printing is slow. If you select **High Priority**, applications will slow down dramatically but the printer will print very fast. In the default **Medium Priority** setting, the Print Manager and applications share the processor approximately equally.

Controlling the Message Display

The second section of the Options menu defines how Print Manager's messages are displayed. You can select any of three modes:

Mode	Action
Alert Always	Always display messages in a dialog box.
Flash if Inactive	If Print Manager is inactive, flash icon. User must then make the Print Manager active to read the message. This is the default mode.
Ignore if Inactive	If Print Manager is inactive, ignore error messages.

Controlling the File Display

You can use the View menu to control the amount of file information displayed for each file in the queue. Use **Time/Date Sent** to display the time stamp for when the file was sent to the queue. Use **Print File Size** to display the size of the file. In the default mode, each of these options is on.

Note: If you attempt to terminate Windows with print jobs still in the queue, Windows displays a dialog box and asks if the print jobs should be ignored or printed. Once Windows terminates, all unprinted print jobs will be lost.

Summary

Windows provides a Print Manager for spooling print jobs from Windows applications. With Print Manager you can continue working while Windows is printing. You can also share the printer between several Windows applications. You can access the Print Manager to control the print queue and, optionally, turn the Print Manager on or off.

Customizing Windows: Using Control Panel and Windows Setup

You can customize Windows for your own needs by using Control Panel and a few clicks of the mouse. For example, if you like fluorescent colors instead of the more subdued default colors, start Control Panel and select the **Colors** icon. Select the fluorescent color configuration and save it. Windows then uses your new default colors. This chapter will show you how Control Panel can be used to install printers, to set the system time and date, to control the mouse parameters, to define the colors of the various Windows elements, and to control many other parameters.

Control Panel Overview

When you install Windows, certain information about how the Windows environment should behave is stored in .INI files. Although Windows includes several .INI files, the one of most interest for customizing Windows is WIN.INI. Control Panel is a Windows application that permits you to change parameters in this file quickly. The WIN.INI file is a text file and can also be printed or edited with Notepad or another editor. Chapter 18 will show you how to do even more extensive customization by editing WIN.INI directly.

You should run Control Panel when you wish to install a printer, install new fonts, change the colors of the window elements, change the system time, or change the mouse parameters. You cannot use Control Panel to change the installed video adapter, change the screen resolution, or install a new mouse. If you need to do any of these, you should run Windows Setup (see "Running Windows Setup" in this chapter).

Starting Control Panel

Start Control Panel by selecting the **Control Panel** program icon on the Program Manager's Main group window. This starts Control Panel, and a small window is displayed (see Figure 17.1). Notice that the window has a border that is only one pixel wide and cannot be resized or zoomed. You can, however, move the window by dragging the title bar. The window has a Control-menu box in the upper left and a Minimize icon in the upper right.

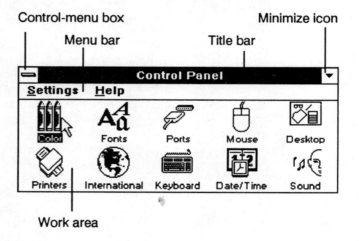

Figure 17.1 Starting Control Panel.

The work area contains ten to twelve icons to control various groups of options. The menu bar contains two options: **Settings** and **Help**. The commands on the **Settings** menu correspond to the icons in the work area. Table 17.1 shows the icons and explains their functions.

You cannot start a second copy (or *instance* in Windows terminology) of Control Panel while one is executing. If you try to start a second copy, Windows makes the first copy active and does not start a second.

Table 17.1 Icons Available from Control Panel's <u>S</u>ettings Menu

Icon	Action
Color	Sets the color of the Windows elements.
Fonts	Adds or deletes fonts for the display or printer.
Ports	Defines serial port parameters.
Mouse	Customizes the mouse setting: double-clicking speed, mouse sensitivity, and whether to use the left or right mouse button.
Desktop	Sets the desktop background pattern, cursor blink rate, and window grid.
Network	Sets network options (available only if a network is used).
Printers	Installs and configures printers.
International	Sets international options such as country, language, number and currency formats, and date/time formats.
Keyboard	Sets keyboard repeat rate.
Date/Time	Sets system clock.
Sound	Turns aural error indicator off or on.
386 Enhanced	Sets parameters for 386 enhanced mode. (Available only in 386 enhanced mode.)

Setting Screen Colors

Use the **Colors** icon to set the color and texture (pattern) of each window element (title bar, scroll bars, background, etc.) to any desired color on an EGA or VGA monitor. On a monochrome monitor, this command allows you considerable control over the texture (patterns) and intensity of the window elements.

When you select this command, a dialog box window is displayed (see Figure 17.2). You can use the **Color Schemes** dropdown list box to choose from any of several predefined color schemes. Scroll to the scheme you want to use. The bottom portion of the dialog box shows how the elements will look if you select this scheme. When you find a selection you want to use, choose **OK**.

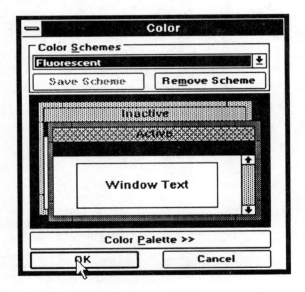

Figure 17.2 Setting the screen colors.

You can define your own scheme by editing an existing scheme. First, select the scheme to edit in the dropdown list. Then choose **Color Palette**. On the next dialog box (see Figure 17.3), click the element to change or select it in the dropdown list at the upper right. Then select the color or pattern desired from **Basic Colors**. The sample window changes to give you a preview of your selection. When all changes are complete, choose **Save Scheme**.

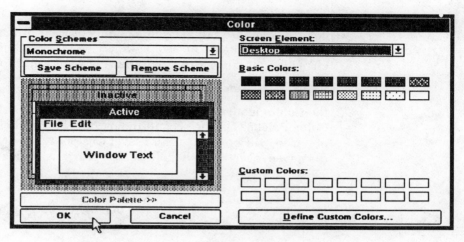

Figure 17.3 Editing a scheme.

Note: Although the **Basic Colors** may show some patterns, some elements such as the Window Frame, Window Text, Window Background, Menu Bar, Menu Text, and Title Bar Text can be set to solid colors only.

To remove a color scheme from the list, select the scheme in the dropdown menu of the first dialog box and select **Remove Scheme**.

Tip: You cannot remove the Windows Default scheme. If you frequently change between color schemes, eliminate those you don't use. Another possibility (if you have enough disk space) would be to install Windows to two directories and define different schemes in each directory. For example, you might keep a fluorescent scheme for your daily work and another scheme for black-and-white screen dumps. If you need both often, install a Windows for each in two separate directories. One would be set to the fluorescent scheme; the other to black-and-white. If you don't change the scheme often, remove the color schemes you don't use. This will keep the list small.

You can also define your own color for any element of a scheme. To understand how to define a color, three terms are important: hue, saturation, and luminosity. *Hue* is the position of the color in the color spectrum (red, blue, etc.). *Saturation* is the purity of the color, and it ranges from gray to pure color. *Luminosity* is the brightness of the color.

Three primary colors are used: red, green, and blue. A custom color is composed of varying amounts of each primary color. As you change the amount of each primary color, the hue and saturation change. After you've tried defining a few custom colors, you will get a better idea of what each term means.

To define a color for a window element, start as before: select the **Colors** icon, and then select the scheme you wish to edit. Choose **Color Palette**. On the second dialog box, choose **Define Custom Colors**. You will now see a third-level Custom Color Selector dialog box displayed over the left half of the previous dialog box (see Figure 17.4).

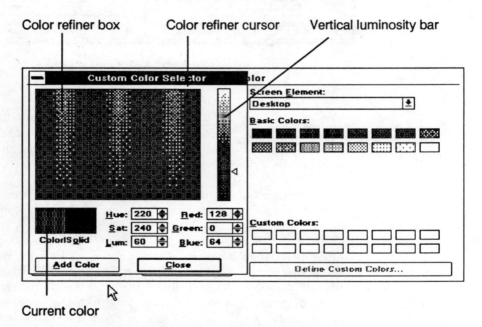

Figure 17.4 Defining a color.

The new dialog box contains a large color matrix known as the *color refiner box*. In the box is a small cursor, called the *color refiner cursor*. To the right is a *vertical luminosity bar*. Dragging the color refiner cursor left and right changes the hue. Dragging the color refiner cursor up or down changes the saturation. Dragging the cursor in the luminosity bar changes the luminosity. The current color is displayed in the left side of the **Color|Solid** box. The right side of the box contains a solid color that approximates the color selected. To choose the solid color, double-click the right side of the **Color|Solid** box. To return to the true color, move the color refiner cursor slightly.

Note: If you don't have a mouse, change the colors by entering the values or by scrolling the values in the boxes at the bottom of the window. Use Alt+O to select the solid approximation.

Once you have defined the color you wish, choose **Add Color**. The color is automatically added to the first empty block under **Custom Colors**, and is now available, as one of the basic colors, for defining window elements.

Tip: If you have a monochrome monitor, you can use the previous strategy to change the texture and pattern of the elements displayed.

Controlling the Desktop

The Desktop icon permits you to define a pattern or image for the desktop surface. You can also use this same option to define a desktop grid for aligning icons and windows or for controlling the cursor blink rate.

Selecting the Desktop icon displays a dialog box for defining its options. The dialog box permits you to define either a pattern or a wallpaper (see Figure 17.5). A *pattern* is a bit-mapped image that is repeated as necessary to fill the desktop area or to cover the desktop. A *wallpaper* is a bit-mapped image that is displayed in the center of the desktop or is tiled to cover the desktop. The wallpaper bit maps are stored as .BMP files. Since they are .BMP files, they can be created, viewed, or edited from Paintbrush. Patterns can be edited from Desktop.

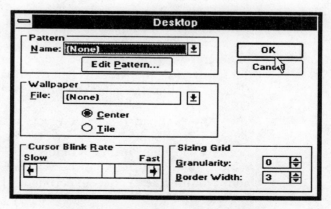

Figure 17.5 Defining the desktop.

To change the desktop pattern, select the desired pattern in the **Pattern** dropdown box and choose **OK**. The desktop will change to the new pattern.

You can edit a pattern by selecting the pattern to edit and choosing **Edit Pattern**. A dialog box is displayed that shows a sample of the desktop and an enlarged working area (see Figure 17.6). Click to toggle the pixels on or off in the enlarged view. When you are satisfied with the sample, choose **Change**. Click **OK**.

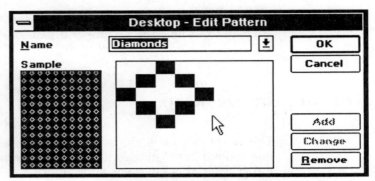

Figure 17.6 Editing a pattern.

Note: You cannot edit patterns from the keyboard.

To add a new pattern, select a pattern that is close to what you want and choose **Edit Pattern**. In the next dialog box, enter the name of the new pattern and edit the enlarged view (click the pixels on or off). Click **Add** and **OK**.

To remove a pattern, select a pattern and then choose **Edit Pattern**. Choose **Remove** and confirm with **Yes**. Then choose **OK**.

With wallpapers, you can use a bit-mapped image of multiple colors and patterns for the desktop. You can even use scanned color photographs. Wallpapers use more memory, however, than patterns. To select a wallpaper, select the wallpaper from the **Wallpaper** box. Choose whether to center the image or tile it to fill the screen. Select **OK**.

Any wallpaper selection you make will overlay any pattern selected. Wallpapers can be created or edited from Windows Paintbrush. Keep them in the Windows directory. To delete a wallpaper, remove the .BMP file from the Windows directory. (If you have VGA and would like a fun experiment, try the sample CHESS.BMP wallpaper.)

Desktop also permits you to define an invisible grid for controlling the placement of icons and windows. The grid acts like a magnet, forcing icons and windows to snap to the invisible grid lines. To turn off the grid, set the **Granularity** value to 0. To define a grid, set the **Granularity** to get the desired grid. Each granularity value is 8 pixels. To set a grid 24 pixels square, for example, set the **Granularity** value to 3. After setting the value, click **OK**.

To set the border width, scroll to the desired width in the **Border Width** box of the **Sizing Grid** section. The window border width is defined in pixels. Select **OK**.

Tip: Use window border widths of 3 to 4 pixels when using a mouse so that you have something to grab for sizing windows. When not using a mouse, use small widths (such as 1 pixel) to get maximum working area.

You can change the cursor blink rate from the initial Desktop dialog box (see Figure 17.5 earlier). To change the rate, drag the scroll box in the **Cursor Blink Rate** section. From the keyboard, you can use Alt+R to select the subwindow and use the direction keys to move the scroll box. The scroll box blinks at the current blink rate. When the rate is set to what you wish, choose **OK**.

Adding a New Printer or Plotter

When you installed Windows, one or more printers or plotters may have been installed at that time. You can use Control Panel to add additional printers or plotters. Once a printer or plotter is installed, it is generally available to all Windows programs. This is not always true for all peripherals, however. A plotter, for example, cannot be used with Paintbrush. Plotters are drawing devices, and Paintbrush uses bit-mapped graphics.

To add a new peripheral to Windows, you must have two items: the driver for that specific peripheral (normally a software file with a .DRV extension) and any special directions for that driver.

The installation involves four steps:

1. Installing the driver file.
2. Selecting the port for the peripheral.
3. Making the peripheral active.
4. Configuring the peripheral.

Installing the Driver File

Windows includes the drivers (.DRV files) for most peripherals. Documentation provided with Windows describes which peripherals are currently supported by these drivers. If you are installing a printer that is not on this list, contact Microsoft for information on additional drivers that they can supply or contact the printer manufacturer.

Note: Software manufacturers may develop special drivers to take maximum advantage of a printer for their software. For example, Aldus developed a special printer driver for the Hewlett-Packard LaserJet for their PageMaker product. When installing such software, you should use the driver that works best with all your applications. (Incidentally, the Aldus driver is a good one.)

Tip: When adding a new printer, check the installation diskettes with Windows. There are README files for many printers on the Windows diskettes that can give you valuable information on installation.

To install a new printer or plotter, select the **Printers** icon from Control Panel. This displays the existing printers in a dialog box (see Figure 17.7). Choose **Add Printer**. The next dialog box displays a list of printers for which drivers are supplied with Windows (see Figure 17.8). Select the desired printer and choose **Install**.

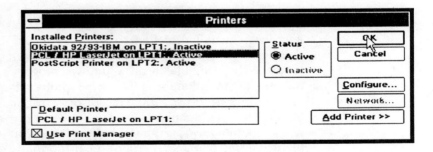

Figure 17.7 Starting a peripheral installation.

Note: If you are installing a peripheral that uses a driver not supplied with Windows, scroll to the end of the list and select **Unlisted Printer**. Follow the directions supplied by the peripheral and driver manufacturer.

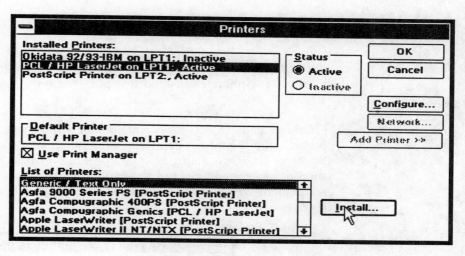

Figure 17.8 Selecting the printer.

Windows will prompt you from this point. In most cases you will be prompted to insert diskettes and told which disk to insert. Printer drivers can be shared by several printers. If you try to install a printer for which a driver is already on the system, Windows will prompt you, indicating this information.

To replace an existing peripheral driver with a newer version, begin as though you were adding a new peripheral and select the printer for which you wish to update the driver. When you select **Install** on the second dialog box, Windows tells you that the driver already exists and requests that you select either **Current** or **New**. Select **New** to install the new driver. Although the new printer driver is now installed, it is not yet configured or active.

Tip: If the system you are working on has only a simple printer and you wish to create a document that you can print later with a PostScript driver on another system, install the PostScript driver to Windows on the first system as another printer, even though you don't have the hardware. Set its **Connections** to **None**. All of the PostScript fonts will then be available in Windows applications and the files will display properly, but you will not be able to print with Postscript on the first system. You can then print the file by using Windows with a PostScript driver on the other system.

Selecting a Port

Once a printer is installed, it must be assigned to a port on your computer and defined as the active device on that port. You can have multiple peripherals assigned to a port, but only one can be active at a time.

To assign a peripheral to a port, select the **Printers** icon on the Control Panel. Select the peripheral for which you wish to assign a port in the **Installed Printers** list and choose **Configure**. On the Printers-Configure dialog box, choose the port (see Figure 17.9). You should also set any desired timeout values. Choose **OK**, and the port assignment will appear in the **Installed Printers** area of the first dialog box.

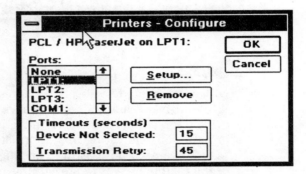

Figure 17.9 Assigning a port.

Some plotters and printers may use a serial port. If using a serial port, you must set the communications settings for the serial port. In this case you must return to the Control Panel and select **Ports**. In the dialog box (see Figure 17.10), select the port you are setting and choose **Settings**. Define the communications settings (see Figure 17.11) and choose **OK**.

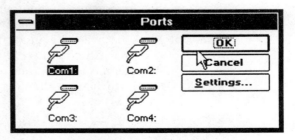

Figure 17.10 Selecting the port to set.

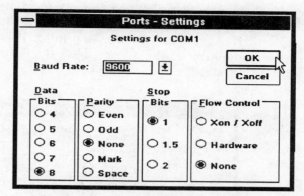

Figure 17.11 Establishing the port settings.

Making the Peripheral Active

Several peripherals may be assigned to a port, but only one can be active at a time. For example, you could have Fifth Generation's Logical Connection print buffer that permits you to share multiple printers with multiple computers. The print buffer is connected to LPT1 and COM1, which, in turn, connect to several printers and a plotter. You then use Windows to define the printer port for each printer as LPT1 and the plotter as COM1. When you are using the printers, however, only one can be set active at a time.

To make a peripheral active, choose the **Printers** icon from Control Panel. In the **Installed Printers** box, select the printer you wish to make active. In the **Status** box, choose **Active**. The **Installed Printers** list will show that printer as active, and all other printers with that port will be set to inactive.

Configuring the Peripheral

As a final step before using a peripheral, you should configure your peripheral. For a laser printer, this means defining a list of variables including paper size, orientation, cartridge, and resolution.

To configure a printer, choose **Printers** from the Control Panel. Select the printer to configure in the **Installed Printers** list and choose **Configure** on the first dialog box. On the next dialog box, choose **Setup**. When the printer dialog box is displayed, select or enter the appropriate options. Figure 17.12 shows the dialog box for a Hewlett-Packard LaserJet printer. This box will vary, depending on the printer. Table 17.2 shows the following options available for this printer.

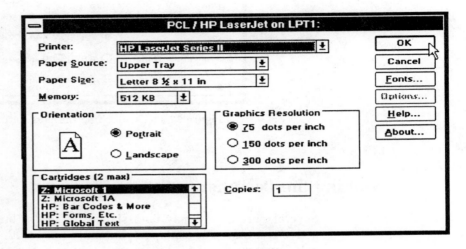

Figure 17.12 Configuring a printer.

Using the Printer

Once a printer is installed, it is ready for use. Most Windows applications have a File menu that permits you to print directly with the current (default) printer and configuration. To print with another printer, use the **Printer Setup** option of the application's File menu to choose the printer. You can choose **Setup** from this option to reconfigure the printer directly from the application without having to use Control Panel.

Note: Printers installed to Windows are available to all Windows applications but are not available to non-Windows applications. For other applications (even when they are running under Windows), the printer drivers in the application are used.

Table 17.2 Options Available for Hewlett-Packard LaserJet Printer

Option	Description
P̲rinter	The printer chosen on the **Installed Printers** list box. Scrolling this box will show other printers supported by this same driver.
Paper S̲ource	The type of paper source (tray or other paper input).
Paper Si̲ze	The paper size. The default is 8½ by 11 inches.
M̲emory	The amount of available memory in the printer.
Orientation	A choice of either normal **Portrait** orientation or sideways **Landscape** orientation. Available fonts will depend on the orientation chosen.
Graphics Resolution	Selection of the resolution in dots per inch. Higher values give better resolution but require more printer memory and printing time is slower.
Cartr̲idges	Selection of the cartridge used for printing.
F̲onts	Selection of soft fonts to be added to the printer.
O̲ptions	Selection of additional options.
H̲elp	Pressing this button displays the version of the printer driver.

Controlling the Print Manager

Windows defaults to using the Print Manager, spooling your printer to a queue from which Print Manager prints in the background (Chapter 16). If you experience printing problems or have a hardware buffer, you may wish to turn off the Print Manager. To print directly from a program without using the Print Manager, choose **Printers** from Control Panel. On the dialog box, clear **U̲se Print Manager**. To use the Print Manager again, toggle **U̲se Print Manager** on.

Other Printer Options

You can define one printer as the default printer. Each time you start Windows, the default printer will be the printer initially chosen for printing. Normally, the first printer you install when you install Windows is chosen as the default printer.

To change the default printer, choose the **Printers** icon from Control Panel. The current default printer is listed in the **Default Printer** box. To change the default printer, double-click the desired default printer in the **Installed Printers** list or select the printer and press Alt+D. The **Default Printer** box will change to show the new default printer. Choose **OK**.

You can control the timeout for a printer. The *timeout* is the amount of time that Windows waits when printing before it sends you a message if something is wrong. This option is set from the **Printers** option of Control Panel. Select the printer for which you wish to set the timing and choose **Configure**. **Device Not Selected** defines the time to wait to send a message if the printer is off-line. The default is 15 seconds. **Transmission Retry** defines the time to wait to indicate that the printer cannot print a character. The default is 45 seconds. You can edit either and choose **OK**. Using a serial port or a PostScript printer may require higher values for these. If you get timeout messages in either case, increase these values.

Deleting a Printer

Occasionally you may want to delete a printer from Windows. As an example, you might want to install a laser printer and then remove your older dot-matrix printer from the system. To delete printers from Windows by using the Control Panel, select the **Printers** icon. Control Panel will display a dialog box of the current printers. Select the printer you wish to delete, click **Remove**, and choose **OK**. This will remove the printer selection from the Windows system and delete the driver file from the Windows directory. The printer will then no longer be available to any Windows application.

Note: Sometimes a single driver file may be used by two or more printers on a system. If this is true, deleting a printer will not delete the driver file. It will, however, remove the printer from the printer list.

Adding and Deleting Fonts

A *font* is a particular graphic design for a set of characters, numbers, and symbols. When preparing a document, the font that you use is part of your message. Certain fonts are more formal and are best in proposals and business correspondence. Others are more personal and informal. Some are easier to read than others.

For each font installed on your system, you should install both the corresponding screen and the printer fonts. The screen font is used for screen displays, while the printer font is a higher resolution and is used for printing. In some cases the printer requires the storing of a separate bit map for each character type, size, and style. Other printers, such as PostScript printers, require the storing of only an outline for each character. The printer sizes the character on printing. When you purchase printer fonts, be sure to also obtain the corresponding printer and screen fonts.

Note: If a screen font does not exist for a particular printer font, Windows will display the text using a font as close as possible to the printer font. Line and page breaks will still be correct for the missing font.

When you install Windows, the installation program automatically installs all the fonts that are needed for the display and for the printers that you are using. Sometimes, however, if you add a printer, you may need to install the basic fonts necessary to support that printer.

Before looking at how fonts are installed, let's take a brief look at the types of fonts that are available. Windows fonts are either of two types: raster (bit-mapped) fonts or stroked fonts. With *raster fonts*, the characters are defined as pixel images. Each character is represented by a matrix of bits of a certain resolution, with each bit either on or off. Raster fonts are used by the video display and by both laser and dot-matrix printers. They vary in quality depending on the resolution of the bit-mapped image, and are difficult to resize except as integer multiples (2X, 3X, etc.). The video fonts are also display-dependent. *Stroked fonts*, also called vector fonts, are defined by mathematical equations that specify the lines that compose the character. Stroked fonts are normally used with plotters, and are easy to resize.

Microsoft supplies a collection of character sets of different sizes. Table 17.3 shows the fonts supplied with Microsoft Windows.

Table 17.3 Fonts Available with Microsoft Windows

Font	Description
Helv	(Helvetica) A proportional sans serif raster font. *Proportional* means that the characters are of varying widths. *Sans serif* means without serifs—short lines that distinguish a character's primary strokes and make the text easier to read. Helvetica is the font used by windows and dialog boxes.
Courier	A fixed-width raster font with serifs.
TMS RMN	(Times Roman) A proportional raster font with serifs.
Roman	A proportional stroked font with serifs.
Modern	A proportional sans serif stroked font.
Script	A proportional vector font.

In addition to the fonts shown in Table 17.3, Windows supports an additional Terminal raster font that cannot be added or removed.

There are two basic situations when you may wish to change the installed fonts:

- When you are installing a new printer or display device to your system. For a new printer, the Windows diskettes generally contain all the files you will need for the default fonts. These are installed by using the **Fonts** option of Control Panel.

- When you are adding soft fonts to an existing printer system. In this case you are purchasing additional fonts for a specific printer and adding them by using the printer driver font installation program.

Adding and Deleting Fonts When Installing a New Printer

When you install Windows, the fonts that are needed for your particular printers and display device are automatically installed. When you add a printer, however, you may need to add the files for its default internal fonts. In most cases these fonts are supplied with Windows (.FON extension). The display fonts normally have a lower resolution than the printer version of the same fonts. Also, you may wish to delete fonts that are no longer in use after you have removed a printer from Windows.

Tip: If you can't decide which fonts to install when adding a new printer, reinstall Windows, selecting the new printer. The fonts for that printer will be automatically installed. Before reinstalling Windows, be sure that you have backed up the WIN.INI file you were using. Installing printer or display fonts may modify this file, and you should keep a backup.

Tip: Before installing fonts, check and print any TXT files on the Windows diskettes that might be relevant for your printer.

To install fonts when adding a printer, choose the **Fonts** icon on the Control Panel. A dialog box shows the current fonts that are installed and shows a sample of the highlighted font at the bottom of the dialog box (see Figure 17.13). You can move the highlight and see samples of other fonts. For raster fonts, you will see a sample of each size available. Stroked fonts are shown in a single size, since they can be scaled as desired. Choose the **Add** button. The next dialog box (see Figure 17.14) requests the filename for the font set to install. Enter the filename and choose **OK**.

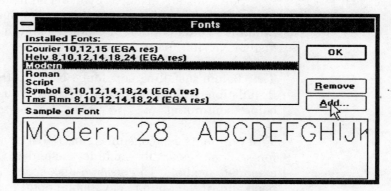

Figure 17.13 Starting to add a font.

If you are no longer using a particular printer, you may wish to delete the font associated with that printer. You can delete a font by choosing **Fonts** from the Control Panel. Select the font to delete and choose **Remove**.

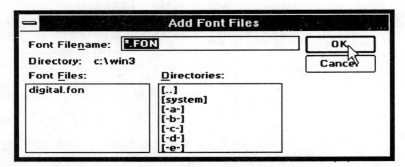

Figure 17.14 Adding a font.

Adding and Deleting Soft Fonts

You many wish to extend the range of your font selection for an installed printer. For example, the Hewlett-Packard LaserJet Series II printers can use cartridges to print Helvetica and Times Roman fonts up to 14 points. For larger sizes, however, you need to purchase and install soft fonts. *Soft fonts* are fonts that are installed on your computer and downloaded to the printer as they are needed. Soft fonts are made by a variety of manufacturers and are generally printer-specific.

Soft fonts are installed by using an installer program provided as part of the printer driver. For this reason, installing soft fonts is done from the **Printers** option of Control Panel. Install both a printer and a display version for each font you install.

Tip: Before installing soft fonts, back up the WIN.INI file. Soft font installation will modify this file, and you should create a backup before continuing.

Tip: Soft fonts can consume a lot of disk space, particularly the larger fonts. Fonts generally include a standard character set as well as extended symbols. To conserve disk space, install only the fonts you need and (if the option is available) don't install the extended portion of the character set unless you plan to use it.

To install soft fonts, select the **Printers** icon from the Control Panel and choose the **Configure** button. Choose **Setup** on the next dialog box. The next dialog box is from the printer driver and is printer-dependent. Figure 17.15 shows this dialog box for a Hewlett-Packard

LaserJet. Choose **Fonts** on this box to get the soft font installer (see Figure 17.16).

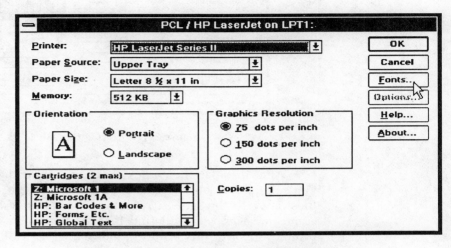

Figure 17.15 The Configuration dialog box.

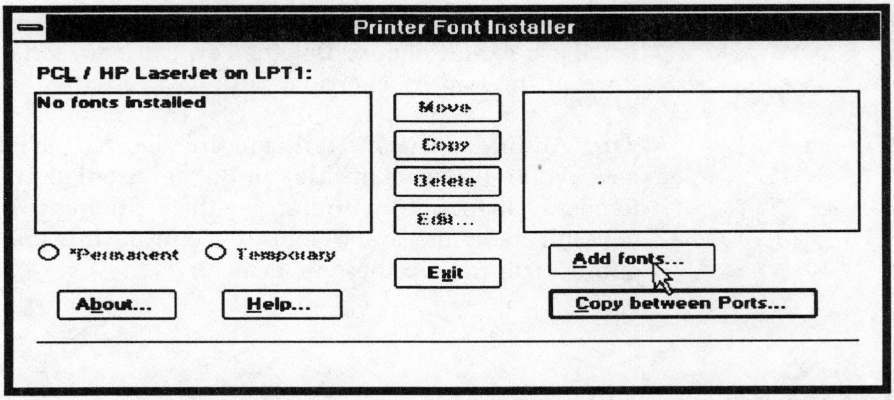

Figure 17.16 The soft font installer.

On the dialog box shown in Figure 17.16, choose **Add fonts**. On prompting, enter the disk with the soft fonts and choose **OK**. The fonts on the disk will be listed. Select the fonts to add and choose **Add** (see Figure 17.17). Repeat for each disk having soft fonts that you want to add. When finished, choose **Exit**. Back out through the dialog boxes by choosing **OK** as necessary.

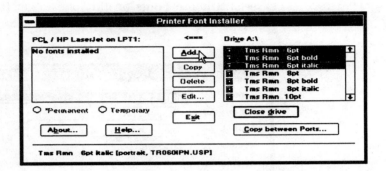

Figure 17.17 Adding the soft fonts.

After installation, a quick check will show that the listing in the **Fonts** option of Control Panel hasn't changed. The system fonts (.FON files) are still the same. If you load Windows Write or another program, however, you will find that the new fonts are available. The printer fonts (for this printer) are installed as .USP files, and the display fonts as .PFM files. Both are placed in a new PCLFONTS directory.

To delete a soft font, use the **Printers** option to return to the same Printer Font Installer dialog box. Select the font to delete in the left list box and choose **Delete**. You can edit certain basic classifications of the font by choosing **Edit**.

Tip: Adding soft fonts will modify the WIN.INI file. Print the file both before (the backup file) and after installation and study the differences. Chapter 18 will describe these differences in depth. You can manually add more soft fonts by editing this file and copying the appropriate files to the new directory.

International Options

The **International** option of the Control Panel permits you to set the date, time, number, and currency format for a particular country (see Figure 17.18). This option will automatically affect all Windows application programs. There are three main uses for this option:

■ You can use it to customize the selections for a particular country. For example, if you live in the United States, you could use this option to customize Windows for the United States formats.

■ If you purchased Windows to use in another country, you could select your country on the list and then customize the settings from that country's defaults.

■ If you travel a lot with a laptop, this option makes it easy to change settings for any particular country.

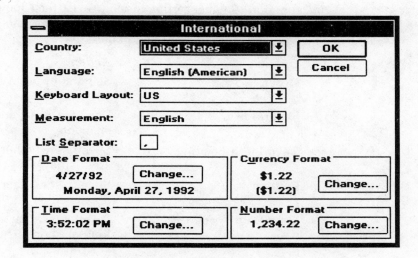

Figure 17.18 Setting the country.

In most cases you need only select the country in the upper list box. The other values will automatically change to the correct values for that country. The rest of the dialog box permits you to customize the following default options for any country:

Option	*Action*
Country	Defines country and sets the remainder of the box to the default values for that country.
Language	Specifies the country's language for language-specific tasks (sorting, case, etc.).
Keyboard Layout	Defines the keyboard layout to use.
Measurement	Defines the measurement system to use (English/Metric).
List Separator	Defines the separator symbol for lists.

In Figure 17.18 notice that the lower part of the box has four sections, each with a **Change** button. The default setting is displayed and can be changed from the **Change** button.

Changing the Date Format

The date option changes the date format for applications having this function. To change this format, select the **Change** button in the **Date Format** subwindow. Set the options in the International-Date Format box (see Figure 17.19) and choose **OK**:

Option	*Action*
Order	Sets the order of the month, day, and year.
Separator	Defines the separator for the date elements.
Day/Month Leading Zero	Specifies whether single-digit months are displayed as one or two digits.
Century	Specifies whether the year is displayed as one or two digits.
Long Date Format	Permits customization of the date to a long or short display.

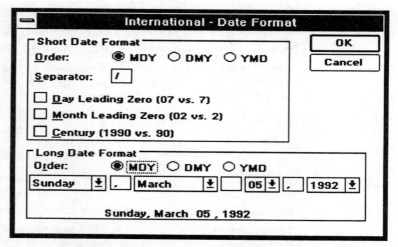

Figure 17.19 International-Date Format dialog box.

Changing the Time Format

The **Time Format** option changes the time format for applications having this function. To change this format, select the **Change** button in the **Time Format** subwindow. Set the options in the International-Time Format box (see Figure 17.20) and choose **OK**:

Option	Action
12 hour/24 hour	Sets the time display in 0–11 hour or 0–23 hour format.
AM/PM	For 12-hour formats, the upper box defines a morning suffix and the lower box defines an evening prefix. For 24-hour formats, the lower text box defines a suffix for all times.
Separator	Defines the separator for time elements.
Leading Zero	Specifies whether to display hours before 10 as one or two digits.

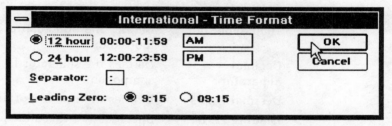

Figure 17.20 Defining the time format.

Changing the Currency Format

The **Currency Format** option changes the currency format for applications having this function. To change this format, select the **Change** button in the **Currency Format** subwindow. Set the options in the International-Currency Format box (see Figure 17.21) and choose **OK**:

Option	Action
Symbol Placement	Defines the placement of the currency symbol.
Negative	Specifies how to display negative numbers.
Symbol	Specifies the currency symbol.
Decimal Digits	Defines the number of digits after the decimal point.

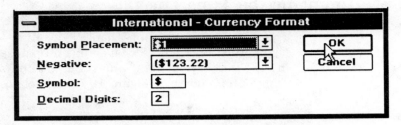

Figure 17.21 Specifying the currency format.

Changing the Number Format

The **Number Format** option changes the number format for applications having this function. To change this format, select the **Change** button in the **Number Format** subwindow. Set the options in the International-Number Format box (see Figure 17.22) and choose **OK**:

Option	Action
1000 Separator	Defines the punctuation used to separate thousands.
Decimal Separator	Defines the separator for the decimal component.
Decimal Digits	Defines the number of digits after the separator.
Leading Zero	Specifies whether numbers less than 1 are to be preceded by a zero.

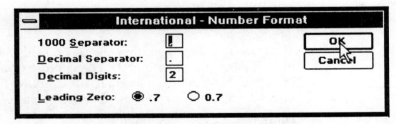

Figure 17.22 Specifying the number format.

Configuring the Mouse

To customize the mouse, select the **Mouse** icon from Control Panel. This icon permits you to change the tracking speed (sensitivity), the double-click speed, and the primary control button of the mouse.

The *double-click speed* defines how fast you must double-click in order for the system to accept your clicks as a double-click (see Figure 17.23). The double-click speed can be changed by using either the mouse or the keyboard:

To change the double-click speed with the mouse, drag the scroll box in the **Double Click Speed** section to increase or decrease the double-click speed. Alternatively, you can click the arrows at either end.

To change the mouse double-click speed from the keyboard, use the Tab or Shift + Tab keys to select the section. Use the left and right keys to move the scroll box and then press Enter to complete the selection.

When the speed is set fast, your fingers will have to be very quick on the mouse to create a double-click. When it's set slow, you will have plenty of time to press the mouse button twice. This window is available only for mouse-driven systems. If you like fast arcade games and have quick reflexes, set this speed to fast. If you have trouble getting double-clicks to work, try the slower speed.

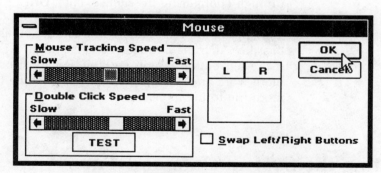

Figure 17.23 Configuring the mouse.

You can test the mouse's double-click speed by double-clicking the TEST box. For each successful double-click, the TEST box will toggle to the opposite state, either turning black to white, or white to black.

You can change the mouse sensitivity from the **Mouse Tracking Speed** section. This option defines how fast the mouse cursor moves when you move the mouse.

To change the mouse sensitivity with the mouse, drag the scroll box in the **Mouse Tracking Speed** section to increase or decrease the sensitivity. Alternatively, you can click the arrows at either end.

To change the mouse sensitivity from the keyboard, use the Tab or Shift + Tab keys to select the subwindow. The scroll box will then be blinking at the current cursor blink rate. Use the left and right keys to move the scroll box and then press Enter to complete the selection.

For painting programs, you will generally prefer a slower mouse (lower sensitivity). For most work, a moderate sensitivity is sufficient.

With the new mice, the question of sensitivity is more complex, since many of them support an automatic variable sensitivity. When you move the mouse slowly, the sensitivity is low. This makes it easy to control the mouse in delicate paint graphics work. When you move the mouse quickly, the sensitivity is high, making it easy to move the mouse cursor large distances.

Clicking the mouse means to quickly press the left button of the mouse. Dragging means to press the left button and move the mouse and then release the button. For special mouse operations, the right button is used. If you wish to switch the roles of the two buttons, select the **Swap Left/Right Buttons** check box. The switch takes place immediately, even while the dialog box is still open. When you are through configuring the mouse, click **OK**.

Tip: If you are left-handed and use the mouse at the left of the keyboard, switch the buttons. You also might wish to switch the buttons if the left button is not working. For most users, the left button gets more work and wears out sooner. Switching the buttons gives a little more life to the mouse.

Setting the System Date and Time

To set the system date or time, select the **Date/Time** icon from Control Panel. Select or scroll to the new date and time (see Figure 17.24). Choose **OK**.

Note: Setting a new system date or time affects the system clock. If you exit Windows, the system date (using the DATE or TIME commands) will be the new date and time.

Figure 17.24 Setting a new date or time.

Setting the Keyboard Speed

Systems using the DOS operating system have a *typamatic* keyboard. If you hold down a key for a period of time, the key begins repeating. Select the **Keyboard** icon of Control Panel to define the period of time that you can hold down a key before it begins repeating. When the dialog box is displayed, drag the scroll box to define the typamatic speed (see Figure 17.25). You can use the **Test Typamatic** area to test the delay.

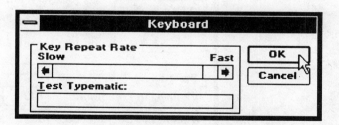

Figure 17.25 Setting the keyboard speed.

Controlling the Beeper

Windows uses a warning beep to give you an audible alarm if you try to do something wrong. You can turn this alarm off or on by selecting the **Sound** icon of Control Panel. Toggle **Warning Beep** as desired and choose **OK** (see Figure 17.26).

Figure 17.26 Controlling the beeper.

Setting the 386 Enhanced-Mode Options

If you are running in the 386 enhanced mode, you will see an icon on Control Panel for setting these options. This dialog box sets the device contention and multitasking options (see Figure 17.27).

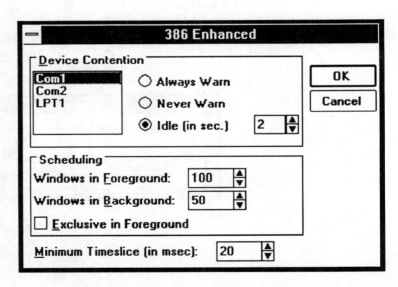

Figure 17.27 Setting the 386 enhanced-mode options.

Setting the **Device Contentions** options defines what happens if two devices try to use the same port at the same time. To set these, select the device and then choose the option for that device:

Option	Action
Always Warn	Causes Windows to display a dialog box if a contention problem occurs. Windows then asks which device should get the port. This option is the one you normally should select.
Never Warn	Eliminates any warning. Could cause garbled data if two programs try to use the same device.
Idle	Specifies the time, in seconds, that must elapse between the time one program stops using a port and another application starts using the same port without providing a warning.

The **Scheduling** section defines how Windows behaves during multitasking. Set the following options as desired:

Option	Action
Minimum Timeslice	Specifies the number of milliseconds an application can have before releasing the processor to another application. Smaller timeslices mean smoother operation, but overall performance declines.
Windows in Foreground	Specifies the amount of processing time shared by all Windows applications.
Windows in Background	Specifies the amount of processing time shared by all Windows applications when a standard (non-Windows) application is running in the foreground.
Exclusive in Foreground	If on, specifies that Windows gets 100% of processing time if a Windows application is active.

After you have selected the desired options, choose **OK**.

Changing the Setup

Although Control Panel enables you to change many parameters, certain options such as the display, mouse, keyboard, or network cannot be altered without some level of reinstallation. To change these parameters, use the **Windows Setup** icon from the Main group window of Program Manager. This icon permits you to change the mouse, display, keyboard, or network.

Selecting the Setup program displays a box with the current parameters (see Figure 17.28). To change the display, mouse, keyboard, or network option, choose **Change System Settings** from the Options menu. From the next dialog box, select the proper list box and change to the desired option (see Figure 17.29). Choose **OK**.

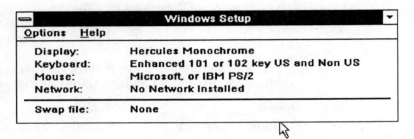

Figure 17.28 Starting Windows Setup.

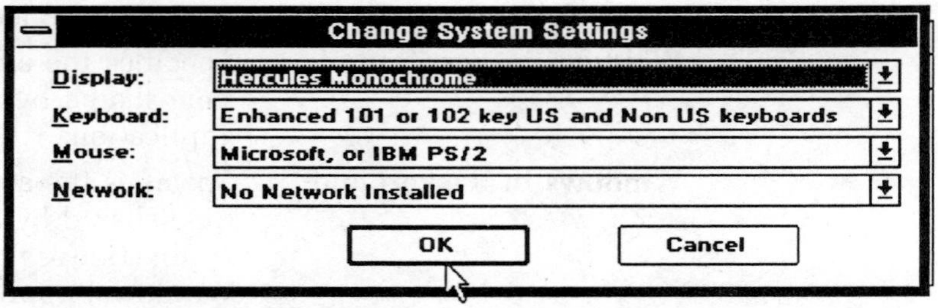

Figure 17.29 Changing Windows Setup.

To change the installation of programs in the group windows, select **Setup Applications**. This option causes the repeat of the application setup steps that were part of the initial installation.

Note: You can also install applications to groups by using Program Manager (Chapter 3).

To terminate the Setup program, double-click the Control-menu box icon, open the Control menu and choose **Close**, or press Alt + F4.

Summary

Control Panel is a Windows application that permits you to quickly alter the Windows environment for your particular system. It is useful for setting the system time or date, installing or uninstalling printers, configuring printers for specific ports, installing fonts, setting the colors of screen elements, and controlling the mouse.

Windows Setup permits you to reinstall portions of Windows without having to install the entire system.

Customizing Windows: Modifying the INI Files

For many users, the Control Panel program provides a sufficient level of customization for Windows. At times, however, you may want to do more than what Control Panel supports. This chapter shows you how to start applications automatically with Windows, how to automatically load data files, how to send printer output to a file, and how to exercise more control over the Windows environment.

Introduction to the WIN.INI File

Windows contains several .INI files that permit you to customize the Windows environment. The file of most interest for customization is the WIN.INI file. The WIN.INI file is a text file that contains the basic configuration information for your Windows environment. When you install Windows, WIN.INI is created with certain basic information based on the display and printer you select. After installation, you can modify the Windows environment by editing this file with any ASCII editor, such as Notepad.

The Control Panel permits you to customize your environment to some extent. When you use Control Panel, WIN.INI is modified based on the changes you specify. Control Panel, however, provides only limited capabilities.

Using an editor and directly modifying WIN.INI give you much more control over your Windows environment. You can use any editor, but you will probably find that Notepad is ideal.

Tip: Before tinkering with WIN.INI, always make a backup. The best way is simply to copy it to a file called WIN.BAK or WIN.OLD:

```
C:\>COPY WIN.INI WIN.OLD
```

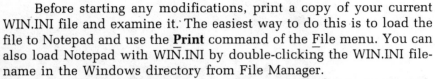

Before starting any modifications, print a copy of your current WIN.INI file and examine it. The easiest way to do this is to load the file to Notepad and use the **Print** command of the File menu. You can also load Notepad with WIN.INI by double-clicking the WIN.INI file-name in the Windows directory from File Manager.

You will find the file composed of a series of sections, with parameter values defined in each section. Each section name is enclosed in brackets ([]). After installation you should find the following sections:

```
[windows]
[desktop]
[extensions]
[intl]
[ports]
[Windows Help]
[fonts]
[colors]
[PrinterPorts]
[devices]
```

These sections will not be in alphabetical order. Table 18.1 shows what each section controls.

Table 18.1. The Sections of the WIN.INI File and Their Area of Control

Section	Description
[windows]	Defines a number of parameters normally set from Control Panel
[desktop]	Controls desktop design and grid
[extensions]	Allows the user to initiate program execution by selecting a corresponding data file
[intl]	Controls international settings
[ports]	Defines available communication ports

Section	Description
[fonts]	Defines font files
[colors]	Defines colors for window elements (this section will exist only if you aren't using the default colors)
[PrinterPorts]	Lists active and inactive peripherals
[devices]	Lists active devices available

In addition to the sections shown in Table 18.1, you should find a section for each printer that you have installed and probably a few sections for various Windows applications:

```
[HPPCL,LPT1]
[Microsoft Excel]
```

You can alter the Windows environment by editing the values of the parameters in the various sections. Comment lines can also be added by starting the line with a semicolon. Comment lines cannot contain an equal sign.

Each section consists of a series of lines in the form

```
keyname=value
```

The keyname is the parameter to set. It is followed by an equal sign and a text string or value.

Tip: Installing a Windows application (such as Excel or PageMaker) can alter the WIN.INI file. Installing Windows applications modifies the [extensions] section and adds a new section for the application. If you reinstall Windows, you can lose these changes. It's a good idea to back up your WIN.INI file to another file on the hard disk before installing a new Windows application. Then print the new WIN.INI file or back it up to a floppy disk. See Appendix A.

The [windows] Section: Defining the Control Panel Parameters

The [windows] section defines a number of parameters that are normally set from the Control Panel. Most of the parameters you will probably recognize from the last chapter. There are, however, a few new parameters. Of particular interest are those that can be used to load and start programs automatically when Windows is started. Here is a sample listing of this section:

```
[windows]
load=
run=
Beep=yes
Spooler=yes
NullPort=None
device=PCL / HP LaserJet,HPPCL,LPT1:
BorderWidth=3
KeyboardSpeed=31
CursorBlinkRate=741
DoubleClickSpeed=452
Programs=com exe bat pif
Documents=
DeviceNotSelectedTimeout=15
TransmissionRetryTimeout=45
swapdisk=
```

The `load` option defines programs that are to be automatically loaded when Windows is started and that will be icons on the initial screen. The `run` option defines programs that are to be loaded and started when Windows is started. You can use multiple programs with either, separating the names by commas or spaces, for example:

```
load=clock,notepad
run=calendar
```

Notice that the file extension is not needed.

You can also use data filenames with these options. Using a data filename will load or start a program with that file. The program loaded for the file is determined by the `[extensions]` section. The extension name must be used. For example, the following would start Calendar with the file MYSCHED.CAL:

```
run=mysched.cal
```

For both the `load` and the `run` options, you must specify the full pathname if the file is not in the current path:

```
load=c:\mw\word.exe
```

The `Beep` option determines whether a warning beep is sounded when something is attempted that is not allowed.

The `Spooler` option permits you to turn the Print Manager off or on. On installation, Windows defaults to using the Print Manager by setting `Spooler=yes`. The Print Manager manages a printer buffer area so that you can continue to work in Windows while a document is printing in the background (Chapter 16). You might want to change this option to `no` if any of the following is true:

- You have a hardware printer buffer and don't need a software buffer.
- You need the Print Manager's memory space.
- You are having printer interface problems and need more direct control of the printer. (Try printing with the spooler on and off. If printing works with the spooler off, leave it that way.)
- You need multitasking printer support.

Note that the spooler option can be changed from the Control Panel by using the Printers option.

The `NullPort` option defines the text that will be displayed in the list box of the Control Panel Printers dialog box and is used to define the null port. The `device` option defines the default printer.

The `Programs` option defines which files are considered applications. File extensions listed here are used to determine which files are displayed by the File Manager when you select **Programs** by using the View menu's **Include** option. The default for the `Programs` option is

```
programs=com exe bat pif
```

The `Documents` option is new with Windows 3, and it defines which files Windows identifies as documents.

The `swapdisk` option defines where Windows should do its swapping. Remember that the Windows environment is a virtual memory machine; that is, only part of the program is in memory at a time. This apparently is a holdover from older versions of Windows, and swapping is now defined in the SYSTEM.INI file (see "Other Initialization Files" later in this chapter). The other options are all controlled from Control Panel.

The [desktop] Section: Controlling the Desktop Design

The [desktop] section controls the appearance of the desktop. It can also define a grid for controlling the placement of icons and windows. This section is normally set from the Control Panel by using the Desktop option.

```
[desktop]
Pattern=
Wallpaper=(None)
TileWallpaper=0
GridGranularity=0
```

The [extensions] Section: Using a Filename to Start an Application

The [extensions] section permits you to start an application by double-clicking a filename of a data file. The application is then started with that file. This section maps various file extensions to corresponding application programs. The application programs do not have to be Windows application programs. With the default installation, this section has the following listing:

```
[extensions]
cal=calendar.exe ^.cal
crd=cardfile.exe ^.crd
trm=terminal.exe ^.trm
txt=notepad.exe ^.txt
ini=notepad.exe ^.ini
pcx=pbrush.exe ^.pcx
bmp=pbrush.exe ^.bmp
wri=write.exe ^.wri
rec=recorder.exe ^.rec
```

This section defines the extensions for the Windows application programs provided with Windows. As an example, double-clicking any filename with the extension .CAL would start Calendar with that file. You can also change this section by using the **Association** command of the File Manager.

Notice that multiple file extensions can be assigned to the same program. In the default mode, either .TXT or .INI files will start Notepad:

```
txt=notepad.exe ^.txt
ini=notepad.exe ^.ini
```

When you install new Windows application programs, the [extensions] section may be modified during installation to permit an application to be started from a data file. For example, installing Excel will add the following lines to this section:

```
xls=excel.exe ^.xls
xlc=excel.exe ^.xlc
xlw=excel.exe ^.xlw
xlm=excel.exe ^.xlm
```

If you use Excel with Lotus 1-2-3 files, you may wish to manually add the lines:

```
wk1=excel.exe ^.wk1
wks=excel.exe ^.wks
```

If the application program is not in the current path, you should specify the pathname:

```
xls=c:\ex\excel.exe ^.xls
xlc=c:\ex\excel.exe ^.xlc
xlw=c:\ex\excel.exe ^.xlw
xlm=c:\ex\excel.exe ^.xlm
```

In the same way, you can start other non-Windows programs from Windows by double-clicking their data files. For example, you can start Microsoft Word version 5 with any .DOC file by using

```
doc=c:\mw5\word.exe ^.doc
```

Tip: For each standard program that you intend to use under Windows, modify the [extensions] section to support loading those programs from data files. During installation of Windows applications, this section is normally modified automatically by the installation program for the application.

Tip: When you are upgrading your version of Windows, it is very easy to lose portions of the [extensions] section during the creation of the new WIN.INI file. For safety, back up the WIN.INI file before you upgrade your version of Windows.

The [ports] Section: Printing to a File

The `[ports]` section defines the available ports in the system and the default configuration for the serial ports. For a typical system, the default might be

```
[ports]
LPT1:=
LPT2:=
LPT3:=
COM1:=9600,n,8,1
COM2:=9600,n,8,1
COM3:=9600,n,8,1
COM4:=9600,n,8,1
EPT:=
FILE:=
```

The serial port settings of this section are normally set from the Control Panel by using the Ports option.

You can print to a file by adding a filename to this section, for example:

```
output.prn=
```

You can use any filename, but the extension must be .PRN. The equal sign must be included, and nothing may follow the equal sign. Once you have added the filename to this section, it will be listed with the other ports when you select the port from the Printers option of Control Panel.

To print to a file, first add the filename to the list of this section. Then use Control Panel's Printers option to select the printer. Select **Configure** and choose the filename as the output port. Now print the file by using the **File** menu and the **Print** option of the application program, and the output will go to the specified file. To print from this file later, use DOS redirection from the DOS prompt, such as:

```
C:\>COPY OUTPUT.PRN > LPT1:
```

Note that you may add as many as eight filenames to this section.

Tip: Use this redirection technique to print a file from a Windows application on another system that does not have Windows.

Tip: To create a text file, install the **Generic/Text Only** printer driver. Use Control Panel to connect it to a filename and then print to that port.

The [fonts] Section: Defining Available Fonts

The [fonts] section defines the available fonts in the system for the display and the printers. You can install new fonts by using the Fonts option of Control Panel:

```
[fonts]
Helv 8,10,12,14,18,24 (VGA res)=HELVE.FON
Courier 10,12,15 (VGA res)=COURE.FON
Tms Rmn 8,10,12,14,18,24 (VGA res)=TMSRE.FON
Symbol 8,10,12,14,18,24 (VGA res)=SYMBOLE.FON
Roman (All res)=ROMAN.FON
Script (All res)=SCRIPT.FON
Modern (All res)=MODERN.FON
```

Note: Any soft fonts that you have installed are listed in a separate section as part of the printer specifications that support those fonts.

The [colors] Section: Controlling the Colors

The optional [colors] section defines the colors of the various window elements. It is set by using the Colors option of Control Panel. The [colors] section is missing in the default installation, but it appears in the WIN.INI file if you change the default colors. Here is an example of a setting:

```
[colors]
Background=0 0 0
AppWorkspace=255 255 255
Window=255 255 255
WindowText=0 0 0
Menu=0 255 0
MenuText=0 0 0
ActiveTitle=255 0 255
InactiveTitle=192 192 192
TitleText=0 0 0
ActiveBorder=128 255 0
```

```
InactiveBorder=192 192 192
WindowFrame=0 0 0
Scrollbar=192 192 192
```

Notice that each window element has a parameter with three values. The three values represent the screen intensity for red, green, and blue. A value of 255 represents full intensity; 0 is black. The color white would be values of 255 255 255. Black would be 0 0 0.

Most users don't try to manually edit this part of the file. It's far easier to set these parameters by using the Colors option of Control Panel. However, you might wish to edit this section if you have saved some special settings and printed the list, but have lost the file. It is easier to reset the settings by editing this list than to use the Colors option again.

Tip: Once you have set the colors you want from Control Panel, keep a copy of the WIN.INI file. You will find it a lot easier next time to copy this section from another file than to tune all the colors the way you want them from the Control Panel.

If you want to print a Windows screen dump and you are using a VGA, create a new monochrome Windows directory for the VGA monochrome version by using the following settings:

```
Background=127 127 127
AppWorkspace=255 255 255
Window=255 255 255
WindowText=0 0 0
Menu=255 255 255
MenuText=0 0 0
ActiveTitle=0 0 0
InactiveTitle=255 255 255
TitleText=255 255 255
ActiveBorder=127 127 127
InactiveBorder=127 127 127
WindowFrame=0 0 0
Scrollbar=63 63 63
```

To capture EGA screens, install Windows as black-and-white and capture the screen. With both VGA and EGA, you can also try the monochrome setting of Control Panel's Colors option.

Now capture the screen you want to print to the Clipboard by using Alt + PrtScrn. Then paste the Clipboard to Paintbrush and print the screen from it.

Tip: This technique isn't ideal. The best way to capture Windows screens is to use a Hercules monitor and a screen capture program or Alt + PrtScrn.

The [intl] Section: Controlling the Country Settings

The [intl] section controls the country settings. It is normally set by the International option of Control Panel. Users in the United States will find this section to be blank except for one entry:

```
[intl]
sCountry=United States
```

The [PrinterPorts] Section: Setting the Printer Ports

The [PrinterPorts] section lists the active and inactive peripherals in the system, specifying the port and timeout parameters for each. These are normally set from the Printers option of Control Panel:

```
[PrinterPorts]
PCL / HP LaserJet=HPPCL,LPT1:,15,45
PostScript Printer=PSCRIPT,LPT2:,15,45
HP Plotter=HPPLOT,COM1:,15,45
```

The [devices] Section: Defining the Devices

The [devices] section defines the current printers in the system, the driver files for each, and the default port. Here is an example:

```
[devices]
PCL / HP LaserJet=HPPCL,LPT1:
PostScript Printer=PSCRIPT,LPT2:
HP Plotter=HPPLOT,COM1:
```

This section is normally set from the Printers option of Control Panel. Each line contains the device name as it will appear in the menus. The device name is followed by an equal sign, the name of the driver file (without the .DRV extension), a comma, and the default port. The default device is defined in the [windows] section.

Adding Printer Drivers

During installation of some printers, Windows may create a new section in the WIN.INI file. For example, if you have an HP LaserJet with soft fonts, you will find a variation of the following section added to your WIN.INI file:

```
[HPPCL,LPT1]
paper=1
prtindex=1
numcart=2
duplex=0
cartindex=23
cartindex1=12
FontSummary=E:\WIN3\SYSTEM\FSLPT1.PCL
sfdir=C:\PCLFONTS
SoftFont1=C:\PCL.FONTS\TRPRO060.PFM,C:\PCLFONTS\TR060RPN.USP
SoftFont2=C:\PCLFONTS\TRPBO060.PFM,C:\PCLFONTS\TR060BPN.USP
SoftFont3=C:\PCLFONTS\TRPIO060.PFM,C:\PCLFONTS\TR060IPN.USP
SoftFont4=C:\PCLFONTS\TRPRO080.PFM,C:\PCLFONTS\TR080RPN.USP
SoftFont5=C:\PCLFONTS\TRPBO080.PFM,C:\PCLFONTS\TR080BPN.USP
SoftFont6=C:\PCLFONTS\TRPIO080.PFM,C:\PCLFONTS\TR080IPN.USP
SoftFont7=C:\PCLFONTS\TRPRO100.PFM,C:\PCLFONTS\TR100RPN.USP
SoftFont8=C:\PCLFONTS\TRPBO100.PFM,C:\PCLFONTS\TR100BPN.USP
SoftFont9=C:\PCLFONTS\TRPIO100.PFM,C:\PCLFONTS\TR100IPN.USP
SoftFont10=C:\PCLFONTS\TRPRO120.PFM,C:\PCLFONTS\TR120RPN.USP
SoftFont11=C:\PCLFONTS\TRPBO120.PFM,C:\PCLFONTS\TR120BPN.USP
SoftFont12=C:\PCLFONTS\TRPIO120.PFM,C:\PCLFONTS\TR120IPN.USP
SoftFont13=C:\PCLFONTS\TRPRO140.PFM,C:\PCLFONTS\TR140RPN.USP
SoftFont14=C:\PCLFONTS\TRPBO140.PFM,C:\PCLFONTS\TR140BPN.USP
SoftFont15=C:\PCLFONTS\TRPIO140.PFM,C:\PCLFONTS\TR140IPN.USP
SoftFont16=C:\PCLFONTS\TRPBO180.PFM,C:\PCLFONTS\TR180BPN.USP
SoftFont17=C:\PCLFONTS\TRPBO240.PFM,C:\PCLFONTS\TR240BPN.USP
SoftFont18=C:\PCLFONTS\TRPBO300.PFM,C:\PCLFONTS\TR300BPN.USP
SoftFont19=C:\PCLFONTS\HVPRO060.PFM,C:\PCLFONTS\HV060RPN.USP
SoftFont20=C:\PCLFONTS\HVPBO060.PFM,C:\PCLFONTS\HV060BPN.USP
SoftFont21=C:\PCLFONTS\HVPIO060.PFM,C:\PCLFONTS\HV060IPN.USP
SoftFont22=C:\PCLFONTS\HVPRO080.PFM,C:\PCLFONTS\HV080RPN.USP
SoftFont23=C:\PCLFONTS\HVPBO080.PFM,C:\PCLFONTS\HV080BPN.USP
SoftFont24=C:\PCLFONTS\HVPIO080.PFM,C:\PCLFONTS\HV080IPN.USP
```

```
SoftFont25=C:\PCLFONTS\HVPRO100.PFM,C:\PCLFONTS\HV100RPN.USP
SoftFont26=C:\PCLFONTS\HVPBO100.PFM,C:\PCLFONTS\HV100BPN.USP
SoftFont27=C:\PCLFONTS\HVPIO100.PFM,C:\PCLFONTS\HV100IPN.USP
SoftFont28=C:\PCLFONTS\HVPRO120.PFM,C:\PCLFONTS\HV120RPN.USP
SoftFont29=C:\PCLFONTS\HVPBO120.PFM,C:\PCLFONTS\HV120BPN.USP
SoftFont30=C:\PCLFONTS\HVPIO120.PFM,C:\PCLFONTS\HV120IPN.USP
SoftFont31=C:\PCLFONTS\HVPRO140.PFM,C:\PCLFONTS\HV140RPN.USP
SoftFont32=C:\PCLFONTS\HVPIO140.PFM,C:\PCLFONTS\HV140IPN.USP
SoftFont33=C:\PCLFONTS\HVPBO180.PFM,C:\PCLFONTS\HV180BPN.USP
SoftFont34=C:\PCLFONTS\HVPBO240.PFM,C:\PCLFONTS\HV240BPN.USP
SoftFont35=C:\PCLFONTS\HVPBO300.PFM,C:\PCLFONTS\HV300BPN.USP
sfdlbat=C:\PCLFONTS\SFLPT1.BAT
SoftFonts=35
fsvers=2
```

You can use this section to support soft fonts for a printer. Soft fonts are stored on the disk until needed and then downloaded to the printer. Installing soft fonts to Windows means that the fonts will be available for that printer in all Windows applications. The actual soft font files in this example are stored in the C:\PCLFONTS directory.

The easiest way to add soft fonts is to use the Printers option of Control Panel (Chapter 17). Select the printer, then **Configure**, then **Setup**, and finally **Fonts**. The Font installer is part of the printer driver.

However, you may wish to edit the WIN.INI file if you want to move the fonts to another directory. In addition, once a few fonts are installed, it is often easier to add new fonts to the font directory and then edit the WIN.INI file to include the fonts. Notice in the preceding listing that each font has both a printer and a display version of the font. Also, the variable `SoftFonts` at the end of the listing contains the total number of fonts in the list. To manually add a font, use the next number in the list and edit the value of `SoftFonts`.

Application Sections

When you are installing some Windows applications, the installation procedure may create a new section in the WIN.INI file for the application. For example, installing Microsoft Excel creates the following new section:

```
[Microsoft Excel]
Options=119
Maximized=0
```

Changing the `Maximized` parameter here to 1 will load Excel with a maximized screen, which for most users is a preferred alternative.

Other Initialization Files

There are several other .INI files in the Windows directory that define the environment while supporting a level of customization:

Filename	*Description*
SYSTEM.INI	Contains the parameters defined at installation based on the hardware or defined by the Windows Setup program on Program Manager's Main group. This file also contains the settings for each of the three modes.
PROGMAN.INI	Contains the parameters for Program Manager.
WINFILE.INI	Contains a single `[settings]` option.
CONTROL.INI	Contains the parameters for Control Panel.

You probably won't need to edit these files very much, but the SYSTEM.INI file does have some important parameters. The size of the swap file (Appendix A) can be controlled from this file.

For the 386 enhanced mode, you can use the `[386enh]` section to define the size of a temporary file. If these parameters are not currently in the file, you can add them:

Parameter	*Action*
`MinUserDiskSpace`	Defines disk space that must be left free when creating a temporary file. A value of 4096 would leave 4096 kilobytes free.
`MaxPagingFileSize`	Specifies the maximum size for a temporary swap file.

In the `[standard]` section, you can use the swapdisk parameter to define the drive for the temporary files in the standard mode.

Summary

Editing of the WIN.INI file gives you a very high level of control over your Windows environment. Experiment with this file by using what you have learned in this chapter, but be sure to back up the file first. You will also find several text files (.TXT) in the Windows directory or on the diskettes that provide more information about each of the .INI files.

Running Windows Applications

Today many products are sold for the Windows environment. These products are known as *WinApps*. This chapter will explain what a Windows application is and define some common characteristics of WinApps. Finally, it will look at examples of Windows applications.

Types of Programs

Four basic types of programs run in the Windows environment:

- Windows applications designed specifically to run under Windows 3.0.
- Older Windows applications designed for previous versions of Windows.
- Standard, or non-Windows, applications.
- Terminate-and-stay-resident (TSR) programs, or memory-resident programs.

This chapter will cover the first two—Windows applications. Chapters 20 and 21 will cover standard and memory-resident programs.

What NOT to Run Under Windows

The following list provides some cautionary guidelines that you should consider when you are running Windows. If you are using Windows, don't try to run any of the programs or commands mentioned in the list. You risk losing data, if not the entire disk contents.

1. Use caution when you are installing disk-caching programs of any type, except for the disk-caching program supplied with Windows. Some products may work with Windows 3 but not as effectively as they would otherwise, some may work perfectly, and some can destroy your disk contents. Check with the manufacturer.

2. Do not run PC Tools Compress and other disk-optimizing programs under Windows.

3. Do not run any program under Windows that physically modifies the disk directly, such as undeletion or disk repair programs.

4. Do not run DOS Format on a hard disk (or other formatters) or the DOS command CHKDSK.

5. Do not run disk backup utilities under Windows.

Besides the programs mentioned in the preceding list, there are still other programs that you would be wise to avoid. These programs will not do any damage to your disk, but they may hang up, not work as they should, or not run at all. These programs fall into the following categories:

■ Programs that are simply too large to run under Windows. So much of Windows would be swapped out that there would be no advantage in using Windows.

■ Programs that use special programming tricks (nonstandard DOS conventions) incompatible with Windows.

■ Some memory-resident programs. Certain of these programs cannot run with Windows. The memory-resident concept is really not a DOS standard, and how each product interfaces with DOS varies in quality.

What Is a Windows Application?

A *Windows application* (WinApp) is an application program that is designed specifically to execute in the Windows environment. The application is developed in C or Pascal using Microsoft WinSDK (Windows Software Development Kit). A WinApp requires that the Windows environment be active before it can be run. Examples of WinApps include Microsoft Excel and Aldus PageMaker.

Windows applications all have the same type of user interface and share similar features. WinApp developers should follow the Application Style Guide that is published with the WinSDK. If this guide has been followed, you can expect the common features described in this chapter and in Chapter 2.

There are many reasons why you should consider purchasing Windows applications. Chapter 1 explains the advantages of Windows, and Appendix G lists many of the Windows applications that are currently available.

Features of Windows Applications

All of the application programs described in this book and the commercially developed Windows applications have a common set of features. This makes it easy to learn a new Windows application after you have had a little Windows experience.

Tip: Windows applications are ideal in businesses with high turnover, since the training time needed to learn most application programs is minimal and the use of the program is naturally compatible with the human thinking process.

Not all Windows applications are easy to use. Just because the application uses the Windows environment doesn't mean that it is easy to learn or use. A good Windows application should tell a story, leading readers through its menus and options (Chapter 1). Commands and menus should form a hierarchy that represents the normal way of solving the problem.

For example, if you have a General Ledger program, you shouldn't have all the reports on one menu. The report commands belong in menus to which they are functionally related. A report that prints the batch should be on a batch processing menu. Income and balance reports should be on a final closing menu.

Most of the general features of Windows applications were discussed in Chapter 2. Now that you have used some applications, however, you may have noticed a few other common features.

Windows Menus

Most Windows applications have a horizontal menu bar. These menu bars generally start with File and Edit menus and often end with a Help menu.

If a File option exists in the menu bar, it is usually the first option. The first four commands of this menu are generally **New**, **Open**, **Save**, and **Save As**, in that order. The **New** command clears the current data and data file selection, restarting the program. The **Open** command opens an existing data file. A dialog box is displayed with a list box at the left, and a second at the right, and often a template text box at the top (see Figure 19.1). The **Files** list box shows all files on the current directory matching the template. The **Directories** list box shows all subdirectories, all drives, and a double period for the parent directory. You can use the mouse or the direction keys to select a file, directory, or drive. Editing the template will change the files listed in the **Files** list box to those matching the new template. Clicking **OK** or pressing Enter will close the box and open the selected file. The **Save As** option saves a file with a user-specified name. The **Save** option saves the file under the current name specified in the title bar. There are often **Print**, **Page Setup**, and **Printer Setup** commands on the menu for printing a file. Most File menus will have an **Exit** command for terminating the program. Table 19.1 shows the mnemonics for these commands.

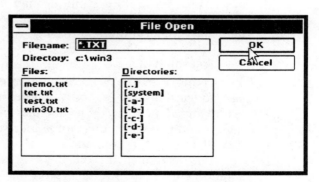

Figure 19.1 A dialog box for the Open command.

Table 19.1 The File Commands

File Command	Mnemonic	Description
New	N	Restarts application
Open	O	Opens a data file
Save	S	Saves current data file
Save As	A	Saves data in a named file
Print	P	Prints the currently active file
Page Setup	t	Defines page layout
Printer Setup	r	Changes or configures printer
Exit	x	Exits the program

Undo	Alt+BkSp
Cut	Shift+Del
Copy	Ctrl+Ins
Paste	Shift+Ins
Delete	Del
Select All	
Time/Date	F5
Word Wrap	

If an Edit menu is used, it will be the second menu option. The first five items on this menu are generally the commands **Undo**, **Cut**, **Copy**, **Paste**, and **Delete**. **Undo** reverses the last Edit menu command. **Cut** copies the selected item to the Clipboard and deletes the item. **Copy** copies the selection to the Clipboard without deletion. **Paste** copies the contents of the Clipboard to the application. **Delete** deletes the selection without copying it to the Clipboard. Table 19.2 shows the mnemonics and shortcuts for these commands.

Table 19.2 The Edit Menu Commands

Edit Command	Mnemonic	Shortcut	Description
Undo	U	Alt + Backspace	Undoes last edit command
Cut	t	Shift + Del	Deletes to Clipboard
Copy	C	Ctrl + Ins	Copies to Clipboard
Paste	P	Shift + Ins	Pastes from Clipboard
Delete		Del	Deletes

Windows Keys

All Windows applications have certain keystroke "rules" in common. They can be summarized as follows:

1. Single keys are used for small, frequently performed operations. For example, F6 switches windows when you are adding a header or a footer in Windows Write.

2. The Shift + *key* combinations are generally the complement of *key* used alone. For example, Tab moves clockwise through dialog-box options, Shift + Tab moves counterclockwise. The Shift key also can be used in selecting multiple items in a list box.

3. The Ctrl + *key* combinations are generally used for large-scale tasks. For example, Ctrl + PgUp scrolls up a screen.

4. The Alt *key* combinations are used for activating menu options. For example, Alt F activates the File menu. You do not need to press the keys simultaneously.

For a complete list of keyboard definitions, see Appendix F.

Selection and Text Editing

Cutting, copying, and deleting involve selecting and then requesting an operation. Windows supports two types of selections: text and nontext. Text selections include characters, words, sentences, and paragraphs. Nontext selections include spreadsheet cells, graphic objects, and a screen area. The selected areas are highlighted or otherwise marked. For text, the marked areas are indicated by the use of reverse video.

When you are selecting and editing text in a window or dialog box, the text is always inserted at the insertion point. The insertion point is indicated by a flashing, vertical line. The insertion point can be moved by clicking the mouse at the new location or by using the direction keys.

Windows applications follow these editing rules:

1. When text is inserted at the insertion point in insert mode, characters to the right are moved over to make room for the inserted text and the insertion point moves to the right.

2. The Backspace key deletes the character to the left of the insertion point.

3. When the Del key is used at the insertion point, it deletes the character to the right of the insertion point.

4. When characters, words, lines, or sentences are selected, the **Delete** command or the Del key will delete the selected text. The **Cut** command places a copy of the selected text in the Clipboard and deletes it. The **Copy** command places a copy in the Clipboard without deleting it.

5. When characters, words, lines, or sentences are selected, inserting text replaces the selected text.

Dialog Boxes

Windows applications use dialog boxes to request information from the user and to output information that is not part of the normal data file. A special type of dialog box, a message box, is used to display error messages and warnings to the user.

Dialog boxes are one of two types: modal and modeless. *Modal dialog boxes* do not permit the user to continue work until some action is taken. Modal dialog boxes are the most common, and are used for command input. *Modeless dialog boxes* permit the user to continue working while the dialog box is displayed. Modeless dialog boxes can be moved and are used for displaying graphics tools in drawing and painting programs or for help windows.

Dialog boxes contain special window types, or *controls*. There are five types of controls (Chapter 2). When a dialog box is initially displayed, the first control in the box is selected for you. You can use the mouse to select other controls. From the keyboard, you can use the Tab key to move forward through the controls and the Shift + Tab key to move backward.

Using the Clipboard

The Windows Clipboard enables you to copy and move data between applications. Chapter 2 describes how to use Clipboard with Windows applications. Clipboard can be used with graphics and text. Chapter 20 describes how to use it with standard, or non-Windows, applications. With standard applications, you can use Clipboard with both text and graphics but there is one limitation: you cannot paste graphics into a document in a standard application.

Windows has a Clipboard utility (see Figure 19.2) that is useful for examining or saving the Clipboard. You can access it from the Program Manager's Main group window. To save the Clipboard contents, start Clipboard and use the **Save As** option of the File menu. To load Clipboard from a file, choose the **Open** option of the File menu. Use the Edit menu to delete the Clipboard contents. The Display menu permits you to display a bit map of the Clipboard contents.

Figure 19.2 The Clipboard.

Using Document Windows

Windows 3.0 supports *multiple document interface* (MDI). This feature allows multiple document windows in an application to be open at the same time. For example, a word processor can open several documents at once or a spreadsheet program can work with multiple spreadsheets at the same time. Another example you are already familiar with is the File Manager's windows, where multiple file (document) windows can be open. To utilize multiple document interface, or MDI, the application must take advantage of Windows' MDI. This section is a review of how the MDI functions.

When multiple document windows are open, each window is contained within the application window. If the application window is too small, you will see only a partial document window. The document windows have no menu bar, but do have an identifying title bar. Each document window will have a Control-menu box, which can access a control menu.

To change the active document window, click the desired window. You can also change document windows by using a Window menu option on the application window. This is useful if the document window you want to make active is hidden underneath another, which is often the case. You can also rotate through available document windows by using F6 or Shift+F6.

The control menu of the active document window can be activated by clicking the Control-menu box or by pressing Alt + -. Once the control menu is displayed, you will notice another difference from the control menu of the application window: the Alt + x accelerator keys have been replaced by Ctrl + x accelerator keys. The Minimize command is often grayed and not available.

If you maximize a document window, an interesting event occurs. The document window zooms to fill the entire application window area and now contains the menu bar of the application. It also contains the title bar of the application. Both control menus are available from the upper left.

If an application uses MDI, you can get some interesting effects. For example, you might switch to a document window that is currently located outside of the application window area. In this case, making the control menu active could give you a floating menu, or a menu that floats outside of the application window area. This is all perfectly normal, and is a part of how MDI operates.

Running Older Windows Applications

Windows 3 is not able to run older versions of Windows applications in the standard or enhanced mode. If you are running in either of these modes and try to start one of these older applications, you will get a dialog box warning you that you are starting an older Windows application. In general, select **Cancel** on this dialog box. Trying to continue to run the program could cause several problems: the hardware could hang up (requiring a reboot), fonts might be displayed incorrectly, or other unusual things could happen.

To use your application with Windows 3, use either of the following techniques:

■ Contact the software manufacturer and obtain an update of the program that will run under Windows 3. This is the best alternative because it will give you a version that can support the extensive virtual memory of the new Windows.

■ Start Windows 3 in real mode, using **WIN/r**. The application will run, but it will not be able to take advantage of any expanded or extended memory.

Windows Applications

There are hundreds of Windows applications on the market, including database managers, spreadsheets, word processors, desktop publishers, graphics design tools, communication software, and utilities. Appendix G lists many of these products. Let's look at a few of them here and see why they are important products.

Aldus PageMaker

Windows made it possible to bring the highly popular Macintosh PageMaker desktop publishing program to the MS-DOS operating system. PageMaker works like an electronic layout board. First you create your text documents with your favorite word processor. Then you create your graphics with any of several drawing or paint tools. Finally you use PageMaker to put it all together as a single document (see Figure 19.3). You can cut and paste various elements and even edit text. Because Windows is really WYSIWYG (What You See Is What You Get), what you see on the screen is what prints. Once you get the design you want, you can print it to a laser printer.

Figure 19.3 Aldus PageMaker.

PageMaker makes it possible to create your own newsletter or magazine. Because it's a Windows application, PageMaker is easy to learn and use and you can concentrate on the more creative aspects of the design.

Drawing Tool Products

Drawing tool products enable you to create graphic images that are limited only by the resolution of your printer. Most of these products have extensive clip art libraries. By editing and combining images from the libraries, you can produce customized art. The most popular products are Corel Draw (see Figure 19.4) and Arts & Letters (see Figure 19.5).

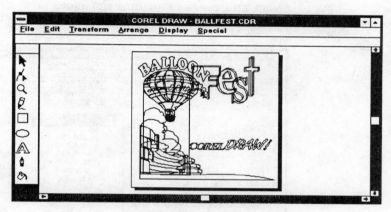

Figure 19.4 Corel Draw.

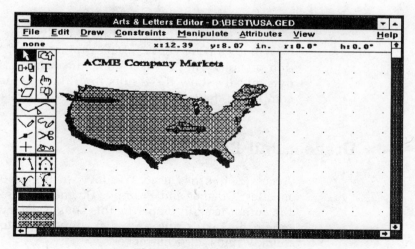

Figure 19.5 Arts & Letters.

Microsoft Excel

Microsoft Excel pioneered a new generation of spreadsheets. Excel is natural and easy for a beginner to use, yet it is so advanced that it appeals to the most experienced user (see Figure 19.6). Presentation features can be defined by the user, making possible the creation of dazzling spreadsheets and graphs for business meetings. Furthermore, you can paste those graphs through the Clipboard to a graphics program and dress them up even more. You can create links between spreadsheets, so you are no longer limited by the computer's memory.

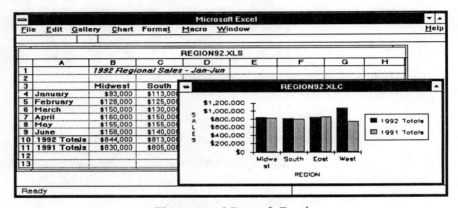

Figure 19.6 Microsoft Excel.

You can even create hot links in Excel by using the DDE feature of Windows (Chapter 22). Data captured by a Windows communication program can be linked to a spreadsheet, making the spreadsheet dynamically show the results from the new data. If stock quotes are coming in, the spreadsheet can do the analysis almost instantly!

Dragnet and Prompt!

Access Softek has used Windows to bring you two important new utilities: Dragnet and Prompt!. Dragnet is a text search program that the author used in preparing this book (see Figure 19.7). The user specifies the text string and disk directories to search, and Dragnet quickly finds all occurrences.

You can set up boolean combinations as well. For example, suppose you are an author and have several megabytes of document files. You are trying to find everything on desktop publishing, PageMaker, or Ventura. Set up the search template by ORing these keywords, and then define the directories to search. Finally, initiate the search. You can do it in the foreground and watch the whole show, or you can shrink Dragnet to an icon, execute it in the background, and read the output file later.

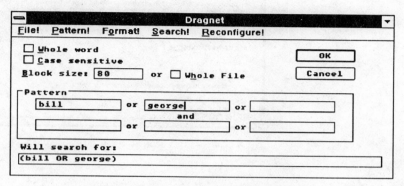

Figure 19.7 Access Softek's Dragnet.

Prompt! is a file manager. It shows a directory tree and does copies and moves. Prompt! will even work with groups of files and requires only a single command.

Word Processing Products

Word processors designed for Windows have the advantage of WYSIWYG; that is, the screen image looks like the final document. This is a big advantage in setting tabs and placing graphics. A Windows-based word processor is much like a low-end desktop publisher. Three popular products are Word for Windows, Ami, and Legend. If you are familiar with Microsoft Word, Word for Windows is a logical step upward (see Figure 19.8). Although Word for Windows uses a different document format, you can read your old documents directly to this new version. Ami is a friendly and fun-to-use product, with cute icons on the screen and a clip art library (Figure 19.9).

Communications Products

Several communications products exist, but Crosstalk for Windows is one of the more popular (see Figure 19.10). It supports an extensive script library, a collection of transfer protocols, and a long list of features. Like other Windows products, it is easy to use.

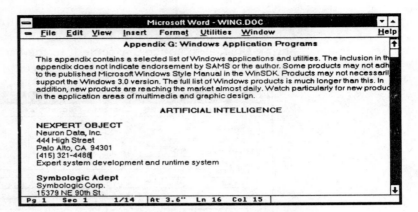

Figure 19.8 Word for Windows.

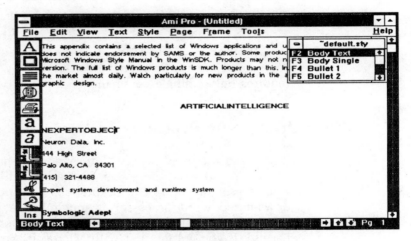

Figure 19.9 Ami.

Games

If you enjoy games, you will probably enjoy Mindscape's new version of Balance of Power: The 1990 Edition. You are the President of the United States (or the top man in Russia), making decisons while various events are happening around you (see Figure 19.11). The goal is to try to prevent a nuclear war. The game runs with extensive databases, and is complex and challenging.

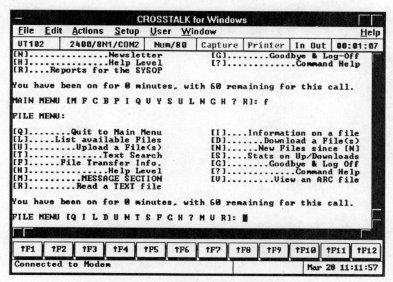

Figure 19.10 Crosstalk for Windows.

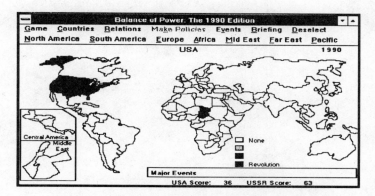

Figure 19.11 Balance of Power: 1990 Edition.

Summary

Windows applications are those specifically designed to run under the Windows environment. All have common features, menu bar options, and shortcut keys. Over a hundred commercial applications have already been developed for the Windows environment: spreadsheets, word processors, graphics design tools, and more.

Running Standard Applications

As a Windows user, you probably have a good library of Windows applications. However, you no doubt have plenty of programs that are not Windows applications but that you still wish to use. These non-Windows applications are known as *standard applications*, and often they can still be run in the Windows environment. You also probably have some memory-resident programs that you would like to run under Windows. This chapter will show you how to use standard and memory-resident applications in the Windows environment.

Why Use Windows?

Why would you want to run a standard application in a Windows environment? There are two basic reasons: Clipboard editing and fast context switching.

Standard applications running in Windows can still access the Clipboard for transferring data (text and graphics) between applications. There may be limitations with some programs, however. For example, some programs support only text transfer. Even with this limitation, the Clipboard is still a useful feature.

Context switching is the ability to move quickly between applications. With the Windows environment, you can have several applications (both Windows and non-Windows) in memory at once. Switching between them is a matter of only a few keystrokes.

Full-Screen versus Window Mode

The Windows environment supports two modes for non-Windows applications: full-screen and window. The choice of mode depends on the application, on the Windows mode (real, standard, or 386 enhanced) that you are using, and on how the application is installed.

In the *full-screen mode*, the application fills the entire screen and looks exactly as it would if running under MS-DOS. There is not even a hint that the program is running under Windows. The program runs at almost full speed, and all features (including graphics) in the program are supported. The familiar title bar, Control menu, and Clipboard are hidden and only a few keystrokes away. Windows gives the system over to the application, saving its own current state. Windows leaves only a small keystroke-trapping routine in memory to enable you to hot-key back to Windows.

In the *window mode*, the standard application looks like a Windows application. The program starts in a window with a title bar. The window can be resized or moved. The window may even have scroll bars.

The mode in which Windows is running determines the mode (window or full-screen) that the application can use:

- If Windows is running in real or standard mode, a standard application must run in full-screen mode. When the standard application is running, other applications are suspended.

- If Windows is running in a 386 enhanced mode, you can run most standard applications in a window. Multiple standard applications can be running simultaneously.

Remember that in any mode the standard application will not use the Windows device drivers or Print Manager. The printer will be driven directly by the device driver that is installed in the application program.

Note: If the standard application must use a mouse, the application must run in a full-screen mode. In a window mode, Windows owns the mouse and it is not available to the application.

Introduction to PIF Files

To use a standard application in the Windows environment, a PIF file is used to communicate basic information about the program to Windows. The *PIF file* tells Windows how much memory is needed and how the screen and keyboard are used. You will need one or more PIF files for each standard application that you are executing under Windows.

The Windows product contains a collection of PIF files for many popular programs, and when you install Windows, these files are put in the Windows directory. Commercial programs often include a PIF file for the corresponding program. For example, if you purchase Microsoft Word version 5.0 (or update an earlier version), the installation disks include a new WORD.PIF file that should be copied to the WORD directory. The next chapter shows how you can create or edit your own PIF files.

Tip: If you have trouble loading a standard application under Windows, make sure that the PIF file is correct (Chapter 21).

If you try to load a standard application for which there is no PIF file, Windows will try to run the program by using default values for the various parameters. In many cases this will work; but if you experience problems, you should create a PIF file.

Installing a Standard Application

Install standard applications in the same way you would install them without Windows. Then follow these three additional steps:

1. Add the PIF file for the program to the Windows directory. Use the PIF file sold with the program, the PIF provided with Windows, or one that you have created by following the directions of the next chapter (in that priority order). If you have several PIF files, you should generally use the one with the latest file date.

2. Put the application subdirectory name in the PATH name of the AUTOEXEC.BAT file.

3. Edit the PIF file (Chapter 21) to indicate the subdirectory of the application program.

Starting the Standard Application

Standard applications can be started with a mouse or from the keyboard in the same way that you start a Windows application. Before starting, you will probably want to add the application to one of the Program Manager's group windows (Chapter 3).

To start a standard application with a mouse, switch to the group window in the Program Manager that shows the application program icon and double-click the program icon or use the **Run** command of the File menu to specify the program or PIF filename. You can also start the program from the **Run** command of the File Manager File menu by using either the filename or the PIF filename. Alternatively, you can add the data file extension name to the WIN.INI file (Chapter 18). If you do this, you can switch to the directory with the data file and double-click the data filename. This will start the program using the PIF file and data file.

To start a standard application from the keyboard, switch to the Program Manager and open the group window that has the application icon. Use the direction keys to highlight the program icon and press Enter. Alternatively, you can add the data file extension name to the WIN.INI file (Chapter 18). If this is done, you can switch to the directory with the data file and use the direction keys to select the data filename. Press Enter. This will start the program with the data file.

Tip: If you hold down the Shift key when starting an application, the application will load as an icon without executing.

You can load multiple copies (instances) of the same application to Windows. Each icon will be uniquely identified by dots placed after the application icon (see Figure 20.1).

Note: You can start programs from batch files, but remember that the PIF file must define enough memory for both the program and the batch file. If you experience loading problems, refer to Chapter 21 for information on how to modify the PIF file.

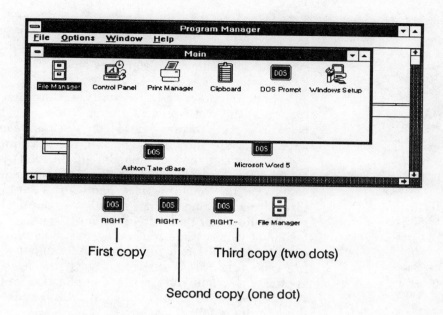

Figure 20.1 Loading multiple copies of the same application.

Context Switching with Standard Applications

The Windows environment makes it easy to switch between applications. This is known as *context switching*. Only one window can be active at a time, but several programs can be in memory at the same time, ready to use.

To use context switching with standard applications, first be sure that the application is in a text mode. Then hold down the Alt key and press and release Tab until the title bar of the desired application is displayed. Release the Alt key. The new application will now be active. The Alt + Tab combination is much like a preview mode, enabling you to scan through all programs that are loaded, including programs that are minimized or represented by icons.

Try using your favorite word processor. The next example uses Microsoft Word, but the directions are the same for WordPerfect or whatever you are using. Before starting:

1. Make sure that the PIF file exists in the Windows directory for the word processor version you are using.

2. Make sure that the word processor is installed to a Program Manager group so that it starts from a PIF file. You can verify this by using Program Manager, selecting the program's icon, and then choosing **Properties** on the File menu.

Start Windows and then start the word processor from Program Manager. The word processor should load and take the full screen. Now press Alt+Tab and release; the Program Manager is active. Press Alt+Tab again, and you are back in the word processor.

Another method of changing applications is to press Alt+Esc. One way to look at this is that Alt+Esc always makes the next application in the chain active, and Shift+Alt+Esc goes backward through the loading chain. For only two applications, this technique is probably better than Alt+Tab, but if you have several applications loaded it can be time-consuming to sequentially activate each program to get to the one you want. Alt+Tab is a preview mode, showing each title bar as the Tab key is pressed, without loading the application. When you get to the application you want, releasing the Alt key makes the application active. Shift+Alt+Tab goes backward through the applications.

A third method of changing applications is to press Ctrl+Esc to access the Task List; then choose the program to make active.

Note: The Alt+Tab, Alt+Esc, and Ctrl+Esc keystrokes are disabled from any use they may have had in the application program.

Using the Clipboard from a Standard Application

Standard applications running under Windows also have access to the Clipboard. This permits you to do copies and moves between applications, including non-Windows applications.

Clipboard Operations in the Window Mode

If the application is running in a window mode, the title bar is displayed with a Control-menu box in the upper left. Clicking this box opens the Control menu, which has the familiar Control menu commands plus a few new ones for editing with the Clipboard. Mnemonics are underlined on this menu. As with any Windows application, you can resize and move the window from the keyboard by using this menu or the mouse.

You can edit from this Control menu by using the mouse or the keyboard:

To edit with the mouse, click the Control-menu box to get the Control menu. On the Control menu, click **Mark**. A small black rectangle will appear on the screen, and the word Mark will appear in the title bar. Click the mouse to indicate the beginning of the area to copy. Hold down the Shift key and drag to select the area. Click the Control-menu box again to get the Control menu and then select **Copy** from this menu. The selected area will be copied to the Clipboard. To paste from the Clipboard, first use the **Mark** command to mark the location for pasting. Then select **Paste** from the Control menu. You can unmark selections by clicking outside of the marked area.

To edit with the keyboard, use the Alt Spacebar keys to display the Control menu. Press **k** to initiate the marking operation. The word Mark will appear in the title bar. Next, use the direction keys to move the black rectangle to the beginning of the area to copy. Then hold down the Shift key and use the direction keys to mark the entire area. Press Alt Spacebar to get the Control menu and then **y** to copy to the Clipboard. To paste, mark the starting location with the **Mark** command and use **p** to paste. You can unmark a selection with the Esc key.

Clipboard Operations in the Full-Screen Mode

In the full-screen mode, you can still use the Clipboard. Because the application takes up the full screen, the title bar is not visible. To get the title bar and Clipboard access, use Alt Spacebar. Notice a difference here, however, from the window mode: there are no mnemonics (underlined letters) in the menu.

The directions for using the mouse are the same as with the window mode. From the Control menu, select **Mark** to mark the area. Click at the start of the area. Drag to mark the entire area. Then select **Copy** from the Control menu. You can unmark selections by clicking outside of the marked area.

To edit with the keyboard, use the direction keys to select the **Mark** command and press Enter. Use the direction keys to move the cursor to the start of the area. Hold down the Shift key and use the direction keys to select the entire area. Now select the **Copy** command by using the direction keys and press Enter. You can unmark a selection with the Esc key. For pasting, mark the starting point and select the **Paste** command from the menu.

Note: The Clipboard can be used for moving and copying text and graphics with Windows and standard applications, with one restriction: you cannot paste graphics to a non-Windows program.

Note: If the application program previously used Alt Spacebar for another purpose, that function will be lost in the program. For example, Microsoft Word uses Alt Spacebar to set character attributes to normal. You will need to turn off the Alt Spacebar combination in the program to have it available for Clipboard use in Windows. Also, if you are using Microsoft Word Version 5.0, you may need to contact Microsoft for a special version if Alt Spacebar does not work.

Practice using the Clipboard with your word processor. Start the processor under Windows and then use Alt Spacebar to get the Control menu. Select **Mark**. Click at the start of a selection to copy. Hold down the Shift key and drag to make the selection. Select **Copy** from the Control menu.

Now let's paste the Clipboard contents to the document. Press Alt + Tab to return to the Program Manager. Load the Clipboard, and you will see your selection. Press Alt + Tab as necessary to return to the word processor. Press Alt Spacebar and select the **Mark** command. Click where you wish to paste the text. Press Alt Spacebar and then select the **Paste** command.

You can capture an entire screen to the Clipboard by using the PrtScrn key (or Print Screen on some keyboards). If this doesn't work (you hear a beep), it's probably for one of these two reasons:

- The PIF file is in error (Chapter 21).
- Not enough memory is available. EGA and VGA images need a lot of memory. Make a smaller selection.

You can capture the active window to the Clipboard by using Alt + PrtScrn.

Scrolling in Standard Applications

Some applications support scrolling. You will find that scrolling works best in the window mode.

If you have a mouse and are in the window mode, you can use the scroll bars just as with a Windows application.

To scroll with the keyboard, select the **Scroll** command from the Control menu. Then use the direction keys to scroll. To turn scrolling off, select the command again.

Terminating a Standard Application

To terminate a standard program execution and remove it from memory, you can use the normal program termination procedures. For Multiplan, for example, you would use Esc Q. For Microsoft Word, select **Quit**. For BASIC, type `system`. To temporarily suspend a standard program, select **Minimize** from the Control menu to reduce it to an icon. Remember that for full-screen mode you will have to press Alt Spacebar first.

Note: If a window remains on-screen after the program has been terminated, the PIF file is not correct. See Chapter 21 for information on editing this file, and be sure that the **Close Window on Exit** option is on. You can temporarily close the window by using Alt F4 or by clicking **Close** on the Control menu.

Running Memory-Resident Applications in Windows

There are two types of memory-resident programs: utility software and popup programs. *Utility software* includes mouse drivers, disk caches, and delete tracking utilities (keeps an audit when deleting files for undeleting). These programs are virtually invisible when running and have no keyboard interface.

Popup programs are programs that remain inactive until a certain *hot key* (a predefined key sequence) is pressed. The program then becomes active and suspends all other programs until it is finished.

Note: Certain memory-resident utilities, such as some disk cache products, can destroy information on a hard disk. Check with the manufacturer before using them with Windows.

Running Utility Memory-Resident Software

If you need a utility over a broad base of programs (such as the mouse driver), start it before you start Windows. It is then available to all Windows programs. The disadvantage is that it is always taking up memory.

If you need a utility for only a few programs that are running under Windows, start the programs from a batch file that loads the utility software and then starts the application. On quitting the application, the batch file should unload the utility. An example would be a program that provides mouse support for dBASE III or IV.

Running Popup Memory-Resident Software

Some popups can be run as stand-alone programs, such as the PC Tools Desktop and PC Shell utilities. If this is the case, start the popup this way and run it as you would any other standard application. You may need to create a PIF file for it (Chapter 21).

If the popup can be run only as memory-resident, follow this procedure:

1. Create a PIF file for the popup program and place the PIF file in the Windows directory.
2. Install the popup to a Program Manager group window.
3. Start the popup as you would any other program. Windows will confirm that it is loaded.

The program's hot keys are now active, and the program can be activated from these keys. If you use the popup with only a few programs, create a batch file that loads the popup when one of the programs is started and that removes it from memory on termination.

Running DOS Commands

To use a DOS utility such as DIR or DISKCOPY, use it as you would any other standard application: Put the utility as a program item in a group window and use the **Run** command of the File menu, or start the utility from File Manager. If you experience problems, you can get a DOS prompt by selecting the **DOS Prompt** icon in Program Manager. Then start the program from the DOS prompt.

Note: Avoid using the JOIN command and the CHKDSK command with the /F option. CHKDSK, for example, modifies the file allocation table, or *FAT* (part of the directory system), on the disk when you use the /F option. For this reason, the command doesn't run properly and may damage the FAT, making it unusable.

Summary

Applications that are not Windows applications are known as *standard applications*. Most standard applications can be executed from Windows just like a Windows application. The application either will run in a window with a title bar and Control menu or will run full-screen with the Control menu accessible using Alt Spacebar.

Running a standard application under Windows offers two advantages. First, the Clipboard is accessible for copying text or graphics between programs. Two, the context switching supported by the Windows environment enables the user to quickly switch between application programs.

Controlling the Execution of Standard Applications

A *PIF file* is used to control a standard (non-Windows) application. This chapter describes how to create and edit PIF files.

What Is a PIF File?

A PIF (Program Information File) file is one that describes the name and location of the program, its memory requirements, and the way that certain system resources are used. The PIF file often has the same filename as the program but has a file extension of .PIF. For example, if the program filename is WP.EXE, the PIF filename is WP.PIF. In some cases you may wish to have multiple PIF files for the same program, each PIF file having a different name and each starting the application in a different way.

Microsoft Windows provides you with a collection of PIF files for many popular commercial programs. You will also find that many application products that you purchase contain their own PIF files. Using the PIF editor provided with Windows, you can modify existing PIF files or create new ones.

The PIF File Editor

The PIF File Editor is a Windows application that can be used to create new PIF files or modify existing files. To start it, select the **PIF**

Editor program icon from Program Manager's Accessories group window. The PIF Editor will then load and start, displaying a working window (see Figure 21.1).

Control-menu box   First control   Title bar

Menu bar

PIF Editor - (untitled)	

File   **Mode**   **Help**

Program Filename:

Window Title:

Optional Parameters:

Start-up Directory:

Memory Requirements: KB **R**equired `128`   KB **D**esired `640`

Display Usage: ◉ F**u**ll Screen   **Execution:** ☐ **B**ackground
          ○ **W**indowed   ☐ **E**xclusive
☒ **C**lose **W**indow on E**x**it   **A**dvanced...

Work area

Figure 21.1 The PIF File Editor.

As you can see from Figure 21.1, the window looks much like that of other Windows applications and can be moved or resized. The menu bar contains a File and a Mode option. The File menu can be used to open PIF files for editing and to save PIF files that you edit or create. The work area contains a variety of dialog box controls. You can click or tab to the item you wish to edit and change it from the keyboard or with a mouse. To change a toggle control state, click the control or press the Spacebar.

If an application is started for which no PIF file exists, the PIF Editor uses the specifications of the _DEFAULT.PIF file. You can edit this file for your own needs.

Tip: The PIF Editor has an excellent help feature for working with these controls. To get help at any time, select the commands of the Help menu.

When you are using the PIF Editor to create a PIF file for an application, the screen that is displayed depends on the mode in which you are running. Windows actually saves one set of parameters for real and standard modes and a completely separate set of parameters for the 386 enhanced mode. You can use the PIF Editor's Mode menu to switch between the two sets. Both sets are saved in a single PIF file. This permits you to run an application one way for real and standard modes and a second way for the 386 enhanced mode.

If you have PIF files created for earlier versions of Windows, they will probably work in Windows 3. Load them into the PIF Editor and then resave them so that they will be in the new PIF format.

Creating a PIF File

Commercial standard programs often contain their own PIF file on their installation disks, but this is not always true. If there is no PIF file for the application with the program or in the Windows PIF directory, you should create your own file to run the application under Windows.

To create a PIF file for an application, start the PIF Editor from Program Manager. The PIF parameter window that is displayed is the one for the current mode. If you are defining parameters for the alternative mode, use the Mode menu to select that mode. Fill in the window (see the next sections).

Once you've defined the parameters, save the file by using the **Save As** option of the File menu. Terminate the editor by double-clicking the Control-menu box icon, selecting **Close** from the Control menu, or by using Alt+F4.

Tip: If you enter a question mark for a control in the Editor, Windows will prompt for that value when starting the application. For example, if you use the same program frequently with different start-up parameters, put a question mark in the field for **Program Parameters**. This will force Windows to prompt you each time for the start-up parameters.

You can create multiple PIF files for an application. If you do, always start the program by clicking or selecting the correct PIF filename instead of the program name. In this way, you know which PIF file is being used. If you click the program name, the PIF file that most closely matches the program name will be used.

PIF File Parameters for Real and Standard Modes

Figure 21.2 shows the dialog box for real and standard modes. Here are some guidelines for filling out this dialog box:

1. **Program Name**. For the program name, be sure to fill in the correct filename with the path and extension. To directly execute a program, the extension must be .COM or .EXE. If you start a program from a batch file, use the .BAT extension. This is the only non-optional entry. The filename and extension must be specified.

2. **Window Title**. Enter the name you want to use for the program's icon when the program is minimized. Keep it short because the display space for the icon is quite small.

3. **Optional Parameters**. Enter any start-up options you wish for the program. For example, you can enter / l with Microsoft Word to start Word with the last document. (If you start the program with the **Run** command on a File menu, any parameters specified in that dialog box will override these.)

4. **Start-up Directory**. Use this entry to define the initial directory that the program should be in when starting.

5. **Video Mode**. Windows has to remember the current display when it is switching between applications. Select **Text** if the program will run only in a text mode. This minimizes the amount of memory used by the application to save the display and also makes swapping faster. Select **Graphics/Multiple Text** if the application uses graphics or multiple text pages. If you are not sure, select **Graphics/Multiple Text**.

Note: If you select **Text** for a graphics application, you won't be able to switch from the application back to Windows. To return to Windows, you will have to quit the application.

6. **Memory Requirements: KB Required**. Specify the amount of memory (in kilobytes) to start the application. This should generally be left at a default 128. Regardless of the value you enter, the program will get all available conventional memory on starting. This value doesn't define the amount of memory that the program actually gets, but rather what Windows needs to have available before it will try to start the program.

7. **XMS Memory**. This option allocates extended memory for programs that can't use Windows own extended memory manager. In most cases, these defaults won't need to be changed unless a nonstandard DOS extender is used, such as with Lotus 1-2-3 version 3.0. Leaving **KB Required** and **KB Limit** at 0 is best for most applications. When using a DOS extender with the Lotus product, set **KB Required** as low as possible (values that are too high will slow down swapping). Set **KB Limit** to −1 if large amounts of extended memory are required.

8. **Directly Modifies**. Set this option to indicate whether the program uses certain system resources that will be locked out to other programs. Only make selections if absolutely necessary, since selecting any parameters will force you to quit the application when you want to return to Windows; i.e., context switching won't work. Select a COM port for communications programs that use a port. Select **Keyboard** if the application takes direct control of the keyboard.

9. **No Screen Exchange**. Selecting this option will save memory, but you won't be able to use the Clipboard. You also won't be able to print the screen to the Clipboard.

10. **Prevent Program Switch**. Selecting this option will prevent context switching. You will have to quit the application to return to Windows.

11. **Close Window on Exit**. This option closes the application's window when you exit the application. Normally it should be toggled on.

12. **Reserve Shortcut Keys**. With this option, you can reserve certain key combinations for an application. If a key combination is reserved, however, it can't be used by Windows. For example, if you reserve Alt Spacebar, you can't use it with the program to get to Clipboard.

Note: If you find that you don't have enough memory, set **Prevent Program Switch** on and **No Screen Exchange** on.

Using PIF Files with 386 Enhanced Mode

| 386 |

If you plan to run the application in the 386 enhanced mode, you should define the parameters for this mode. This mode uses two dialog boxes: the basic PIF box and an Advanced options box.

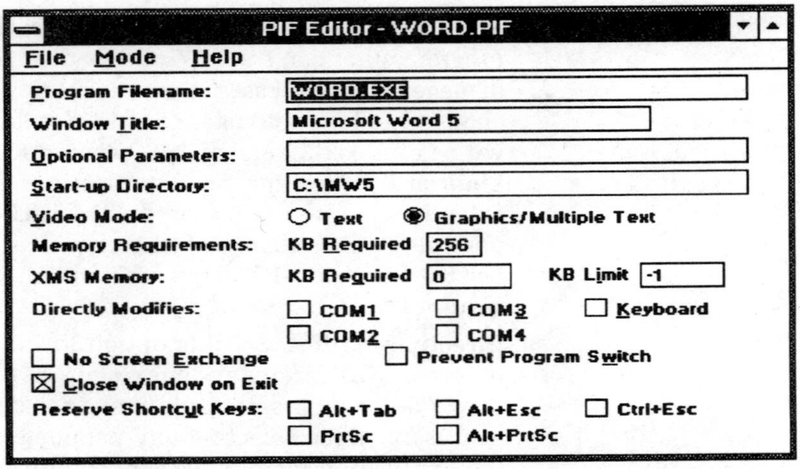

Figure 21.2 Defining the parameters for real and standard modes.

Basic Options

Figure 21.3 shows the initial dialog box that defines the basic parameters for the 386 enhanced mode. Here are some guidelines for filling out this dialog box:

1. **Program Name**. For the program name, be sure to fill in the correct filename with the path and extension. To directly execute a program, the extension must be .COM or .EXE. If you start a program from a batch file, use the .BAT extension. This is the only nonoptional entry. The filename and extension must be specified.

2. **Window Title**. Enter the name you want to use for the program's icon when the program is minimized. Keep it short because the display space for the icon is quite small.

3. **Optional Parameters**. Enter any start-up options you wish for the program. For example, enter / l with Microsoft Word to start Word with the last document. The parameters you enter here apply only to the 386 enhanced mode. (If you start the program with the **Run** command on a **F**ile menu, any parameters specified in that dialog box will override these.)

4. **Start-up Directory**. Use this option to define the initial directory that the program should be in when starting.

5. **Memory Requirements: KB Required**. Specify the amount of conventional memory (in kilobytes) needed to start the

application. This should generally be left at a default 128. Regardless of the value you enter, the program will get all available conventional memory on starting. This doesn't define the amount of memory that the program gets, but rather what Windows needs to have available before it will try to start the program. Set **KB Desired** to define the maximum amount of conventional memory that the application can use. Set **KB Required** to –1 to give the application all conventional memory. Set **KB Desired** to –1 to give the application as much memory as possible to a maximum of 640K.

6. **Display Usage**. Use this option to define whether the application should run in a window or full-screen mode. Running the application in a window requires more memory than running it full-screen, but the application is much easier to use. Once the application is running, you can toggle the mode with Alt + Enter.

7. **Execution**. Use this option to define how the application runs with other applications. If **Background** is on, the program can be run in the background with other programs. If **Exclusive** is on, the application owns all the system resources with Windows and will not release them to a program running in the background, such as a communications program. This will give the application more speed and memory; other applications will be suspended. Each option can be toggled on or off individually.

Tip: Run **Exclusive** applications full-screen because in this mode Windows will release the resources that it needs for running other programs.

8. **Close Window on Exit**. This option closes the application's window when you exit the application. It should normally be toggled on. You might wish to leave it untoggled if you are tight on memory in a full-screen mode and need to use the Clipboard. Quitting the application releases the memory, but the window will not be closed. You can then copy to the Clipboard from the window.

Advanced Options

The Advanced Options give you more support for fine-tuning the execution of the application. In most cases you won't need to adjust

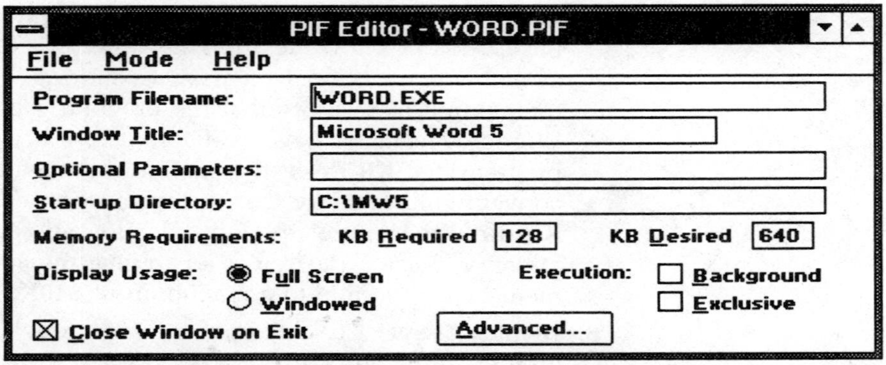

Figure 21.3 Defining the parameters for the 386 enhanced mode.

these parameters. If you do need to change them, select **Advanced** on the first PIF dialog box. Figure 21.4 shows the dialog box that is displayed for Advanced Options. Notice that the options are grouped into four subgroups: **Multitasking Options**, **Memory Options**, **Display Options**, and **Other Options**. The following sections will look at each subgroup separately.

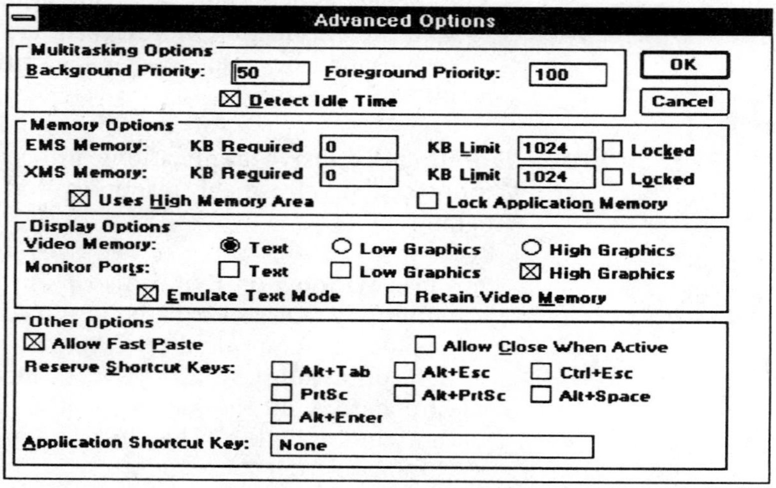

Figure 21.4 Setting the Advanced Options.

Multitasking Options

The **Multitasking Options** allow you to change the priority of the application when it is running with other applications. You can specify a priority when the application is running in the background and a second value for running in the foreground. The value can be any number from 0 to 10000. The default background priority is 50. The default foreground priority is 100.

To understand how this option works, assume that a background communications program is running at 50 and a foreground program is running at 100. The total is 150. The foreground program gets two clock cycles (100/150 of the time) for every one that the background program gets.

If **Detect Idle Time** is on, the foreground application will give the system's resources to other applications when it is idle, such as when it is waiting for input from you. Leave this option on for most applications.

Memory Options

You can control how the application uses the memory resources from the **Memory Options**. Windows can allocate extended or expanded memory to an application. These options define the memory for both of these.

Note: See Appendix B for information on how Windows uses expanded and extended memory.

Windows (in 386 enhanced mode) can simulate expanded memory for those applications that need it. Use the **EMS Memory** options to specify the amount of extended memory to reserve for this simulation. **KB Required** specifies the amount of expanded memory needed to start the application. Leave this setting at 0 unless expanded memory is needed. **KB Limit** specifies the maximum amount to allocate. Set it to 0 if no expanded memory is needed. **Locked** prevents Windows from swapping out the expanded memory when changing applications. Locking out the expanded memory will improve the application's performance but will slow down the system.

Use the **XMS Memory** options to define the options for managing extended memory. The options are similar to those for configuring expanded memory. **KB Required** specifies the minimum amount needed to start the application. Set this value to 0 if no extended memory is required. **KB Limit** defines the maximum amount of extended memory that the application can use. Setting this value to 0 prevents any extended memory from being used. Selecting **Locked** prevents the extended memory from being swapped to disk. This improves the performance of the application but slows down the rest of the system.

The **Uses High Memory Area** toggle defines whether the application can use the first 64K page of extended memory. Keep this option selected for most applications.

The **Lock Application Memory** defines whether the conventional memory portion of the application can be swapped. Notice that separate toggles are used to lock the swapping of the expanded, extended, and conventional memory portions of the application.

Display Options

The **Display Options** define how Windows will appear on the screen and how the display memory will be handled. The **Video Memory** option defines how much memory is reserved for swapping the screen image. **Text** mode requires the least amount of memory, normally less than 16K. Use it if the application runs only in text mode. **Low Graphics** sets enough memory aside for low-resolution graphics, such as a CGA. This uses about 32K of memory. **High Graphics** sets enough memory aside for EGA and VGA adapters, usually about 128K. The **Video Memory** option sets enough memory aside only for the initial display. After you start the application, the amount of memory needed is defined automatically.

The **Monitor Ports** option enables Windows to monitor the display operations (display ports) to ensure that the display is restored properly when you are switching applications. If you have a problem restoring a screen on swapping applications, set this option. Set it only as needed, however, because it will slow down the application. **Text** requests Windows to monitor the ports if the application is running in text mode. Few applications require this option. **Low Graphics** requests monitoring when the application in running in low-resolution video mode. **High Graphics** requests monitoring when the application is running in an EGA or VGA mode. Most applications require this option.

Emulate Text Mode controls the rate at which text is displayed. If this option is on, text is displayed faster. For most applications, leave this option on. Turn it off if the text becomes garbled or if the cursor is displayed at the wrong place.

Select the **Retain Video Memory** option to prevent extra video memory from being released to other applications. Some applications (such as Microsoft Word) can run under Windows in a text or a graphics mode. If **Retain Video Memory** is not selected, Windows automatically adjusts the display buffer to whatever mode is currently in use. Switching to a text mode and then back to graphics could lose some of the display if another application took the released memory when Word left the text mode.

Other Options

With **Other Options** you can control the pasting speed, tell Windows to close the application without exiting it, and reserve shortcut keys.

Windows defaults to a fast pasting mode that most applications can use. If a slower paste is necessary, Windows can generally detect this condition and adjust accordingly. You may find, however, that a paste doesn't work sometimes. If this happens, quit the application and load the PIF Editor. Turn off the **Allow Fast Paste** option. Then start the application and try the paste again.

The **Allow Close When Active** option permits Windows to close the application without exiting the application. In most cases you will want this option to be off, since closing the application from Windows can cause a loss of data if you forget to save the file you are working on.

The **Reserve Shortcut Keys** option allows you to ignore certain key combinations. Use it if a certain key combination is used by an application program. For example, Alt Spacebar is used by Microsoft Word to restore normal attributes. Under Windows, this key combination activates the menu from the keyboard. The **Application Shortcut Key** option permits you to assign a shortcut (or hot) key to a particular application that is loaded to memory and running. Pressing the shortcut key immediately makes the application active. To set a shortcut key, select the option and then the key combination you wish, and choose **OK**. Use caution in selecting your shortcut keys. The first key should be Ctrl or Alt, and you should avoid key combinations used by Windows. Alt + F4 and Ctrl + Shift + F11 are valid. Alt + F is not a good selection, since it is used by most applications to activate the File menu.

Editing a PIF File

Although many commercial programs are sold with PIF files, you may want to modify these files. Or you may want to edit a file that you have created. As an example, IBM Writing Assistant comes with a PIF file, but it is set to run the program full-screen. You may want to modify this file so that you can run the program in a window. You can use the PIF Editor to change it.

Start the PIF Editor from the Program Manager's Accessories group window. Use the **Open** command of the File menu to open the existing PIF file. Edit the file. Save it again by using the **Save** command of the File menu (or the **Save As** command if you want to save it with a different filename). Be sure to save it to the directory of the application program. Terminate the editor by double-clicking the Control-menu box icon, by selecting **Close** from the Control menu, or by using Alt + F4.

If the program will run in a window mode, you may wish to create two PIF files: one for the full-screen mode and one for the window mode. In this way, you can start the program in either mode. The full-screen mode is faster but not as versatile. Use it when you are running the program by itself. Run the program in the window mode when you are running it with other applications and need to use the Clipboard. Some programs, such as Microsoft Multiplan, are sold with both PIF files.

Tip: When using multiple PIF files, always start the program by selecting the PIF file.

Using PIF Files

PIF files are the management instructions for your program in the Windows environment. If the instructions are wrong, the program may not load, or it may load but lock up the computer. If you find that the computer is doing unusual things when loading or using a standard application, check the PIF file.

You can force Windows to remove itself from memory in order to give a standard application as much memory as possible. To perform this trick, enter – 1 as the **KB Desired**. This will prevent context switching and use of the Clipboard, but it will give the maximum amount of memory for a large application. When you exit the program, Windows will be restored.

Note: This swapping cannot be done if the application uses a communications port.

As another alternative, you may wish to give an application the maximum amount of available memory. To do this, enter 640 for the **KB Required** and set **Prevent Program Switch** on. To run the application now, you must close all applications except the Windows Program Manager.

Changing Settings While a Program Is Running

If a program is running with Windows in a 386 enhanced mode, you can change the PIF settings dynamically while the program is running. The new settings will be in effect only while the program is loaded, and they do not alter the PIF file. You also can change only a limited number of PIF settings: the display options (window/full-screen), the tasking options (exclusive and background), and the priority. There is also an emergency **Terminate** command on this dialog box. Use it to terminate an application if the application locks up and won't terminate by the normal means. By using this command, you can get back to Windows and close files in other applications.

To change these options, select **Settings** from the Control menu. Select the new settings and choose **OK**. You can also toggle between window and full-screen mode by using Alt + Enter.

Summary

Learning how to create PIF files is important if you want to optimize your use of standard applications under Windows. The PIF file lets you control how the application uses the system's resources. Creating a few PIF files for the applications you use with Windows will give you valuable experience for using Windows most effectively.

Miscellaneous Topics

This chapter discusses miscellaneous Windows topics that are important to users: transferring data between applications, using Windows on a network, and writing your own Windows applications.

Transferring Data between Applications

One of the most important features of Windows is that it makes possible the transfer of data between applications. Four important transfer methods are available: the Clipboard, DDE, libraries, and messages. A full discussion of all four techniques is beyond the scope of this book, but we will briefly discuss two of the methods that are important to you as a user: the Clipboard and DDE.

Clipboard Techniques

The Clipboard has already been mentioned in earlier chapters, and in most cases the Clipboard is the easiest method of transferring data between applications—both Windows and standard applications. The Clipboard supports text and graphics, and is simple and easy to use.

Occasionally you may want to paste data between an older version of a Windows application and an application designed for Windows 3.0. You can't do a paste directly through the Clipboard in real mode because of memory constraints. However, you can accomplish a paste indirectly by using the following techniques:

1. Start the source application containing the data to be pasted. If the application was designed for an earlier version of Windows, start Windows in the real mode.
2. Paste the data to the Clipboard.
3. Start the Clipboard and save its contents as a file.
4. Exit Windows and start it again in a mode that supports the destination application.
5. Start the Clipboard and load the data from its file.
6. Load the application and paste the data to it from the Clipboard.

Introduction to DDE

DDE is an abbreviation for Dynamic Data Exchange. Available in many Windows application programs, DDE enables several programs to access and use a common pool of data. Excel, Word for Windows, Crosstalk for Windows, and other applications support DDE. Although DDE is complex to understand and even to use, the basic commands are available in many applications.

As an example of how DDE works, consider a communications program and spreadsheet both loaded to memory. Stock market quotations arrive to the communications program, and are immediately available to the spreadsheet program. You can watch totals and graphs change dynamically as the data coming into the communications program updates the stock prices. At the same time, a word processor document can pull up the current data from the spreadsheet each time that it is printed.

Using Windows on a Network

Windows can be used on many popular networks. To install Windows to a network, the system administrator must first put a shared copy of Windows on the network. Once this is done, you can install

Windows on your system by using the network version of Windows Setup, which is on a separate diskette from the normal Setup program.

To install Windows on a network, follow this procedure:

1. Identify any local network procedures, such as where you should store your files on the network server. Be sure that the network is up and operational.
2. Connect your system to the network.
3. Change to the directory on the server containing Windows.
4. Insert the network Setup diskette and type `setup /n`.
5. Follow the directions on the screen. Windows should now be operational.

Note: Each time you connect to the Windows directory on the server, always use the same disk designator.

The network version offers many features that can make you more productive on the network. For example, File Manager will support network drives and enable you to work with them as well as with the files on your computer. The Print Manager will support the network printer and allow you to direct documents to it.

Writing Your Own Windows Applications

If you are interested in writing your own applications, you need two additional products:

- The Windows Software Development Kit (WinSDK), which is available commercially from software supply houses. You will need a version specifically for Windows 3.0.
- A C or Pascal compiler that is compatible with the WinSDK. You can use the Microsoft C compiler.

You will also find it advantageous to locate books and other materials with example software listings. Some example source code can be found on the CFS BBS. You can access it at (503) 284-5130.

Appendixes

The eight appendixes found here contain helpful information on a variety of topics:

- *A—Installing and Optimizing Windows*
- *B—Managing Memory for Speed and Performance*
- *C—Increasing Execution Speed*
- *D—Troubleshooting Common Problems*
- *E—ASCII Character Set*
- *F—Windows Application Keys*
- *G—Windows Application Programs*
- *H—Glossary*

Installing and Optimizing Memory

This appendix includes installation notes for Windows 3.0. Even if you plan to use your Windows manuals for installation or have already installed Windows, you will probably find that this appendix contains many useful tips and you may wish to reinstall your Windows.

What You Will Need

Before starting, be sure that you have everything you will need for the installation:

- An MS-DOS compatible computer with a processor that supports the particular version of Windows you are installing. It should have 640K of conventional memory.
- A hard disk with at least 8 megabytes of free memory.
- DOS 3.2 or later.
- The Microsoft Windows product.
- A printer and video terminal supported by the Microsoft Windows environment.
- A mouse is optional, but highly suggested.

■ An optional Hayes-compatible modem if you want to use the Terminal application.

■ For maximum productivity with Windows, you should have a 386-type processor with 1024K or more of extended memory.

Note: Some systems require special versions of Windows.

Planning

Before installing Windows, be sure that your hard disk is organized the way you want it. Here are some general guidelines that work for many users:

1. Use subdirectories, but don't make the levels too deep. In most cases, the root directory should contain only the bootup routines (AUTOEXEC.BAT and the SYS files).

2. Put all the DOS routines in a \DOS directory.

3. Put all batch files in a \BAT directory.

4. Put each application program (including each Windows application) in its own directory.

5. Separate data files by project, and create subdirectories for each project. (This is where you may want more hierarchical levels.)

6. Put utilities in their own \UTIL subdirectory.

7. Create a \TEMP subdirectory for Windows to use for disk swapping. (Other programs, such as Microsoft Word, also use this same directory for temporary files.)

8. Anticipate how you will do your backups, and design your directories to support this. For example, temporary projects could have their own directories so that they can be backed up easily. Program files, which are seldom backed up, should be on separate directories.

Modify the AUTOEXEC.BAT file to contain a PATH command that includes the Windows directory; the \DOS, \BAT, and \UTIL directories; and the directories for the application programs. Also add a line to define a \TEMP directory to enable file swapping in Windows.

Tip: When DOS searches for a file, it starts in the current directory and then proceeds down the directories of the PATH command left to right. Directories used most frequently should be first so that you can maximize speed. Since Windows is highly disk intensive, you generally should put its directory early in the list.

As an example, you might have the following commands in your file:

```
PATH D:\WIN3;D:\DOS;C:\BAT;D:\UTIL;C:\
VERIFY ON
SET TEMP=D:\TEMP
PROMPT $p$g
CLS
```

These commands set the path, turn on the verify option to improve disk-writing reliability, define a symbolic name for the D:\TEMP subdirectory that Windows will use, define a new DOS prompt that will include the current directory, and clear the screen.

After modifying the AUTOEXEC.BAT file, you will need to modify the CONFIG.SYS file in order to increase the number of files and buffers in use at one time. Add the following lines to your CONFIG.SYS file:

```
FILES=30
BUFFERS=10
```

Note: Refer to Appendix B for a discussion of memory management in Windows, and use that as a guideline for defining your CONFIG.SYS file.

Most of the modifications of the AUTOEXEC.BAT and the CONFIG.SYS files are automatic during Windows installation. You should, however, have some understanding of what is happening and be able to tune the installation to your specific needs.

Windows 3.0 Installation

If you are upgrading from a previous version of Windows, keep your current version on its current directory for a period of time. You may find that some applications will not run on the new version and you will need your old version for them. In addition, you will need information from the old WIN.INI file to modify files in Windows 3.0 for any applications you already have installed. Create a new directory for Windows 3.0.

Tip: Before installing Windows, compress the disk that will contain the Windows routines by using a compression utility such as PC Tools Compress. Compressing the disk will ensure the most efficient operation of Windows.

To install Windows 3.0, place the first disk in the drive that you want to use for the installation and switch to that drive. Type the command:

    SETUP

and then follow the directions on the screen.

Note: Do not install Windows into a directory with existing files or over a previous copy of Windows. Install Windows to an empty directory. Do not try to install Windows by copying the disk files to the directory because the files are not in a usable form. Use the SETUP program to install Windows.

Setup Options

When you are installing Windows, various options are supported for optimizing the operations of Windows for various systems. Refer to Appendix B for a discussion of how Windows manages memory.

Modes

Windows supports three modes: real, standard, and 386 enhanced. The *real* mode assumes that no expanded or extended memory is installed. This mode is supported by all processors. The *standard* mode assumes that at least 256K of extended memory is installed. This mode is supported by all processors. The *386 enhanced* mode assumes that at least 1024K of extended memory is installed and that the processor is an 80386 or 80486.

When you install Windows, one of these modes is selected automatically as the default mode. The decision is based on the system resources. During installation, Windows senses the available resources and sets up the default mode (real, standard, or ^l386 enhanced) based on these. You can find out which mode is installed by selecting **About Program Manager** on the Program Manager's Help menu.

You can force Windows to start in a particular mode by using a specified start-up parameter:

WIN / r   Start in real mode
WIN / s   Start in standard mode
WIN /3   Start in 386 enhanced mode

For example, if you install Windows for a default 386 enhanced mode, you could use WIN / r to start in real mode. Windows will start only in the mode specified as a start-up parameter if there are sufficient resources to support the mode.

Using Swap Files

Windows uses the disk as an extension of memory, swapping applications and even parts of executing programs to disk as necessary. This swapping is done through the use of *swap files*. Swapping in the 386 enhanced mode is managed differently than swapping in the real or standard modes.

To find out how your swap file is currently configured, choose the **Windows Setup** icon from the Program Manager's Main group window. The current information on your swap file is displayed.

Swapping in 386 Enhanced Mode

In the 386 enhanced mode, swapping can be done by using either a permanent or a temporary swap file. A *permanent swap file* is a hidden file created on the disk as an extension of memory. It is a permanent file that is never deleted, and can use a large amount of space. Using a permanent swap file is the fastest and most efficient way to install Windows.

If disk space is at a premium, use a *temporary swap file*. You do not need to create this file. If no permanent swap file has been created, Windows automatically creates a temporary swap file on starting. When you exit Windows, the temporary swap file is deleted.

Tip: If possible, install Windows with a permanent swap file. This ensures maximum speed, secure swapping, and better control. Windows can access this file without using DOS. You cannot use a permanent swap file on a network drive or on a RAM disk.

To create or edit a permanent swap file, use the following steps:

1. Compress the disk by using a compression or defragmentation utility. The permanent swap file can be installed only to *contiguous disk clusters* (clusters that are sequential).

2. Start Windows in the real mode by using the command `WIN /r`.

3. Close all applications except Program Manager.

4. Choose **Run** from the File menu.

5. Enter `swapfile` in the dialog box and choose **OK**.

6. If a permanent swap file already exists, you will see a message. Choose to delete the current file and create a new one.

7. You will see a dialog box showing the largest possible permanent swap file size that you can build and recommending a file size. For the initial installation, it is generally best to use the recommended value. The swap file will use no more than half of the available disk space.

8. Select **Create**. The permanent swap file will be created or changed.

To delete a permanent swap file, follow the previous procedure until the first dialog box is displayed. On this box, choose to delete the current file and choose **OK**.

If you choose not to use a permanent swap file, Windows will create a temporary swap file on starting. By default, this file will be in the Windows directory. You can define the drive for the temporary file by editing the `PagingDrive` parameter of the SYSTEM.INI file (Chapter 18). Set this parameter to your fastest disk. Do not set it to a RAM disk. The size of this file defaults to 1024K on starting. To change this value, refer to the discussion on the SYSTEM.INI file in Chapter 18. You must restart Windows after editing the SYSTEM.INI file because it is read only upon starting.

Swapping in Real and Standard Modes

When Windows is running in a real or standard mode, swapping still occurs, but *application swap files* are used instead. There is no permanent or temporary swap file. When you switch away from a particular application, a portion or all of the application is put in the application swap file. Multiple application swap files can be created for different applications. When you exit Windows, all application swap files are deleted. To control the location of the swap files, edit the `Swapdisk` parameter of SYSTEM.INI (Chapter 18).

Using a Disk Cache

Windows is highly disk-intensive. Unless it is running in 386 enhanced mode with megabytes of extended memory, you will see the disk doing a lot of work as you use Windows.

You will almost always find that a disk cache will improve the system's speed and your productivity. A *disk cache* acts as a memory buffer for disk reading and writing. Several sectors of the disk can be read to the cache at a time. If Windows needs more data from the same sectors, it can get the data faster by accessing the cache than by reading the disk again. Instead of writing to the disk, the program has to write only to the cache. The cache software can then write to the disk in the background.

Windows includes its own disk-caching utility, SMARTDrive. If possible, you should use SMARTDrive for caching because it is specifically designed to work with Windows.

Note: In older versions of Windows, do not use the SMARTDrive provided with Windows 3.0. It can corrupt the hard disk.

To install SMARTDrive, add the SMARTDRV.SYS driver to the Windows directory. Enter the corresponding installation line into the CONFIG.SYS file anywhere after the line defining the extended memory driver (HIMEM.SYS):

```
DEVICE=C:\WIN3\SMARTDRV.SYS 1024 256
```

The first number is the memory size (in kilobytes) allocated to the disk cache when the system is started. Windows will reduce this, as necessary, to gain memory for Windows. The second size defines the minimum size (in kilobytes) to which Windows can reduce the cache.

The starting cache size should be between 256K and 1024K. If memory space is available, the larger size is better. Increasing the cache size beyond 1024K generally does not improve performance much.

Using RAMDrive

RAMDrive is a memory-resident utility that manages a specified memory area as if it were a drive. The RAM drive has a drive letter, and it acts—to the system—like a disk drive with two exceptions: it is much faster than a disk and it is *volatile*. If you turn off the power to the computer, the contents of the RAM drive are lost.

There are two situations when you might wish to use a RAM drive. One would be when you are using a diskless workstation where you have plenty of memory. The second situation would be when you are using the RAM drive as a storage location for swap files if an application uses many small temporary files.

If you do need a RAM drive, use the RAMDrive memory resident software to manage the memory. Avoid using other RAM drive software because the software may conflict with Windows. Copy the RAMDRIVE.SYS driver to the Windows directory and add a line to the CONFIG.SYS file to install it:

```
DEVICE=C:\WIN3\RAMDRIVE.SYS 256
```

The number specifies the amount of memory (in kilobytes) to allocate to the RAM drive.

Using Expanded Memory

When you are using expanded memory with Windows 3.0, keep in mind the following guidelines:

1. If you are running in the real or standard mode and wish to use a program that needs expanded memory, you will need to install an expanded memory board and the driver that comes with your memory board.

2. If you are running in the 386 enhanced mode and need to use a program that uses expanded memory, Windows simulates expanded memory in the extended memory and no board or driver is needed.

3. If you have a 386/486 computer and wish to use a program outside of Windows that requires expanded memory, you should install the EMM386 Expanded Memory Emulator (with Windows) to simulate expanded memory in your extended memory.

4. If you have a 386/486 computer and wish to use a program requiring expanded memory in standard mode, you should install the EMM386 Expanded Memory Emulator (with Windows) to simulate expanded memory in your extended memory.

5. Do not substitute other expanded memory drivers on a 386/486 system. The QEMM, 386MAX, CEMM, and MEMM products do not work with Windows 3.0 at the present time.

To install the EMM386 Expanded Memory Emulator, add the EMM386.SYS driver to the Windows directory and enter the following line to the CONFIG.SYS file:

```
DEVICE=C:\WIN3\EMM386.SYS 640
```

where the path for the driver is specified and the number represents the amount of memory to allocate for expanded memory in kilobytes. Assign the minimum amount of expanded memory needed to support your programs.

Managing Memory for Speed and Performance

One of the most important ways to improve Windows' speed and operation is to use as much memory as possible and to configure it correctly. The configuration method for your system depends on your processor and the mode and type of applications that you are using.

Types of Memory

The 8086 and 8088 processors used in the early XT-compatible machines were limited to addressing a maximum of 1 megabyte of memory. The operating system used approximately 360K of this amount, leaving a maximum of 640K of memory for applications. This 640K of memory is known as *conventional memory*.

As programs became larger, program developers sought a method of getting more memory for applications. To solve the problem, they developed a memory extension method known as *expanded memory*. The standards for this method were developed jointly by Lotus, Intel, and Microsoft (LIM).

To use expanded memory, you must purchase an expanded memory board with some appropriate software. Once the board and software are installed, any program that uses expanded memory can use the memory on the board. Examples include Lotus 1-2-3 and Ventura. Since the expanded memory standard is published (as the LIM 4.0), any software developer can take advantage of it (see *Advanced MS-DOS: Expert Techniques for Programmers* by Carl Townsend, published by Howard Sams).

The advantage of expanded memory is that it can be used by almost any type of PC-compatible computer. The disadvantage is that it is a rather clumsy approach to solving a difficult problem and is slow. The expanded memory is viewed by the system as partitioned into 64K pages. The expanded memory driver manages these pages by making the computer think they are in lower memory; that is, the manager moves each upper page into a conventional memory area as it is needed. The data is not moved; it is just that the upper memory page is addressed as if it were a lower memory page. A 64K memory area in the lower DOS 360K area is used for the alternate addressing. Another problem is that expanded memory is difficult to use for program execution, and is used primarily to support data storage while a program is executing.

When Intel released the 80286 processor, it supported two modes (or methods) for memory addressing. In the *real mode*, the 80286 was exactly compatible with the older 8088 and 8086 and was limited to addressing 1 megabyte of memory. The 80286 also was capable of supporting a new protected mode method that could address megabytes of memory. This new processor mode was known as *protected mode*, and the addressing method was known as *extended memory*. In protected mode, several programs can be loaded to memory at a time and each executed. The memory used by each is protected from being used by other programs in memory. If Lotus 1-2-3 is in memory, nothing else executing in memory can alter data or that program. There is nothing clumsy or tricky about using extended memory—it is a clean solution, although DOS does not support it.

Since the MS-DOS operating system does not support extended memory, DOS cannot execute any programs written to take advantage of extended memory. If a DOS program wants to run in extended memory, it has to shut down interrupts and exit DOS, do its memory addressing, and then return to DOS. The clock and any real-time processing are stopped during that time. Various DOS extender products have been developed to enable DOS programs to take advantage of extended memory. In essence, each product is a type of environment that enables the program to exit DOS to complete its memory addressing, after which the program returns to DOS.

Also, the 80286 processor was crippled in the sense that it could not switch easily between the two processor modes without rebooting the computer. The proper support of extended memory was not available until Intel released the 80386 processor. With the 80386, for the first time, users could use extended memory practically. There was no operating system, however, that could run current DOS applications with the 80386's extended memory.

OS/2 was Microsoft's vision of an operating system that could take full advantage of extended memory and the 80386. However, Microsoft was slow to develop OS/2 and users grew impatient. In addition, users were not willing to throw away their extensive investment in DOS application software. Also, Microsoft crippled OS/2 development by designing the early OS/2 to support the 80286 processor as well as the 80386.

Microsoft took a different approach with Windows 3.0. If you have an 80386 or 80486 processor and are running Windows applications, the Windows 3.0 environment converts the DOS computer to an extended memory system. Windows and standard applications can run together under DOS, limited only by the amount of physical memory that you have. As far as individual Windows applications are concerned, they are running in a virtual memory environment with megabytes of memory if the physical memory is there. With the introduction of Windows 3.0, program developers at last could write large programs for the DOS environment as long as the programs were Windows applications. Microsoft also realized that this virtual memory would bring many software developers into the Windows fold (new Windows applications) as well as build a bridge to the eventual 386 version of OS/2. This virtual memory is one of the most important facts that makes Windows 3.0 stand out from any previous release.

Windows and Your Computer

Now let's look at each of the three basic types of PC compatibles and see how the Windows environment is installed in each.

Use this section as a guide to planning your system. Then refer to Appendix A for specific directions for installing the disk cache, the EEM386 Expanded Memory Manager, or a RAMDrive.

Configuring 8088 and 8086 Computers

If you are using an XT-compatible system (8088/8086 processors), you can use Windows' real or standard mode. To use the standard mode, you will need to install an expanded memory board. The expanded memory must conform to the LIM EMS 4.0 specifications. The processor will run only in the real mode. You should have 640K of conventional memory.

The CONFIG.SYS file must contain the following:

- A FILES command line that sets FILES to at least 20
(`FILES=20`).
- A BUFFERS command line that sets BUFFERS to 20. If using a
SMARTDrive, set BUFFERS to 10.
- If using an EGA monitor for standard applications, you will
need to add the driver for the EGA device. This driver is called
EGA.SYS. Specify the full path for the driver:

```
DEVICE=C:\WIN3\EGA.SYS
```

- If you are using expanded memory, install the memory. Install
the device driver that came with it in the CONFIG.SYS file.
Don't use the EMM386 expanded memory driver with
Windows.
- If you are using expanded memory, install the SMARTDrive
disk-caching utility.

Configuring 80286 Computers

If you have a computer with an 80286 processor (AT-compatible),
configure it based on the applications you are running, the physical
memory that you have, and the Windows mode you intend to use.
Windows can be used in the real or standard mode with the 286 processor.

If you are running applications that require expanded memory,
you will need to install the expanded memory for those applications
to use when they are running under Windows or from the DOS
prompt.

For other Windows applications, you will need extended memory to take advantage of Windows' standard mode. Many memory
boards can be used as either expanded or extended memory. Sometimes you can partition a board so that part of it is expanded and
another part extended. Whatever your choices, put just enough
expanded memory in your computer to keep those applications that
need it operational. Then use all of the rest as extended memory.
Windows uses only extended memory. You need 640K of conventional memory to use the real or standard modes. You will need at
least 256K of extended memory if you wish to use the standard mode.

When creating the CONFIG.SYS file, you will need to insert the
following:

■ A FILES command line that sets FILES to at least 30
(`FILES=30`).

■ A BUFFERS command line that sets BUFFERS to 20. If using a
SMARTDrive, set BUFFERS to 10.

■ If using an EGA monitor for standard applications, you will
need to add the driver for the EGA device. This driver is called
EGA.SYS. Specify the full path for the driver:

```
DEVICE=C:\WIN3\EGA.SYS
```

■ A line adding the Windows driver for the extended memory:

```
DEVICE=C:\WIN3\HIMEM.SYS
```

Note: Do not substitute other extended memory drivers.

■ If you need expanded memory for any application, add a line
for the expanded memory driver that came with the expanded
memory board. Don't use the EMM386 expanded memory
driver with Windows.

■ For maximum disk speed, add a line for the SMARTDrive disk-
caching driver.

Configuring 80386 or 80486 Computers

The 80386 and 80486 processors are capable of supporting the real
and standard modes of other processors as well as an advanced 386
enhanced mode. To take full advantage of Windows and use the 386
enhanced mode, you will need 640K of conventional memory and at
least 1024K of extended memory. You can run these processors in a
standard mode if you have at least 256K of extended memory.

In the 386 enhanced mode, Windows can simulate expanded
memory from extended memory for a program that needs it. This is
not true for other modes. You will need to install an expanded memory driver for a program that needs it if you plan to run the application in real or standard mode or if you will be running it outside of
Windows. Otherwise, don't install expanded memory or a driver. If
you do need expanded memory with a 386/486 processor, instead of
its normal driver you should install the EMM386 expanded driver
with Windows.

When creating the CONFIG.SYS file, you will need to insert the
following:

■ A FILES command line that sets FILES to at least 30
(`FILES=30`).

■ A BUFFERS command line that sets BUFFERS to 20. If using a
SMARTDrive, set BUFFERS to 10.

■ If using an EGA monitor for standard applications, you will
need to add the driver for the EGA device. This driver is called
EGA.SYS. Specify the full path for the driver:

```
DEVICE=C:\WIN3\EGA.SYS
```

■ A line adding the Windows driver for the extended memory:

```
DEVICE=C:\WIN3\HIMEM.SYS
```

Note: Do not substitute other extended memory drivers.

■ Add the Windows driver for the expanded memory
(EMM386.SYS) if you plan to run any expanded memory
application in real or standard mode or outside of Windows.
This line should be after the HIMEM.SYS installation line.

Note: Do not substitute other expanded memory managers. At the
current time, no other expanded memory manager will work under
Windows 3.0.

■ For maximum disk speed, add a line for the SMARTDrive disk-
caching driver.

General Guidelines for Managing Memory

If Windows gives you an error message telling you that you have
insufficient memory, don't panic. Here are some guidelines for resolving your memory problems:

■ If you are using a 286/386/486 processor, add additional
extended memory.

■ Free as much memory as possible before starting Windows.
Remove memory resident programs.

Guidelines for Windows Applications

To recover memory space when you are using Windows applications, follow these guidelines:

- Make sure that you have configured Windows properly. If you are using expanded memory, be sure that the expanded memory is active.
- Close or minimize applications not in use.
- Remove unused icons.
- Turn off the spooler (Chapter 15).
- Load large applications first.
- If you are using a wallpaper for the desktop, change to a pattern.

Guidelines for Standard Applications

To recover memory space when you are using standard applications, follow these guidelines:

- Install additional expanded memory if you have an XT-compatible system or if you have a 286/386/486 system and wish to run applications that require expanded memory.
- Make sure that you have configured Windows properly.
- Make sure that the PIF Editor has been used to tune the PIF file effectively. Adjust the **Memory Requirements** option in real or standard mode. In the 386 enhanced mode, adjust **Memory Options** on the Advanced Options dialog box.
- If you have expanded memory, be sure that you are not running in the real mode.
- Turn off the spooler (Chapter 15).

Increasing Execution Speed

This appendix suggests ways that you can increase the speed of Windows execution. They can be grouped into two categories: hardware and software.

Hardware

To increase Windows' execution speed, follow these guidelines for hardware:

- When purchasing hard disks, look for disk access times of 30 milliseconds or less and disk interleaves of 2:1 or 1:1.
- Use a system with a 386 or 486 processor.
- Use plenty of extended memory with 286/386/486 systems. For XT-compatible systems, use plenty of expanded memory.
- Use a disk cache. Windows includes a SMARTDrive to use for caching if you have extended or expanded memory.
- Install a RAMDrive. Set the TEMP environmental variable to the RAMDrive.

Software

To increase Windows' execution speed, follow these guidelines for software:

■ Windows is very disk intensive; that is, it does a lot of disk reading and writing. Use a disk-organizer software utility frequently (such as PC Tools Compress) to reduce disk fragmentation. Run the utility outside of Windows.

■ If running in 386 enhanced mode, use a permanent swap file instead of a temporary one.

■ Fine-tune the use of memory when using standard applications with the PIF Editor.

Troubleshooting Common Problems

Here are suggestions for troubleshooting and resolving various kinds of problems that may occur when you are using Windows. The problems are organized into the following categories:

General
Printing
Running Standard Applications
Communications Problems (Terminal, Cardfile)
Networks

General Problems

Windows fails to start in a standard or 386 enhanced mode.

Windows may not be installed for this mode. Reinstall or use a lower mode.

A standard application is locked up and won't terminate by normal means.

Choose **Settings** from the Control menu and select **Terminate** on the dialog box. Close any open files in other applications immediately. Then reboot.

I can't use my extended memory in an enhanced 386 mode.

Make sure that you don't have any memory drivers installed except those provided by Windows and that the Windows drivers are installed properly (Appendix B).

I can't delete fonts by using Control Panel.

Check WIN.INI to see how many fonts are installed. Control Panel works only if 40 or fewer fonts are installed. If you have more than 40 installed, delete the extra fonts from WIN.INI by using Notepad.

Sometimes, I can't get double-clicks with the mouse to work.

Use the Control Panel to set the mouse for a slower double-click speed.

How can I get screen dumps of a Windows application screen?

You must use a capture program that supports Windows 3 or later. Various capture programs are being modified to work with Windows 3. These include Hotshot, Hijaak, and a capture utility provided with PC Paintbrush. Try using Alt+PrtScrn to capture the window to the Clipboard or PrtScrn to capture the screen. Then paste it to Paintbrush and save it as a PCX file or print it.

Printing

The printer doesn't print at all.

Exit Windows and try to print from a non-Windows program. If this fails, make sure that the printer is correctly connected and on-line. When using a serial printer, make sure that the serial port is set correctly. If the problem occurs only when you are printing from Windows, check for the correct driver (use **Change Printer** on the File menu) and check the Control Panel setting for the printer (Chapter 17).

The printer is advancing the page but nothing prints.

Make sure that the correct printer driver is selected. Check the printer settings to be sure they are correct.

The screen fonts don't match the printed fonts.

If you installed a printer font but did not install a corresponding display font of the same type and size, Windows will try to match the printer font as closely as possible, but the match may not be an exact one.

I changed printer font cartridges in my HP Laser printer, but the new fonts are not available.

Use the **Change Printer** command of the program's File menu and its **Setup** button to select the proper cartridge. (Also see Chapter 17.)

My printer times-out when printing long jobs.

Select **Retry** on the message box as a temporary fix. For a more permanent fix, install hardware or software handshaking, or use Control Panel to set the timeout values higher (Chapter 17).

I can't get spooling when using a standard application under Windows.

Standard applications don't use the Print Manager and can, in fact, interfere with spooler printing. Use a hardware print buffer.

The printer output is garbled or the text is lost.

Try to print a document outside of Windows to verify that the printer and its connection are correct. If this works, check to be sure that Windows is installed for the correct printer. If the printer is a serial one, check for the correct baud rate and other serial settings.

The page is not correctly formatted.

Make sure that the correct printer and font are selected. When installing the printer, be sure to specify the correct paper source and size. Check the printer switches in the printer to see if they are set correctly.

The printer mixes the output of two files.

Windows is trying to print the output of a standard application while another print job is active. If running Windows 386 enhanced mode, you will get a message about the device contention problem.

The printer does not recognize a particular font.

If you are using a cartridge for the font, turn off the printer and verify that the cartridge is plugged in all the way. (Don't check this with the printer on.) If using a soft font, make sure that it is properly installed.

I have an HP LaserJet and can't install soft fonts.

Only the HP LaserJet Series II, HP LaserJet +, HP LaserJet II, LaserJet III, and HP LaserJet 2000 support soft fonts. The HP LaserJet does not. Select the right printer from the setup.

My laser printer won't print a full graphics page.

Either you don't have enough memory installed in the printer or the installed memory is not recognized by Windows. Reconfigure the printer by using Control Panel (Chapter 17). Select the **Printers** icon, then select the printer, and choose **Install** and then **Setup**. On this dialog box, make sure that the memory specified is the same as the memory installed. If there is not enough hardware memory installed, use this same dialog box to print at a lower graphics resolution.

Boxes and lines on the screen print as funny characters on the printout.

The screen fonts support an extended ASCII set that includes the characters needed to draw boxes and lines. To print these on the printer, you must be using a corresponding printer font set that includes these extended ASCII characters. For example, with a Hewlett-Packard LaserJet printer, you can select at the printer a default character set. You should choose one that supports the extended ASCII characters.

Running Standard Applications

I just updated a standard application (or my Windows version), and the application no longer will work with Windows.

The old PIF file is probably no longer correct. First, check to see if a new PIF file was provided with the update. If so, copy it to the directory with the program. Another alternative is to edit the old PIF file to support the new version. In some cases, you may find that the new version requires so much memory that it will not run under Windows. Also, be certain that you access the correct PIF file. If you are using Windows with a PIF file that supports Micorsoft Word version 5, the PIF file won't work if you are using the older version 4.

The system locks up when I use a particular standard application.

This situation generally means that the PIF file for the application has an error, particularly if the standard application is running in a window.

I can't switch from the application back to Windows.

Edit the PIF file so that the **Video Mode** is **Graphics/Multiple Text**.

When I switch between graphics applications, the screen is not restored properly.

If you are running in real or standard mode, make sure that the **Video Mode** of the PIF file is set to **Graphics/Multiple Text**. In the 386 enhanced mode, access the advanced options to make sure that the **Video Memory** is set to **High Graphics** and the **High Graphics** option of **Monitor Ports** is on.

An application doesn't load when I click the PIF file for it.

The PIF file is incorrect. Check the program name to see that it is spelled correctly and that it designates the correct path and extension.

An out-of-memory error message is displayed when I run a standard application.

Change the memory specifications in the PIF file. If the application won't start, change the **KB Required**. If the application starts but later displays the message, then change **KB Desired** and **KB Required** (Appendix B).

I can't switch from a standard application.

Make sure that the shortcut keys you need are not reserved by the PIF file. Check for the correct video mode in the PIF file. If you are running in a real or standard mode with an EGA display, make sure that the EGA display driver is installed in CONFIG.SYS (Appendix B). Check the PIF file for other options that might prevent switching, such as the **Prevent Program Switch** option.

A standard application's display is lost.

If you are running in enhanced 386 mode, make sure that the **Monitor Ports** option in the PIF file is selected for your video mode. Also select **Retain Video Memory**.

An application runs very slowly.

If you are running in 386 enhanced mode, try adjusting the **KB Required** and **KB Desired** settings to larger values in the PIF. You might also try clearing the **Detect Idle Time** option in the PIF. Also try using Control Panel to improve Scheduling.

Windows cannot paste properly.

If you are pasting to a standard application, make sure that the data to paste is in text format and not graphics. Another possibility is that the pasting is too fast. If running in the 386 enhanced mode, clear the **Allow Fast Paste** option.

A standard application remains on the screen when I close it.

Press any key, click the mouse, or double-click the Control-menu box icon. The **Close Window in Exit** option in the PIF file is not set. Edit this to close the window next time.

I can't quit an application.

First, try using Ctrl+C or Ctrl+Break to terminate. If this doesn't work, use Alt+Tab to return to Windows. Press Ctrl+Esc to see the Task List. Select the application and **End Task**. Reboot the computer. Another method is to press Alt+Spacebar, if necessary, to get a window. Choose the **Settings** option of the Control menu. Select **Terminate** on the dialog box. Reboot the computer.

Communications Problems (Terminal, Cardfile)

I can't establish a connection.

For Terminal, make sure on the **Communications** parameters that the correct port is selected. On the same dialog box, try the connection with and without **Carrier Detect** toggled on.

I can't communicate on a local line between two computers.

Make sure that you are using a null modem cable instead of a standard RS-232 cable and that the correct serial ports on both machines are connected. Make sure that the two computers are using identical parameters.

The incoming text is double-spaced or not spaced at all (the lines are on top of each other).

Use Terminal's **Terminal Preferences** command of the Settings menu to change the **CR→CR/LF** option.

When I type, I get double-characters or no characters at all.

Use Terminal's **Terminal Preferences** command of the Settings menu to change the **Terminal Modes** option.

I get garbled data using a standard application with Windows.

Try running at a lower baud rate. If you are using 386 enhanced mode, use Control Panel to access the **386 Enhanced** icon. Adjust the **Contention** options.

Networks

Windows fails to start in a standard or 386 enhanced mode.

The network Windows may not be installed for this mode. Another possibility is that Windows needs a larger DMA buffer. Edit the `NetDMASize` in the SYSTEM.INI file for a larger size. The default is 16. Try changing the size to 32. You may also wish to change the `EMMExclude` parameter to prevent Windows from scanning a particular memory range. Be sure to adjust the parameters in the `[386enh]` section.

Network-specific applications don't run on the network.

Try running the application in real mode. Also contact the application vendor to see if there is a special version for Windows. If the problem occurs on program switching, adjust the PIF file to prevent program switching and run in exclusive mode.

Programs don't run properly in standard or 386 enhanced modes.

Increase the `NetHeapSize` parameter in the `[standard]` or `[386enh]` sections of SYSTEM.INI. The default is 8. You might try 16.

I can't run any standard applications.

Try running the applications in a lower mode. Try adjusting the PIF file to make the application **Exclusive**.

I can't connect to network printers.

Try connecting to them before starting Windows.

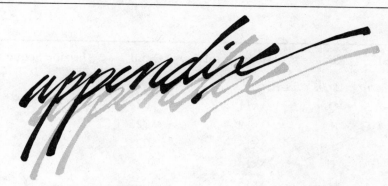

ASCII Character Set

Decimal	Key	Hexadecimal	Octal	Escape Sequence	Name
Nonprinting ASCII Characters					
0	^@	'\x00'	'\000'		NULL
1	^A	'\x01'	'\001'		SOTT
2	^B	'\x02'	'\002'		STX
3	^C	'\x03'	'\003'		ETY
4	^D	'\x04'	'\004'		EOT
5	^E	'\x05'	'\005'		ENQ
6	^F	'\x06'	'\006'		ACK
7	^G	'\x07'	'\007'		BELL
8	^H	'\x08'	'\010'	'\b'	BKSPC
9	^I	'\x09'	'\011'	'\t'	HZTAB
10	^J	'\x0a'	'\012'	'\n'	NEWLN
11	^K	'\x0b'	'\013'	'\v'	VTAB
12	^L	'\x0c'	'\014'	'\f'	FF
13	^M	'\x0d'	'\015'	'\r'	CR
14	^N	'\x0e'	'\016'		SO
15	^O	'\x0f'	'\017'		SI
16	^P	'\x10'	'\020'		DLE

Decimal	Key	Hexadecimal	Octal	Escape Sequence	Name

Nonprinting ASCII Characters

Decimal	Key	Hexadecimal	Octal	Escape Sequence	Name
17	^Q	'\x11'	'\021'		DC1
18	^R	'\x12'	'\022'		DC2
19	^S	'\x13'	'\023'		DC3
20	^T	'\x14'	'\024'		DC4
21	^U	'\x15'	'\025'		NAK
22	^V	'\x16'	'\026'		SYN
23	^W	'\x17'	'\027'		ETB
24	^X	'\x18'	'\030'		CAN
25	^Y	'\x19'	'\031'		EM
26	^Z	'\x1a'	'\032'		SUB
27	ESC	'\x1b'	'\033'	.	ES C
28		'\x1c'	'\034'		FS
29		'\x1d'	'\035'		GS
30		'\x1e'	'\036'		RS
31		'\x1f'	'\037'		US

Decimal	Key	Hexadecimal	Octal

Printing ASCII Characters

Decimal	Key	Hexadecimal	Octal
32	(Space)	'\x20'	'\040'
33	!	'\x21'	'\041'
34	"	'\x22'	'\042'
35	#	'\x23'	'\043'
36	$	'\x24'	'\044'
37	%	'\x25'	'\045'
38	&	'\x26'	'\046'
39	'	'\x27'	'\047'
40	(	'\x28'	'\050'
41	)	'\x29'	'\051'
42	*	'\x2a'	'\052'
43	+	'\x2b'	'\053'
44	,	'\x2c'	'\054'

Decimal	Key	Hexadecimal	Octal
Printing ASCII Characters			
45	-	'\x2d'	'\055'
46	.	'\x2e'	'\056'
47	/	'\x2f'	'\057'
48	0	'\x30'	'\060'
49	1	'\x31'	'\061'
50	2	'\x32'	'\062'
51	3	'\x33'	'\063'
52	4	'\x34'	'\064'
53	5	'\x35'	'\065'
54	6	'\x36'	'\066'
55	7	'\x37'	'\067'
56	8	'\x38'	'\070'
57	9	'\x39'	'\071'
58	:	'\x3a'	'\072'
59	;	'\x3b'	'\073'
60	⟨	'\x3c'	'\074'
61	=	'\x3d'	'\075'
62	⟩	'\x3e'	'\076'
63	?	'\x3f'	'\077'
64	@	'\x40'	'\100'
65	A	'\x41'	'\101'
66	B	'\x42'	'\102'
67	C	'\x43'	'\103'
68	D	'\x44'	'\104'
69	E	'\x45'	'\105'
70	F	'\x46'	'\106'
71	G	'\x47'	'\107'
72	H	'\x48'	'\110'
73	I	'\x49'	'\111'
74	J	'\x4a'	'\112'
75	K	'\x4b'	'\113'
76	L	'\x4c'	'\114'

Decimal	Key	Hexadecimal	Octal
Printing ASCII Characters			
77	M	'\x4d'	'\115'
78	N	'\x4e'	'\116'
79	O	'\x4f'	'\117'
80	P	'\x50'	'\120'
81	Q	'\x51'	'\121'
82	R	'\x52'	'\122'
83	S	'\x53'	'\123'
84	T	'\x54'	'\124'
85	U	'\x55'	'\125'
86	V	'\x56'	'\126'
87	W	'\x57'	'\127'
88	X	'\x58'	'\130'
89	Y	'\x59'	'\131'
90	Z	'\x5a'	'\132'
91	[	'\x5b'	'\133'
92	\	'\x5c'	'\134'
93	]	'\x5d'	'\135'
94	^	'\x5e'	'\136'
95	—	'\x5f'	'\137'
96	'	'\x60'	'\140'
97	a	'\x61'	'\141'
98	b	'\x62'	'\142'
99	c	'\x63'	'\143'
100	d	'\x64'	'\144'
101	e	'\x65'	'\145'
102	f	'\x66'	'\146'
103	g	'\x67'	'\147'
104	h	'\x68'	'\150'
105	i	'\x69'	'\151'
106	j	'\x6a'	'\152'
107	k	'\x6b'	'\153'

Decimal	Key	Hexadecimal	Octal

Printing ASCII Characters

Decimal	Key	Hexadecimal	Octal
108	l	'\x6c'	'\154'
109	m	'\x6d'	'\155'
110	n	'\x6e'	'\156'
111	o	'\x6f'	'\157'
112	p	'\x70'	'\160'
113	q	'\x71'	'\161'
114	r	'\x72'	'\162'
115	s	'\x73'	'\163'
116	t	'\x74'	'\164'
117	u	'\x75'	'\165'
118	v	'\x76'	'\166'
119	w	'\x77'	'\167'
120	x	'\x78'	'\170'
121	y	'\x79'	'\171'
122	z	'\x7a'	'\172'
123	{	'\x7b'	'\173'
124	|	'\x7c'	'\174'
125	}	'\x7d'	'\175'
126	~	'\x7e'	'\176'
127	DEL	'\x7f'	'\177'

IBM Graphic	Dec	Hex	IBM Graphic	Dec	Hex

Extended ASCII Set

IBM Graphic	Dec	Hex	IBM Graphic	Dec	Hex
Ç	128	80	ç	135	87
ü	129	81	ê	136	88
é	130	82	ë	137	89
â	131	83	è	138	8A
ä	132	84	ï	139	8B
à	133	85	î	140	8C
å	134	86	ì	141	8D

IBM Graphic	Dec	Hex	IBM Graphic	Dec	Hex
Extended ASCII Set					
Ä	142	8E	¡	173	AD
Å	143	8F	«	174	AE
É	144	90	»	175	AF
æ	145	91	░	176	B0
Æ	146	92	▒	177	B1
ô	147	93	▓	178	B2
ö	148	94	│	179	B3
ò	149	95	┤	180	B4
û	150	96	╡	181	B5
ù	151	97	╢	182	B6
ÿ	152	98	╖	183	B7
Ö	153	99	╕	184	B8
Ü	154	9A	╣	185	B9
¢	155	9B	║	186	BA
£	156	9C	╗	187	BB
¥	157	9D	╝	188	BC
P_t	158	9E	╜	189	BD
ƒ	159	9F	╛	190	BE
á	160	A0	┐	191	BF
í	161	A1	└	192	C0
ó	162	A2	┴	193	C1
ú	163	A3	┬	194	C2
ñ	164	A4	├	195	C3
Ñ	165	A5	─	196	C4
ª	166	A6	┼	197	C5
º	167	A7	╞	198	C6
¿	168	A8	╟	199	C7
⌐	169	A9	╚	200	C8
¬	170	AA	╔	201	C9
½	171	AB	╩	202	CA
¼	172	AC	╦	203	CB

IBM Graphic	Dec	Hex	IBM Graphic	Dec	Hex
Extended ASCII Set					
╠	204	CC	μ	230	E6
═	205	CD	τ	231	E7
╬	206	CE	Φ	232	E8
╧	207	CF	Θ	233	E9
╨	208	D0	Ω	234	EA
╤	209	D1	δ	235	EB
╥	210	D2	∞	236	EC
╙	211	D3	φ	237	ED
╘	212	D4	ε	238	EE
╒	213	D5	∩	239	EF
╓	214	D6	≡	240	F0
╫	215	D7	±	241	F1
╪	216	D8	≥	242	F2
┘	217	D9	≤	243	F3
┌	218	DA	⌠	244	F4
█	219	DB	⌡	245	F5
▄	220	DC	÷	246	F6
▌	221	DD	≈	247	F7
▐	222	DE	°	248	F8
▀	223	DF	·	249	F9
α	224	E0	·	250	FA
β	225	E1	√	251	FB
Γ	226	E2	η	252	FC
π	227	E3	²	253	FD
Σ	228	E4	■	254	FE
σ	229	E5	(blank)	255	FF

Windows Application Keys

Key	Description
Alt + F4	Close window or application
Alt Spacebar	Select Control menu of active window
Alt –	Select Control menu of document window
Alt + Tab	Select next active application (includes icons)
Shift + Alt + Tab	Select last active application (includes icons)
Alt + Esc	Select next active window
Shift + Alt + Esc	Select last active window
Alt + Enter	Toggle standard application full-screen/ windowed
Alt + PrtScrn	Capture active window to Clipboard
PrtScrn	Capture screen to Clipboard
Ctrl + Esc	Start Task List
F10	Set menu mode
Alt	Set menu mode
Enter	Initiate command
Esc	Cancel menu
F1	Help key
F6	Switch to next window within an application

Key	Description
Shift + F6	Switch to last window in an application
Ctrl + F6	Switch to next document window in application
Shift + Ctrl + F6	Switch to last document window in application
Alt + F6	Switch to next modeless dialog box
Shift + Alt + F6	Switch to last modeless dialog box
←	Move one character left
→	Move one character right
↑	Move up one line
↓	Move down one line
Ctrl + ←	Move to beginning of field, group, or selection

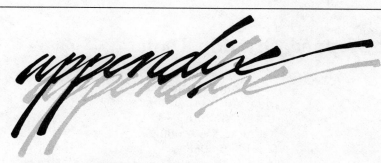

Windows Application Programs

This appendix contains a selected list of Windows applications and utilities. The inclusion of a product in this appendix does not indicate endorsement by Howard W. Sams or the author. Some products may not adhere to the published Microsoft Windows Style Manual in the WinSDK. Products may not necessarily support the Windows 3.0 version. The full list of Windows products is much longer than this. In addition, new products are reaching the market almost daily. Watch particularly for new products in the application areas of multimedia and graphic design.

Artificial Intelligence

NEXPERT OBJECT
Neuron Data, Inc.
444 High Street
Palo Alto, CA 94301
(415) 321-4488
Expert system development and runtime system

Symbologic Adept
Symbologic Corp.
15379 NE 90th Street
Redmond, WA 98052
(206) 881-3938
Expert system

Bit-Mapped Graphic Tools

Microsoft Paintbrush
Microsoft Corporation
16011 NE 36th
Redmond, WA 98073
(206) 882-8088
Inexpensive paint program

PC Paintbrush
ZSoft Corporation
450 Franklin Road, Suite 100
Marietta, GA 30067
(404) 428-0008

Communications

Crosstalk for Windows
Crosstalk Communications
1000 Holcomb Woods Parkway
Roswell, GA 30076
(404) 998-3998
Very popular communications program

DynaComm
Future Soft Engineering, Inc.
1001 S. Dairy Ashford
Houston, TX 77077
(713) 496-9400
Communications package

DaVinci eMAIL
Da Vinci Systems
P.O. Box 5427
Raleigh, NC 27650
1-800-DAVINCI
Messaging system for networks

MicroPhone II
Software Ventures Corporation
2907 Claremont Avenue, #220
Berkeley, CA 94705
(415) 644-3232
Communications program

Microsoft Mail
Microsoft Corporation
16011 NE 36th
Redmond, WA 98073
(206) 882-8088
Network mail system

Multex Quote
Multex Inc.
254 West 31st Street, 9th Floor
New York, NY 10001
(212) 629-8169
Works with Excel and Lotus Signal as financial workstation

Multiplex/XL
Network Innovations Corporation
20863 Stevens Creek Blvd.
Cupertino, CA 95014
(408) 257-6800
Links Excel spreadsheets to corporate computers, supporting SQL queries

The Network Courier
Consumers Software, Inc.
314 Holly Street, Suite 106
Bellingham, WA 98225
(604) 688-4548
LAN electronic mail system

Tempus-Access/Windows Interface
Micro Tempus, Inc.
440 Dorchester Blvd. West
Suite 1700
Montreal, QC, Canada H2Z 1V7
(514) 397-9512
Excel interface to Tempus Access on host system

VIEW/PC
DB/ACCESS
2011 Stevens Creek Blvd, Suite 200
Cupertino, CA 95104
(408) 255-2920
SQL interface for mainframe data

Windowlink for Irma
Digital Communications Associates, Inc.
1000 Alderman Drive
Alpharetta, GA 30201-4199
(404) 442-4000
(800) 241-IRMA, ext. 560
Enables PC to emulate 3278/79 terminal and interface with Irma

Windows InTalk
Palantir
4455 S. Padre Island Drive, Suite 43
Corpus Christi, TX 78411
(512) 854-8787
Communications package

Database

Access SQL
Software Products International
(619) 450-1526
SQL database query system

FormBase
Columbia Software, Inc.
18908 Muirkirk Drive
Northridge, CA 91326
(818) 363-2574
Forms editor and relational database manager

Guide 2 and Guidance
OWL International, Inc.
14218 NE 21st Street
Bellevue, WA 98007
(207) 747-3203
(800) 34-HYPER
Creates hypertext documents

IPS
Pacific Image Communications
1111 South Arroyo Parkway
Pasadena, CA 91105
(818) 441-0104
Document management system

Omnis Quartz
Blyth Software, Inc.
2929 Campus Drive, Suite 425
San Mateo, CA 94403
(415) 571-0222
Relational database

Opus 1
Roykore Software, Inc.
749 Brunswick Street
San Francisco, CA 94112
(415) 333-7833
Hyperdrawing database

Q&E
Pioneer Software
5540 Centerview Drive, Suite 324
Raleigh, NC 27606
(919) 859-2220
Query system for dBASE files

SQLWindows
Gupta Technologies, Inc.
1040 Marsh Road, Suite 210
Menlo Park, CA 94025
(415) 321-9500
SQL applications generator

Superbase 2
Precision Software, Inc.
8404 Sterling Street, Suite A
Irving, TX 75063
(800) 562-9909
(214) 929-4888
Flat-file database, but doesn't follow Windows conventions

Windows Filer
Palantir
4455 S. Padre Island Drive, Suite 43
Corpus Christi, TX 78411
(512) 854-8787
Flat-file database and report writer

Xerox FormBase
Xerox Corporation
9745 Business Park Avenue
San Diego, CA 92123
(800) 822-8221
(619) 695-7891
Forms program and database

Fonts

Fontware
Bitstream, Inc.
Athenaeum House
215 First Street
Cambridge, MA 02142
(617) 497-6222
Creates soft font files for Bitstream fonts

PostScript Fonts
Adobe Systems, Inc.
1585 Charleston Road
P.O. Box 7900
Mountain View, CA 94039-7900
Fonts by family for Windows

Publisher's Type Foundry
ZSoft Corporation
450 Franklin Road, Suite 100
Marietta, GA 30067
(404) 428-0008
Creates a family of fonts or special symbols

Soft Type
ZSoft Corporation
450 Franklin Road, Suite 100
Marietta, GA 30067
(404) 428-0008
Designs outline fonts

WYSIfonts
SoftCraft
16 N. Carroll Street, Suite 500
Madison, WI 53703
(800) 351-0500
(608) 257-3300
Fonts and font installer

Games

Balance of Power
Mindscape, Inc.
3444 Dundee Road
Northbrook, IL 60062
Popular Windows game in which the player tries to make political decisions and affect world events

Presentation Tools

Show Partner
Microsoft Corporation
16011 NE 36th
Redmond, WA 98073
(206) 882-8088
Creates video presentations for computer monitor

Slidewrite Presenter
Advanced Graphics Software
333 W. Maude Avenue, Suite 105
Sunnyvale, CA 94086
(408) 749-8620
Creates video presentations for computer monitor

Programming

ABC Flowcharter
Roykore
749 Brunswick Street
San Francisco, CA 94112
(415) 333-7852
Flowcharting program

Actor
The Whitewater Group
Technology Innovation Center
906 University Place
Evanston, IL 60201
(312) 491-2370
Object-oriented programming system

Bridge
Softbridge, Inc.
125 Cambridge Park Drive
Cambridge, MA 02140
(800) 955-9190
(617) 576-2257
Good for developing Windows applications, but runtime cost is high

Case:W
Caseworks, Inc.
One Dunwoody Park, Suite 130
Atlanta, GA 30338
(800) 635-1577
(404) 491-2370
Program template generator for Windows applications

Resource Scrapbook and Control Paks
Eikon
989 East Hillsdale Blvd., Suite 260
Foster City, CA 94404
(415) 349-4664
Resources and resource manager

Resource Toolkit
The Whitewater Group
600 Davis Street
Evanston, IL 60201
(800) 869-1144
(312) 328-3800
Creates, edits, and copies Windows resources

System Architect
Popkin Software & Systems, Inc.
111 Prospect Street, Suite 505
Stamford, CT 06901
(203) 323-3434
CASE development tool

WinTrieve
The Whitewater Group
600 Davis Street
Evanston, IL 60201
(800) 869-1144
(312) 328-3800
ISAM data file manager for Windows

Scanning

ScanDo
Hammerlab
938 Chapel Street
New Haven, CT 06510
(203) 624-0000
Scanning interface and editor for Windows/386

Scanning Gallery
Hewlett-Packard Company
Personal Software Division
3410 Central Expressway
Santa Clara, CA 95051
Scanning software for Hewlett-Packard scanner

Spreadsheet and Financial

CFO Advisor
Financial Feasibilities, Inc.
9454 Wilshire Blvd.
Penthouse Suite
Beverly Hills, CA 90212
(213) 278-8000
(800) 752-5556, in CA: (800) 247-4452
Decision support system

Excel
Microsoft Corporation
16011 NE 36th
Redmond, WA 98073
(206) 882-8088
Advanced spreadsheet program

Micro Control
IMRS Inc.
1600 Summer Street
Stamford, CT 06905
(203) 323-6500
Financial reporting system

TaxView 2.00
SoftView, Inc.
4820 Adohr Lane, #F
Camarillo, CA 93010
(805) 388-2626

Tutorial

Demo II
Software Garden, Inc.
P.O. Box 373
Newton Highlands, ME 02161
Creates tutorials combining Windows screens and text screens

IconAuthor
AIMTECH Corporation
77 Northeastern Blvd.
Nashua, NH 03062
(800) 289-2884
(603) 883-0220
Creates computer-based training for the Windows environment

Utilities

Bridge/386 & Toolkit 1.1
Softbridge Microsystems
125 Cambridge Park Drive
Cambridge, MA 02140
(617) 576-2257
Batch processor

Clearview
Wang Laboratories
1 Industrial Avenue
Lowell, MA 01851
(508) 459-5000
Windows organizer

Current
IBM Desktop Software
472 Wheelers Farms Road
Milford, CT 06460
(203) 783-7000
Desktop PIM (Personal Information Manager)

Desktop Set 2.01
Okna Corporation
285 Van Buren Street
P.O. Box 522
Lyndhurst, NJ 07071
(201) 460-0677
Desktop utility set

File Manager
Distinct Corporation
14082 Loma Rio Drive
Saratoga, CA 95070
(408) 741-0781
File manager

Hammer and Vise
R
2170 Georgina Avenue
Santa Monica, CA 90402
(213) 393-9992
Creates help files

hDC Windows Express and Windows Manager
hDC Computer Corporation
15379 NE 90th Street
Redmond, WA 98052
(206) 885-5550
(800) 321-4606
Application launching program

OnTrak: The Information Organizer
Active Software Corporation
1208 Apollo Way, Suite 507
Sunnyvale, CA 94086
(408) 732-1740
Personal information manager

Packrat
Polaris Software
613 West Valley Parkway, Suite 323
Escondido, CA 92025
(619) 743-7800
Personal information manager

Prompt!
Access SoftTek
3204 Adeline Street
Berkeley, CA 94703
(415) 654-0116
File management utility

PubTech File Organizer
Publishing Technologies, Inc.
7719 Wood Hollow Drive, Suite 260
Austin, TX 78731
(800) PUBTECH
(512) 346-2835
File management utility

Windows Manager 1.0
hDC Computer Corporation
15379 NE 90th Street
Redmond, WA 98052
(206) 885-5550
Application launching program

Vector-Graphic Drawing Tools

Arts & Letters: Graphic Composer and Editor
Computer Support Corporation
2215 Midway Road
Carrolton, TX 75006
(214) 661-8960
Graphic editor with large clip art collection

ClickArt EPS Illustrations and ClickArt Scrapbook
T/Maker
1390 Villa Street
Mountain View, CA 94041
(415) 962-0195
Clip art and clip art organizer

Corel Draw!
Corel Systems Corporation
1600 Carling Avenue
Ottawa, Canada K1Z 7M4
(613) 728-8200
Highly rated drawing program

Design/2.0 and Design/OA
Meta Software Corporation
150 Cambridge Park Drive
Cambridge, MA 02140
(800) 227-4106
(617) 576-6920
Object-oriented drawing tool

Designer
Micrografix Inc.
1303 Arapaho
Richardson, TX 75081
(214) 234-1769
(800) 272-3729
Very high quality graphic art designer; supports tracing, scanning, and rotation of text and graphics

EasyCAD
Microsoft Corporation
16011 NE 36th
Redmond, WA 98073
(206) 882-8088

In*a*Vision
Micrografix Inc.
1303 Arapaho
Richardson, TX 75081
(214) 234-1769
(800) 272-3729
Drawing and CAD drafting tool

Instinct 2.0
Cadlogic Systems Corporation
2635 N. First Street, Suite 202
San Jose, CA 95134
(408) 943-9696
Drawing tool

MGX/Port
Micrografix Inc.
1303 Arapaho
Richardson, TX 75081
(214) 234-1769
(800) 272-3729
Captures graphics from drawing programs for certain color printers

Pixie
Zenographics
19752 MacArthur Blvd., Suite 250
Irvin, CA 97215-9976
(714) 851-6352
Graphing program

Windows ClipArt
Micrografix Inc.
1303 Arapaho
Richardson, TX 75081
(214) 234-1769
(800) 272-3729
Vector-graphic clip art

Windows Convert
Micrografix Inc.
1303 Arapaho
Richardson, TX 75081
(214) 234-1769
(800) 272-3729
Converts between AutoCAD and Micrografix file formats

Windows Draw
Micrografix Inc.
1303 Arapaho
Richardson, TX 75081
(214) 234-1769
(800) 272-3729
Creates vector graphics or enhances Lotus 1-2-3 charts

Windows GRAPH and GRAPH PLUS
Micrografix Inc.
1303 Arapaho
Richardson, TX 75081
(214) 234-1769
(800) 272-3729
Graphing program--probably the best of current graphing products

Xerox Graph and Xerox Presents
Xerox Corporation
9745 Business Park Avenue
San Diego, CA 92123
(800) 822-8221
Graphing and presentation programs

Word Processing, Desktop Publishing, and Text Management

AMI Professional
Samna Corporation
5600 Glenridge Drive
Atlanta, GA 30342
(800) 831-9679
(404) 851-0007
Word processor

Dragnet
Access SoftTek
3204 Adeline Street
Berkeley, CA 94703
(415) 654-0116
Supports boolean searches of disk text files

Guide
OWL International, Inc.
14218 NE 21st Street
Bellevue, WA 98007
(207) 747-3203
Creates hypertext documents

NBI Legend 2.0
NBI
3450 Mitchell Lane
Boulder, CO 80301
(800) 922-8828, ext. 560
Word processor

PageMaker
Aldus Corporation
411 First Avenue South, Suite 200
Seattle, WA 98104
(206) 622-5500
Desktop publisher

PageView
Microsoft Corporation
16011 NE 36th
Redmond, WA 98073
(206) 882-8088
Previews pages of Microsoft Word before printing

ReadySetGo
Manhattan Graphics Corporation
401 Columbus Avenue
Valhalla, NY 10595
(800) 451-1668
Desktop publisher

Windows Spell
Palantir
4455 S. Padre Island Drive, Suite 43
Corpus Christi, TX 78411
(512) 854-8787
Spell checking utility

WinText
Palantir
4455 S. Padre Island Drive, Suite 43
Corpus Christi, TX 78411
(512) 854-8787
Word processor

Word for Windows
Microsoft Corporation
16011 NE 36th
Redmond, WA 98073
(206) 882-8088
Word processor

Miscellaneous

GeoGraphix Exploration System
GeoGraphix, Inc.
1350 17th Street, Suite 200
Denver, CO 80202
(303) 595-0596
Oil exploration software

Geovision Desktop Geographic Information System
Geovision, Inc.
270 Scientific Drive, Suite 1
Norcross, GA 30092
(404) 448-8224
Mapping system

Hijaak & Inset
Inset Systems Inc.
71 Commerce Drive
Brookfields, CT 06804
(203) 775-5866
TSR screen capture for WinApps

Hotshot Graphics
SymSoft
444 First Street
Los Altos, CA 94022
(415) 941-1552
Screen capture tool

Inertia
Modern Computer Aided Engineering, Inc.
Cumberland Technology Park
1231 Cumberland, Suite A
West Lafayette, IN 47906
(317) 497-1550
Modeling system that interfaces with AutoCAD

Micro Planner
Micro Planning International
235 Montgomery Street, Suite 840
San Francisco, CA 94104
(415) 788-3324
Project management

Project OUTLOOK
Strategic Software Planning Corp.
One Athenaeum Street
Cambridge, MA 02142
(617) 577-8800
Project management

Glossary

Active application The application that appears in the window and that has the current focus for any keyboard input. The window's title bar will be in a different color from an inactive application.

Active printer The printer to which a port is assigned.

Application swap files Files used in real or standard modes for swapping applications to disk.

ANSI character set A numeric coding standard for characters and other symbols defined by the American National Standards Institute.

Application A program that supports a functional role for the user. Spreadsheet programs, word processors, and desktop publishing software are all examples of application programs. Application programs that require Windows are called Windows Application Programs, or *Winapps*.

Application icon An icon used to represent an application when no windows of the application are open.

Bit map An image stored as a bit array.

Buffer A storage area that holds data to be printed.

Cascading windows A method of arranging the windows on the desktop so that they overlap, with the title bar of each visible.

Cascading menu A submenu that can be dropped down when the user initiates a command from the menu bar. The display of both the menu bar and dropdown menus is handled by Windows. The menus are defined in the resource file.

Check box In dialog boxes, a type of control that acts as a toggle, either on or off.

Click To press and release the mouse button quickly. For a right-handed person, the left mouse button is normally the one that is clicked.

Client area The portion of a window available to the application program. The title bar, menu bar, and scroll bars are all outside of the client area. Also called the work area.

Clipboard A temporary storage area used by Windows to transfer data between programs or documents. Clipboard can also be used for moving or copying data within an application.

Close To remove an application or document from the desktop.

Command button A type of dialog box control used to initiate action.

Controls In dialog boxes, objects having predefined behaviors that are consistent for all Windows applications. The five basic control types for input are command buttons, option buttons, check boxes, list boxes, and text boxes.

Control menu A menu activated by clicking the Control-menu box. It is common to all application windows and provides options to minimize, maximize, move, and size the window. It can be altered by the application program.

Control-menu box A box located at the upper left of the window and identified by a horizontal bar. Clicking the control-menu box causes the system menu to be displayed.

Conventional memory The first 640K of memory used by MS-DOS for applications.

Default printer The active printer when Windows is started.

Desktop The screen background on which the various windows are displayed.

Dialog box A type of predefined window that contains controls. Dialog boxes are one of the primary methods of receiving user input in a Windows application program.

Disk cache An area of memory used to manage and improve disk access.

Document window A window used within an application for documents. In Word for Windows, the working document is displayed in a document window. In Excel, a document window is used for the spreadsheet.

Drag To move a screen object by pressing a mouse button on an object and moving the mouse. For example, you can move a window by dragging the title bar.

Dynamic Data Exchange (DDE) A name used by Microsoft to signify the process of passing data between Windows applications.

Elevator A small box within the scroll bar that can be clicked and moved by the mouse to affect the window display. Also called a *thumb box*.

Expanded memory A type of memory supported by all Intel processors (XT and AT compatible machines) in which pages of memory above 1 megabyte are temporarily placed in the 1-megabyte address space (see Appendix B).

Extended memory The physical memory beyond the 1-megabyte limitation of conventional memory. Only the 80286 and 80386 processors or later can use extended memory, and then only when running in protected mode. Windows supports extended memory in standard or enhanced modes.

Focus The area on the window where keyboard input will be received. Which window has the focus is normally determined by the mouse, but location of the focus can also be controlled by the user within the program. For example, an application program can set the focus to any control in a dialog window.

Font family A graphic design common to all symbols of a set (characters, numbers, punctuation, etc.). A single font is supported in multiple sizes and styles (bold, italics, etc.). An example would be *Tms Rmn* (Times Roman).

Grouped controls Controls in a dialog box that are grouped to act as a unit, such as command buttons and check box controls.

Full-screen application A non-Windows application that occupies the entire screen when executing rather than using a window.

Group A collection of programs treated as a unit by the Program Manager.

Group icon An icon that represents a group.

Group window A window used by the Program Manager to display the items in a group.

Icon A small pictorial representation of an object, application, or process.

Iconic A program state in which no window of the application program is visible, although the application is still in memory. Iconic programs are represented by a small icon at the bottom of the screen.

Inactive window An open window that is not currently in use. Only one window can be active at a time.

Insertion point The place where text will be inserted when the user begins typing.

Instance A currently active copy of the application. Windows can have several copies of the same program in memory at one time, with each copy an *instance* of the program. Windows can share program code and data between instances.

List box A type of dialog box control permitting selection from a list, such as a collection of filenames.

Macro A series of actions stored as a unit that can be activated from a single action. In effect, a macro is a type of program.

Maximize box A box located at the upper right of a window and identified by an Up Arrow that permits a user to zoom the window to maximum size.

Menu Command options that are displayed to the user. Windows supports a first-level menu selection in a menu bar, and each item in the menu bar can support a pulldown menu as a second-level menu selection. As a third level, cascading menus can be supported from the pulldown menu items. Menus can be dynamically created or altered by a program. In addition, menu items can be altered dynamically.

Menu bar A first-level menu displayed as a horizontal bar. It is displayed above the client area and below the title bar.

Messages The primary method used within Windows applications for communicating with another program and the system.

Message box In a program, a popup window that contains a brief message, with an optional icon, variable display, title bar, buttons, and response options.

Minimize box A box located at the upper right of a window and identified by a Down Arrow that permits a user to reduce the window to an icon appearing at the bottom of the screen.

Modal dialog box A dialog box that is activated by the system (system modal) or application (application modal) and that must be responded to before execution can continue. Modal dialog boxes are used for input.

Modeless dialog box A dialog box that permits the user to continue to use other windows while the box is displayed. Modeless dialog boxes are normally used for output only.

Multitasking An environment in which several applications execute simultaneously and share a single processor and other resources.

Nonclient area The area of a window that contains the menu bar, title bar, size box, minimize box, maximize box, and scroll bars. The artwork for the nonclient area is controlled by Windows, not the application program. However, the application can define some aspects of the nonclient area, such as the options of the menu bar.

Object A related group of items.

Option button A type of dialog box control used to select one item from a group, such as the modem speed or serial port in a communication program.

Permanent swap file A file used in 386 enhanced mode for swapping applications if memory becomes full. Access is directly from Windows, bypassing DOS. See **Temporary swap file**.

PIF file A file that is used when you are executing standard applications from Windows and that defines how the program should be managed.

Protected mode A mode supported by 80286 processors, or later, that can address extended memory.

Real mode A processor mode that is supported by all Intel processors and is used by Windows and MS-DOS.

Restore box A box that appears at the top right of a window when the window is maximized and that permits the user to restore the window to its previous size. It can be identified by a double arrow.

Scroll bar An optional horizontal or vertical bar that is displayed in a window (at the right or bottom) and that permits the user to control the view of the logical window.

Scroll box A small movable box within the scroll bar that can be moved by the mouse to control the view of the logical window.

Shrink To iconize (minimize) an application.

Shortcut key Predefined keystrokes that can be used as an alternative for menu commands.

Spooling A technique in multitasking systems that permits more than one task to use the printer. Print output is queued to a disk file, from which a spooler utility program prints the tasks in a FIFO (first-in, first-out) manner.

Task An open application.

Temporary swap file A default file created in the 386 enhanced mode for swapping applications to disk if the memory becomes full. See **Permanent swap file**.

Text box A type of dialog box control permitting text entry and editing.

Thumb box A small box within the scroll bar that can be clicked and moved by the mouse to affect the window display. Also called an *elevator*.

Tiled window A window that is placed on the screen adjacent to, but not overlapping, other windows. Early versions of Windows supported a tiled concept.

Title bar An optional bar at the top of a window that contains the program's title.

TSR (terminate-and-stay-resident) software Memory-resident software. TSR software is a program that can remain in memory while another program is executing. Normally, a TSR program is activated with a special, or *hot key*, sequence.

Virtual machine An engine that does not interface directly to any physical input or output. The Windows enhanced 386 mode is a virtual machine. Memory, disks, keyboard, and display are addressed logically instead of physically.

WinApp A Windows application program, or a program that runs under, and is dependent upon, the Windows environment.

Window A rectangular area of the screen that is under the control of the user's application program.

Work area See **Client area**.

Index

real, 354-358, 362-367, 377-379, 409
standard, 354-358, 363-367, 377-379
text, 120-121
mouse, 25, 372
click, 26
configuring with Control Panel, 279-280
double-click, 26
drag, 26
editing documents, 188-189
move, 26
point, 26
selecting blocks of text, 188-189
Move Picture selection (Edit menu), 174
Move selection
Control menu, 29, 52
File menu, 57, 68, 73-74
Move to Beginning (Ctrl + ←) keys, 390
moving
cursor, 189-191
directories, 68
files, 73-74
graphics within a Write document, 174
mouse, 26
objects in Paintbrush, 216
with Clipboard, 215-216
programs among groups, 57
windows, 29
MS-DOS operating system, 62
MSP file extension, 200
Multex Quote program, 393
multiple document interface (MDI), 310-311
Multiplex/XL program, 393
multitasking, 12, 42-43, 413
options (386 enhanced mode PIF files), 338-339

N

naming macros, 236-237
NBI Legend 2.0 program, 406
nesting macros, 240
networks
printers, 380
troubleshooting, 379-380
Windows, 346-347

New selection
File menu, 130, 142, 169-170, 306-307
Game menu, 161
NEXPERT OBJECT program, 391
next active application (Alt + Tab) key, 389
next active window (Alt + Esc) key, 389
next modeless dialog box (Alt + F6) key, 390
next selection, 97
Non-Windows Applications program group, 49
nonclient area, 413
Notepad, 128-135
editing text, 129
starting, 127
null modem cable, 137
NullPort option, 291
number
bases
changing, 108
functions, 110-111
format, 278
numbering pages, 183-185

O

objects, 413
octal mode, 108
Omnis Quartz program, 395
one character left (←) key, 390
one character right (→) key, 390
one line down (↓) key, 390
one line up (↑) key, 390
OnTrak: The Information Organizer program, 401
opaque move, 216
Open selection (File menu), 76, 130-131, 142, 169-171, 306-307
opening
appointment files, 90
existing card files, 118
group windows, 51-52
Microsoft Word document, 170-171
Recorder file automatically, 235
operating modes
386 enhanced, 18-19
changing, 19